Advance Praise for
Life at The Edge of Chaos

"*Life at the Edge of Chaos* contains an amazing wealth of science, philosophy and business know-how. I know this book is going to become one of my few favorite reference books. If Mark doesn't help you get ready for the Quantum Organization, at least you will have learned what you'll be missing!"

> — Perry Pascarella, author and speaker, former Editor-in-Chief of *Industry Week* magazine, and Vice President Editorial of Penton Publishing

"*Life at the Edge of Chaos* provides a truly visionary framework for managing organizations through these times of continuous change."

> — Brent Magnuson, Senior Vice President, The Bombay Company

"This is the book that I've been waiting for—a system's approach to business that even a layperson can relate to!"

> — Marc W. Schwartz, Chairman, Spectra Communications, Inc.

"*Life at the Edge of Chaos* is inspirational! Youngblood's insights have helped me to finally understand what is going on in my company and in the greater business environment. So simple yet so profound. Thank you!"

> — Greg Stromberg, Vice President Marketing, INX International Ink Co.

"*Life at the Edge of Chaos* is an incredible synthesis of the new thinking that is so necessary for organizations to make the leap over the chasm of chaos so prevalent today. Mark Youngblood has done an outstanding job of making the task more understandable and inviting. If you only have one business book to read this year, this would be a great pick!"

> — John E. Renesch, editor/publisher of *The New Leaders* newsletter

"Youngblood has done it again. *Life at the Edge of Chaos* is a brilliant and insightful look at the 'biological' way organizations must adapt themselves in order to survive in the 21st century—now just around the corner. It's must reading for every businessperson."

> — Jessica Keyes, President of New Art, Inc., author of *InfoTrends and Technology Trendlines*

"This book offers an innovative, yet pragmatic perspective on managing in the 21st century and leading organizations in the information age."

> — Paul R. Ray, Jr., President and CEO, Ray & Berndtson

"*Life at the Edge of Chaos* points us in the direction we need to go and tells us how to get there. I am extremely impressed with Mark Youngblood's comprehension and powerful insights into the technologies of personal and organizational transformation."

> — Bill DeFoore, Ph.D., co-editor of *Rediscovering the Soul of Business* and *The New Bottom Line*, author of *Anger: Heal it, Deal With It, Stop It From Killing You*

"Mark Youngblood gives us a thorough historical perspective on how we got into our current business chaos, then offers well formulated alternative ideas to move us out of crisis and into functioning, harmonious and workable companies. His explanation of Quantum Organizations based on the EcoSystem Model is masterful! This book is a must read for anyone interested in being in business in the next century. Magnificent!"

> — Margery Miller, author of *Sound Business Bites: A Common Sense Approach to Customer Service and Management*, and contributing-author to *The New Bottom Line*

"As the primary author of the only organization theory textbook with a transformational perspective, I appreciate Mark's courage and boldness in articulating this new paradigm of organization. But, beyond that, I was greatly impressed by his lucid, friendly prose, his great stories, and his ability to make such arcane subjects as 'the new science' come alive! Mostly, I feel that this book takes up where mine (and others) leave off: he clearly spells out a 'road map' of where we are organizationally, how we got there and what to do about it. A stunning achievement!!"

> — Dr. David K. Banner, The Napoleon Hill Professor of Leadership
> (Emeritus) University of the Pacific, co-author of *Designing
> Effective Organizations: Traditional and Transformational Views*

"Say good-bye to the Organization Man! Now is the era of the self-organizing men and women. Whether you are cultivating a business or re-engineering your life, this is the book to read!"

> — Martha Finney, business writer, co-author of *Callings*

"Today's business world demands that managers deal effectively with change in order to build a successful organization. This book is an excellent resource in challenging managers to accept change as a fundamental part of their leadership. It is easy to understand and is a useful resource on the complete subject of change.

> — Dr. Harry J. Ashenhurst, Executive Vice President-Human Resources,
> Lennox International, Inc.

"Mark describes in a very unique way the journey that successful organizations must undertake, because the true 'quantum leap' in customer service and shareholder value must ultimately come from employees."

> — Michael Kruklinski, Director of Business Process Innovations,
> First American Corporation

"This book is worth buying, reading, highlighting, and using. . . . If you want your organization to have meaningful purpose, then this book offers insights into how to get it done. Bravo Mark!"

> — Niki McCuistion, Executive Director, Foundation for Responsible
> Television, producer of the PBS program *McCuistion:
> Talking About Things That Matter With People Who Care*

Life at the Edge of Chaos

Creating the Quantum Organization

By Mark D. Youngblood

Perceval Publishing

Perceval Publishing

9330 LBJ Freeway Suite 900
Dallas, TX 75243

Phone: (972)783-2070
Fax: (972)783-2040
Email: QuayAll@aol.com

Ordering Information

Orders by individuals and organizations. Perceval Publishing publications are available through bookstores or can be ordered direct from the publisher. For details, see the order form at the back of this book.

Quantity sales. Perceval Publishing publications are available at special quantity discounts when purchased in bulk by corporations, associations, and others. For details, please contact the publisher at the address above or call (972)783-2070, fax (972)783-2040.

Orders by U.S. trade bookstores and wholesalers. For Distributor information, please contact the publisher at the address above or call (972)783-2070, fax (972)783-2040.

Orders for college textbook/course adoption use. Please contact the publisher at the address above or call (972)783-2070, fax (972)783-2040.

Publisher's Cataloging-in-Publication
(Provided by Quality Books, Inc.)

Youngblood, Mark D.
      Life at the edge of chaos : creating the quantum organization /
by Mark D. Youngblood.
        p. cm.
        Includes bibliographical references and index.
        Preassigned LCCN: 97-65406
        ISBN: 1-889847-40-2

        1. Organizational change. 2. Management. 3. Leadership. 4. Complexity (Philosophy)
        5. Interpersonal relations. I. Title.

   HD58.8.Y68 1997   658.4'063
                        QBI97-40210

Printed in the U.S.A. on acid-free paper
Edited by John Renesch and Janet Reed
Cover Illustration by Angelica Collantes, Perfect Page Publishing (Richardson, Texas)
Desktop Publishing by Perfect Page Publishing (Richardson, Texas)

"Before the beginning of great brilliance,
there must be chaos."

I-Ching

Table of Contents

Part Two
Powerful New Ways of Working

Chapter Three
The Quantum Organization 75

DON'T READ THIS BOOK!
(The way you normally would....)

I know many people who have shelves full of unread books. They never quite found the time to read these books or quickly became disinterested and put them away. I do not want the same fate to fall on this book. There is important material in here for you—it is your job not only to find it, but to have a good time in the process!

The key to getting value out of a book is to find the parts that you are most interested in, and read them first. Here are a few suggestions:

⊠ Think about a problem or opportunity that you want the material in this book to address (some immediate issue facing you or your organization).

⊠ Scan through the book, reading the headings and pull-out quotes on each page. Mark the sections that catch your attention.

⊠ Read chapter one because it establishes the basic premise of the book.

⊠ Go back and read the sections that caught your attention. Let your curiosity lead you around the book from there.

⊠ Don't feel like you have to read the entire book—just focus on the parts that are interesting and relevant to you.

Happy reading!

Preface

Writing a book is either an act of love or an act of insanity . . . or maybe a little of both. I really struggled as I started to write this book. I knew in my heart that the message was important. In fact, it had become the driving influence in my life. Then I realized that I had to write out of my passion, not for you, the reader, but for me. Inspiration is not about pleasing others, but about staying true to yourself—living your life authentically. When I finally accepted this law of Nature, the book literally flowed out of me. There were times when I would look up and notice that I had written ten pages with barely any memory of having done so.

I once heard a radio interview with philosopher Joseph Campbell wherein he gave a masterful response to a caller's question. When the interviewer asked him to repeat it, Campbell said that he couldn't. He explained that the answer had been given out of inspiration, and he did not remember what he had said only seconds earlier! That is how I feel about the experience of writing much of this book.

Leadership and Organization for the Twenty-First Century

I have been helping organizations through large-scale transformative change for the past twenty years. Early in this experience I learned that "change" was a unique creature, one that followed its own rules. The tried-and-true techniques that I had mastered for managing line organizations failed miserably when I applied them to organizational change. I had to experiment with entirely new management techniques, and I had to develop a different view of the organization.

Gradually, a consistent and workable approach emerged. I developed a systemic model of organizations called the Organizational EcoSystem Model and a holistic approach to change called the Integrated Change Methodology. These new models and techniques acknowledged that organizations are highly complex and interdependent systems, change is mostly about people and their mind-sets, change cannot be forced or controlled, and successful change requires employees to take ownership of the outcome. Managing during periods of change was inclusive, participatory, relational, and democratic.

The struggle that organizations have with transformative change is that the democratic techniques required for success are like an island in the greater sea of industrial-era command-and-control management practices and organizational structures. As a result, organizational change is a tremendous struggle and frequently fails. In the last few years, many companies have finally acknowledged that change management requires new skills, mind-sets, and approaches. The problem is that we live in a world of constant change—there is never a time anymore when we aren't going through a major change of some sort. What place, then, do the traditional command-and-control structures have in this fast-paced and complex age? Practically none.

The successful company in the next century will be what I call a Quantum Organization. These companies are characterized by openness, flexibility, responsiveness, resilience, creativity, vitality, balance, and caring. The study of living systems in the new science provides us with a model for developing these organizations. I have identified seven principles that characterize these systems and use them as the basis for the Quantum Organization. The result is a substantially different organization from that developed to succeed using the mechanistic principles of industrial-era management—one that is much more appropriate and effective for the twenty-first century world in which we live.

Finding Your Way Around This Book

Life at the Edge of Chaos was written for business people who are seeking new and simpler ways for managing complexity and change in their organizations. However, the material presented here is relevant to *any* organization—whether it is a church, social group, governmental body or agency, not-for-profit group, or even a family. The concepts, principles and skills are
the same.

Part 1: Powerful New Ways of Thinking. The two chapters in this section provide the theoretical cornerstones for the book. They highlight the need for changing the prevailing mechanistic worldview and describe a vision of what the quantum worldview would mean for organizations and for society as a whole. Chapter 1, "A New Order," begins by exploring how and why our experiences today are so remarkably different from those of just twenty-five years ago. It then looks into the consequences our outdated worldview has had on attempts to improve organizational performance. Chapter 2, "The Way of Living Systems," provides an in-depth description of the seven principles of living systems and explains why this is a superior model for managing complexity and change.

Part 2: Powerful New Ways of Working. This section answers the questions: "What would an organization developed to operate as a living system look like?" and "How do we make the changes needed to become such an organization?" Chapter 3, "The Quantum Organization," describes the Organizational EcoSystem Model and what needs to change for it to operate as a living system. Chapter 4, "Shared Vision," describes the importance of and methods for creating an organization's shared vision. Chapter 5, "Transforming Corporate Culture," presents the Integrated Change Model. This comprehensive methodology embodies systems concepts and applies them to large-scale organizational change.

Section 3: Powerful New Ways of Being. In order to be effective, organizational change needs to address three different levels: the personal, organizational, and inter-personal. Part 2 addresses the changes needed at an organizational level. Part 3 discusses the changes in core skills required at the personal and inter-personal levels.

The first two chapters in this section describe the personal skills required to prosper in an Quantum Organization. Chapter 6, "Personal Leadership," is about understanding ourselves at a deep level, taking full responsibility for our lives, discovering our inner sources of power and happiness, and living authentically. Chapter 7, "Personal Mastery," explores how we perceive, think, and react to situations and events, and provides practical methods for increasing our ability to learn.

The final two chapters in this section describe the interpersonal skills people need in order to be successful in our complex world. In the quantum worldview, relationships are vital to success. Chapter 8, "Relationship," describes the attitudes and skills required to create and maintain strong interpersonal relationships. Chapter 9, "Dialogue," describes the importance of—and practical methods for—creating shared meaning in organizations.

Epilogue. The final chapter, "For Our Children," takes a look at the consequences of our current behavior and practices and the impact they will have on our children and the world they will inherit. It is a call to look outside of our own concerns and recognize how we are going to hurt those we care for the most—our children—if we don't change our self-destructive behaviors.

Appendix A. "The Wonders of Quantum Physics," describes the scientific discoveries in this century regarding the characteristics and behavior of atomic phenomena. It uses easily understood language and presents the concepts in ways that most people should be able to comprehend. The world that quantum physics describes is absolutely fascinating and radically different from what most of us learned in school. These concepts will eventually have a powerful impact on the thinking of our society and so I highly recommend your taking the time to read this material.

My Hopes

I think that it is important to know something about an author's intentions to understand the natural bias that is inherent in every communication. Before I started writing, I sat down and developed a list of hopes. These were the seeds for the vision that has culminated in this publication.

* I hope this book will make a profound difference in the lives of millions of people. It will speak to people's hearts, guiding them to greater peace in their lives. They will be able to act with more wisdom, more confidence, and more faith that the world supports them.

* I hope businesses and organizations of all kinds will transform how they operate to become more life-affirming, participative, and enjoyable.

* I hope people will learn to embrace change—to let go of their anxiety and view change calmly.

* I hope people will gain a greater ability to manage their thoughts and emotions. They will view the world more clearly, make decisions consciously, and choose their responses from a wider range of options.

* I hope people will develop a profound reverence for relationships of all kinds along with better skills for developing and maintaining them.

* I hope this book will support my own learning, providing rich opportunities for me to gain insights into my thoughts and behaviors, and helping me to consistently choose my actions through wisdom and love.

Changes of the sort described in this book do not occur overnight. They may take years to implement in companies and decades to filter through the greater social system. A colleague once told me that truly great things cannot be achieved in a single lifetime. For this reason, I am dedicating this work to our children, to their children, and to all of the generations to follow.

April, 1997   Mark D. Youngblood
Dallas, Texas USA

Acknowledgments

No major accomplishment was ever achieved without the efforts—known and unknown—of very many people. And so it is with the creation of this book.

First and foremost I am grateful to the One True Source for the opportunity to participate in such a grand endeavor.

As always, I am deeply indebted to my beautiful wife, Connie, and my precious son, Ryan, for their love, support and patience with me as I struggled to give birth to this 800 pound gorilla.

To my parents, Steve and Sandra: thank you for the gifts—intentional and unintentional, pleasant and painful—that launched me on this path.

A number of generous and thoughtful people provided their time and insights as reviewers of early drafts of the book. Without you this book may never have come into being. A big thank you to: Brian Skinner, Carole McAvoy, Connie Youngblood, David Chase, David McClure, Gail McDonald, Greg Stromberg, Jay Cober, Jean Johnson, Karen Lymon, Kent Odland, Marc Schwartz, Margery Miller, Martha Finney, Michael DiAngelo, Molly Hanchey, Niki McCuistion, Perry Pascarella, Tom Marinelli, and Viki Hurst.

Thank you to the people who provided those wonderful, glowing endorsements—your votes of confidence mean a lot to me!

I am grateful to all of the wonderful people at Ray & Berndtson for their courage in taking on such far-reaching change, and in having confidence in me to guide them in their effort. In particular, I want to thank Paul Ray Jr., Reece Pettigrew, and Carrie Ham for making the long hours and late nights such a pleasant and enriching experience—you're the best!

And finally, my appreciation goes out to you, the Reader, for your interest in this material. I urge you to learn it, share it, live it!

PART ONE

POWERFUL NEW WAYS OF THINKING

*Man's mind, once stretched
by a new idea, never regains
its original dimension.*
    — Oliver Wendell Holmes

Chapter One
A New Order

Nothing is more powerful than
an idea whose time has come.

        — Victor Hugo

A colleague of mine—a retired senior executive of a Fortune 1000 company—recently voiced his deep concern about the condition and direction of our society. The problems that he sees facing our world seem insurmountable to him. He wants to believe in a positive future for the human race, but it gets harder for him to do so with each day that passes. Our social institutions, which we have relied on to solve these problems in the past, have become ineffective and paralyzed in bureaucratic gridlock. Leaders can't lead. Governments can't govern. Schools can't educate. Churches can't create meaning. Health care can't provide healthy lives. Judicial systems can't bring about justice. And economies can't prevent poverty.

Many people in our society are searching for someone to emerge with *The Answer* to all of our problems. Some people look to a divine intervention, others hope that science will devise an answer, and still others believe that our current approaches will solve the problem if we give them a little more time, try a little harder, and spend a little more money. I think all of us know in our hearts that there will be no miracle cure.

Our current methods can't solve the complex problems facing our society. Our traditional approach to addressing such issues has been to isolate the problem and treat its visible symptoms with external, event-based remedies.

This reductionist approach may have worked fairly well when the world was a simpler place. However, our global environment has changed dramatically, and these techniques are no longer effective. Today's problems are *systemic*, highly interdependent and interwoven, and cannot be solved by merely addressing the *parts*. We can only hope to fix them by addressing the system as a *whole*.

This book is based on the premise that the majority of our social and organizational problems cannot be dealt with using traditional concepts and methods. Problem-solving which applies mechanistic approaches to complex systems does not work and can even create new problems. We have already tried those tired old solutions, and tried them again, and then tried them some more . . . and they *simply do not work*. How many prisons do we have to build before we recognize that incarceration doesn't deter crime? How much must we spend on the drug war before we finally grasp that we had a better chance of winning the Vietnam War? How many times will we tweak our government's monetary and social policies before we accept that they do not improve people's lives? How many more hospitals, doctors, and drugs do we need before we realize that we are not bettering our population's health? How much moralizing will we do before we admit that our preaching and judging isn't reducing childhood pregnancy or the spread of AIDS? How many more layoffs will businesses try before conceding that brutal staff reductions don't improve long-term performance?

> *It is the mode of handling problems, rather than what they are about that assigns them to an age.*
>
> — Susanne Langer, author of *Philosophy in a New Key*

Most of our deepest beliefs and assumptions are grounded in a mechanistic worldview—outdated scientific principles and management practices adopted in the early days of the Industrial Revolution. We are still operating out of this unconscious mental programming despite the fact that it is no longer suitable or effective for the challenges that we face today. This is true both for business and for society at large.

The Classical Worldview: The World As a Machine

The classical worldview emerged more than 300 years ago when Sir Isaac Newton led a revolution in scientific thought that was unparalleled in human history. Building on the ideas of René Descartes, Newton articulated an entirely new, mechanistic view of the universe that ultimately overthrew the Nature-centered, holistic outlook that had prevailed for more than a millennia. Since both Newton and Descartes were products of the existing patriarchal culture, the prevailing mind-set of dominance, control, and separateness provided the cornerstones of their new ideas.

The Newtonian-Cartesian model of the world as a machine was a stunning success, and the new scientific approach of Newton's classical physics immediately insinuated itself into the physical sciences. In the centuries that followed, the newly founded social sciences—economics, psychology, sociology, anthropology, and others—followed suit. By the early 1800s, a comprehensive worldview based on Newtonian science dominated Western thought.

It still does to this day.

Newton's ghost haunts the corridors and boardrooms of our corporations, the classrooms of our educational institutions, the assembly rooms of our governing bodies, the operating rooms of our hospitals, and even the sanctuaries of our religious organizations. But a lot has changed since the 1600s when Newton formed what Descartes called "this marvellous science."

> *The modern scientific paradigm has become as difficult to maintain in the late twentieth century as was the religious paradigm in the seventeenth.*
>
> — Morris Berman, author of
> *The Reenchantment of the World*

Fifty years ago, scientists knew that Newton was wrong about the way the world worked. When Einstein and other scientists first explored the exotic world of atomic physics, they were not happy about what they found. As they struggled to understand, one pre-eminent physicist asked, "Can nature possibly be so absurd as it seemed to us in these atomic experiments?" They realized that their basic concepts, their language, their *whole way of thinking* were inadequate. The Newtonian-Cartesian model was almost completely invalidated by what these path-breaking scientists discovered. Their findings were irrefutable—the universe is definitely *not* a machine. Recent explorations into the behavior and organizing principles of complex adaptive systems has further validated the quantum physicist's organic view of nature. Nature is very much alive and actively organizing itself into ever-higher levels of complexity and order.

Modern scientists have long since left behind the Newtonian-Cartesian model. But the rest of society, including business, has not. Margaret Wheatley tells us, "We have not in any way abandoned [classical] science as the source of our operating principles." She goes on to say, "We social scientists are trying to be conscientious, using the methodologies and thought patterns of seventeenth-century science, while the scientists, traveling away from us at the speed of light, are moving into a universe that suggests entirely new ways of understanding."

> *It is foolish for a society to try to cling to old ideas in new times, just as it is foolish for a grown man to try to squeeze into a coat that fit him in his youth.*
>
> — Thomas Jefferson

The cold legacy of Newton's ghost—his ancient mechanistic worldview—still pervades almost every aspect of modern civilization. But our world is not Newton's world—seventeenth century concepts don't work for us on the eve of the twenty-first century. I believe that the breakdowns in our social institutions, the inability of organizations to respond effectively to new challenges, and the dreadful state of the human experience in business relate directly to the obsolete mechanistic worldview that has given rise to our society's policies, systems, and structures.

If we are to prosper—to create a sustainable future for our children—we must break the bonds of our mental captivity. We must find and embrace new and more effective ways of understanding and relating to our world.

The Age of Complexity

Profound changes start quietly. We may not be aware of them when they first take root, so they grow unattended and unnoticed for years. Then one day they surface fully developed . . . and take us completely by surprise. This is how it came to pass that one morning, sometime in the early 1980s, we awoke to a world that we no longer understood. That is when we first realized that the "Age of Complexity" had emerged around us without our noticing. Although our awakening was not as startling as Dorothy's experience in *The Wizard of Oz*, we each had a moment when we felt as Dorothy did when she said, "Toto, I don't think we are in Kansas anymore."

We have always lived in an environment of incredible complexity and global interdependencies, but for the past several hundred years we have succeeded in ignoring this fundamental truth. However, exponential increases in information, technological advancements, and interactions between diverse people and cultures have made it impossible to continue with our self-deception. We are now realizing that our local issues are really global ones. Even small policy decisions carry world-wide implications. It is clear that our Newtonian-Cartesian thought system—based on the linear and predictable behavior of machines—cannot cope with the realities of today's fast-paced, complex environment.

Many of us have felt a growing uneasiness as the effectiveness of our traditional approaches to personal and organizational success has slowly eroded. Few people and even fewer organizations have grasped the full implication of the changes that have taken place in the past two decades or understand how deep our own changes must go if we are to operate effectively in this new environment. Richard Callahan, chief of U.S. West International, captured the sense of this when he said, "We're talking about a new order, a sea change, that will go on for the rest of my career. It's almost like Haley's Comet arriving unannounced."

Margaret Wheatley, writing in her lyrical style in *Leadership and the New Science*, mused about the powerful changes that are challenging our most fundamental beliefs:

> I too can feel the earth shaking. I hear its deep rumblings. Any moment now, the earth will crack open and I will stare into its dark center. Into that dark caldera, I will throw most of what I have treasured, most of the techniques and tools that have made me feel competent. I cannot do that yet; I cannot just heave everything I know into the abyss. But I know it is coming.

Strange Changes: Life in 1970 vs. Today

As part of a management seminar that I lead, I ask the participants to describe the world as it was leading up to the year 1970. I ask them to discuss both business and personal aspects of their lives.

The most frequently mentioned points regarding life in the decade prior to 1970 are listed below:

※ *The pace was much slower.* There were fewer changes and much more time to prepare for them. Also, there were long periods of stability between major changes.

※ *The authority of managers was rarely challenged.* Managers were expected to know more, to be able to identify the right answer, to organize activities and deliver results. Their authority was complete and people did as they were told. This asked people to give up a lot of their personal autonomy and thinking, but for most, the bargain was worth it because of the security that was offered in return.

✠ *Jobs were more certain.* Each day at work, people knew pretty much what activities to expect, and what was required of them. Jobs were clearly defined and rules and procedures governed everything. Life-long employment with the company was a given so long as you performed.

✠ *The business environment was more predictable.* There were fewer competitors and most of them were well known. Concerns were local and national—rarely did international issues surface.

✠ *Home life was simpler.* Family roles were fairly constant and duties were well separated between men and women. People could expect to leave the stress of work behind at the end of the day.

✠ *Information technology was vastly different.* Computer programs were still typed painstakingly onto punch cards, and scores of data entry clerks keyed each day's transactions. CRTs didn't begin to show up on desks until nearly 1980. Phones, typewriters, adding machines, and desk calculators were the primary office machines. Hand calculators were expensive and bulky, and fax machines and personal computers were unknown.

✠ *There was much less information.* There were three commercial channels on television. Memos were typed on paper, and copies were made via carbon paper—white-out corrective ink was a *huge* time-saving invention. Phones had one feature—they rang. There was no voice mail, call forwarding, or beepers.

When asked to describe the equivalent experiences today, seminar participants offer the following views:

✠ *We are being bombarded by change.* Changes pile up on top of changes. We are so busy dealing with interruptions that there isn't enough time to do any "real" work. And the challenges are unfamiliar—at home and at work we are coping with situations that we have never before faced.

✠ *Employees often know as much or more than their supervisors.* They have access to much of the same information and make their own informed decisions. As a result, employees have a lot of questions—they want to know the reasoning behind key decisions. People want to be included; they want to participate; they want and expect more from their work than just a paycheck.

People want to be included; they want to participate; they want and expect more from their work than just a paycheck.

- *The phrase "job security" has become an oxymoron—there is no longer any such thing.* Job expectations are vague and subject to constant change. Rules and regulations (although they are often still in effect) are outdated, restrictive, and basically useless for conducting daily business.
- *Business has become global for even the smallest companies.* World-wide markets, competitors, and suppliers all now fall into the mix of considerations for operating organizations. And business is broadening in more ways than just geography. Competitors and suppliers are emerging from non-traditional sources as companies increase their range of products and services and as new distribution channels open up. Changing demographics have added the challenge of managing and integrating people of diverse cultures and social backgrounds. The participation of women has changed the face of business at every level except the boardroom (and that last bastion will fall soon).
- *Life at home has also become chaotic, stressful, and uncertain.* Traditional household roles for men and women have changed with the entry of large numbers of women into the workplace. More than 50 percent of households are led by only one parent. The challenges for children are greater than ever: lower quality education, unavailable parents, increased violence and drug use, the threat of sexual diseases. The challenges of raising children is greater now because parents have less time and children have more options (and thus more demands). And money is tighter than ever for most families. Home is no longer a refuge where working parents can release stress—demands at home just add to stress.
- *Information technology has had an enormous impact on our lives.* Fax machines, mobile phones, beepers, the Internet, voice mail, e-mail, miniaturized computing, cable and satellite access, software of every kind, and rapid air

travel have made a local community of the entire world, leveraged our mind power, and reshaped virtually every aspect of human society.

- *The increase in access to—and the volume of—information has also had a huge impact on our lives.* Each day we must dig out from under an avalanche of information that buries us in trivia and overwhelms our senses. Statistics indicate that there is more information in one edition of a major metropolitan newspaper today than a person 100 years ago encountered in an *entire lifetime.* There are more than 200 television channels available today, and news from anywhere in the world can reach us in less than 10 minutes. The advent of the hand-held video recorder has had a tremendous effect as witnessed by such events as the Rodney King trial. Magazines are available (in print and on the Internet) for almost every conceivable special interest. Added to this is the increase in personal communications that the new technologies have made possible. Some seminar participants report that they receive 50 to 100 e-mail and voice mail messages *every day.*

Turbulence in Society

These lists demonstrate clearly that the world has changed dramatically since 1970. Today's social and business environment is characterized by staggering complexity, rapid change, and unpredictability. We have the feeling that we are barely holding back the floodwaters of chaos. Order seems to hang by a thin thread, and only our frantic efforts to impose control keep us from being completely overwhelmed. Peter Vaill, author and professor at George Washington University, uses the metaphor of "permanent white water" to describe this feeling. In his recent book, *Learning As a Way of Being*, he describes our subjective experience of all this confusion:

> [People] talk about "being on a roller coaster," a "see-saw," or a "merry-go-round," about "being in the theater of the absurd," about "arranging the deck chairs on the *Titanic*." They wonder, "who's on first," and "Are the patients running the asylum?" They feel "the situation unraveling," "things coming apart at the seams," "the train leaving the tracks," "a meltdown

happening." . . . They compare their activities to "something in a puzzle palace" or "something out of *Alice in Wonderland*" or "a Keystone Kops movie" and they whistle the theme from *The Twilight Zone*.

Our pre-1975 management experience was that of "calm water"—an environment characterized by certainty and predictability. The tools, techniques, and mind-sets that were developed for managing in calm water conditions (currently referred to as *bureaucratic, classical,* or *industrial era* management), worked extremely well for most of this century. The problems and conditions that we faced lent themselves to simple, linear analysis and solutions, and a command-and-control management style. These were *convergent* problems, where application of analytical problem-solving techniques converged on a single "right" solution. However, these same approaches are inadequate and even destructive when used in today's complex environment.

> *To everything there is a season, and a time for every purpose under heaven.*
>
> — Ecclesiastes 3:1,
> *The Bible*

The word *complexity,* which comes from a Latin root meaning "to entwine," is formally defined as "intricately interconnected or interwoven." We cannot predict the behavior of our current systems because there are too many interrelated factors—too much uncertainty. The challenges of complexity are *divergent* problems; analysis only leads to more and more possible solutions, none of which is "best." In complexity, the links between cause-and-effect are lost and problems become "un-figure-out-able" using classical management tools. The times have changed, and our mental models, tools, techniques, and skills have not kept up.

A Case of Newtonian Despair

"Sally" was exhausted. She put her face in her hands and shook her head in defeat—a victim of "Newtonian despair."

The time was midnight, and the scene a warehouse in Dallas. A team of people were swarming over the building counting inventory for a system conversion scheduled for the next day. I was the Big-6 consultant leading the effort; Sally was the client manager. I knew this project was going to be a challenge when I first learned that the warehouse had never been fully inventoried. We had no way to know what to expect, so our planning document could serve as a rough outline at best. The counting was going to be chaotic and the reconciliation a nightmare. Because of the number of problems we could expect to encounter, I knew that the only way to get through the effort was for all team members to think for themselves. We would have to improvise and learn as we went.

The project started out well enough, but before long we ran into our first problem. Sally, who had been uncomfortable with the approach all along, used this opportunity to step in and seize control. Her method was to control all the activities, telling each person what, when, and how to do each task. She was responsible, so all problems came to her. Individual team members were nothing more than physical extensions of Sally. This was classical management at its best.

At first, things seemed to run smoother with the centralized control. But then the number of problems started to multiply. Because the problems were unfamiliar, each took a substantial amount of time to analyze and solve. Delays built up as people sat around waiting while Sally solved another person's problems. She was overwhelmed by a never-ending stream of interruptions and demands on her time. After several hours of this, the project had come to a standstill, and Sally had collapsed in exhaustion. Her attempts to control the process and to separate intrinsically related activities into discrete parts had only made matters worse. After she relinquished control, team members stepped in and followed the original approach. Soon the effort gained momentum and the team's collective learning led to increased productivity. By morning, the project was complete.

Traditional management is based on the scientific principles of Newtonian physics—the view that the universe is a machine. However, modern science has determined that the machine model is ineffective in dealing with complexity. We are now realizing that our modern organizations and institutions are so interconnected, both internally and externally, that we can never expect to follow all of the intricate connections in the hope of sorting out linear causes and effects. When we use classical management techniques in a complex environment (which describes most of our modern experience in organizations), we find ourselves in a vicious circle where we must expend ever-increasing energy and get ever-decreasing results. This is the experience of Newtonian despair, and this is what happened to Sally.

There is a veritable epidemic of Newtonian despair in modern organizations. The desperate call-to-arms, "Change or die!" can be heard echoing down the corridors of businesses everywhere. We are being challenged to find new responses, and we are failing. In 1994, I wrote that "most companies are ill-equipped to manage organizational change." This is still true. Our industrial-era organizations are simply not capable of dealing with the chaos of our modern environment.

> The desperate call-to-arms, "Change or die!" can be heard echoing down the corridors of businesses everywhere.

Organizational Change: A Core Incompetence

The *Harvard Business Review* reports, "The problem for most executives is that managing change is unlike any other managerial task they have ever confronted. When it comes to change, the model he uses for organizational issues doesn't work." *Business Week* magazine notes that, "Thriving in this fast-paced environment requires *a new kind of company* and *a new kind of CEO*." (Italics added.) Ronald E. Compton, CEO of Aetna Life and Casualty, understands this point: "Change is not something that happens. It's a way of life. It's not a process, it's a value. It's not something you do, it engulfs you." Just as "quality" became a basic requirement for corporate viability in the 1980s, the ability to adapt—to change quickly and easily—has become a core requirement for all businesses in the 1990s.

No one can say that companies aren't trying. Businesses everywhere are engaged in a frantic whirlwind of activity in search of ever-increasing operational efficiency and competitive fitness. They are trying desperately to cope with the changes being forced on them by our rapidly evolving environment. Unfortunately, most organizations are not succeeding. We see the evidence in the non-stop smorgasbord of management techniques that are being served up to many organizations. Figure 1.1 lists just a few of the programs being foisted onto weary employees.

The Efficiency Squeeze

Figure 1.1

Business Process Reengineering
Total Quality Management
Continuous Improvement
Core Competencies
Benchmarking
Outsourcing
Downsizing
Teamwork
Mergers
Automation
Restructuring
Empowerment
Pay-For-Performance
Time-Based Competition
Activity-Based Management
Mission and Value Statements

Frustrated and anxious management teams try on and discard these management approaches like people do clothes at a bargain basement sale. It is evident that leaders feel frustrated and stymied at every turn. The classical management model that made them successful no longer seems to work. So they feel lost. In a senior staff meeting at a high-tech firm, one executive confided to me that the CEO suffered from "MBMA." When I asked what MBMA was, he responded: "Management By Magazine Article." Cartoonist Scott Adams, author of the enormously popular comic strip *Dilbert* has made a fortune exploiting the employee cynicism that has built up in response to what many see as the "management fad du jour."

In the 1992 presidential campaign, U.S. President George Bush acknowledged that he wasn't very good at the "vision thing." If corporations were as forthright, they would admit that they aren't very good at the "*change* thing." The shortcomings of the traditional management model are most evident when we attempt to make structural changes. Until then, the systemic interdependencies that characterize complexity go unnoticed and undisturbed. But making organizational modifications requires changing systemic interconnections. Living systems—which include business organizations—are intrinsically organic. They must be developed, grown, and nurtured from the ground up following a general structural pattern. Our traditional concepts and tools, however, are geared for making changes to an inorganic machine. We identify the faulty parts, pull them out, and replace them with new ones. Our mechanistic models for "building," "engineering," and "architecting" organizations are wholly inadequate for making systemic changes. The results bear this out; the statistics regarding success and failure of organizational change are abysmal. We are exerting enormous amounts of energy trying to achieve organizational change, and we are getting little or nothing for it.

> *Eighteen months after Peter's and Waterman (1982) published their list of "excellent" companies, one-third of them had dropped off the list. An examination of the fallen shows that the majority failed to respond adequately to changes in the external environment.*
>
> — Geary Rummler and Alan Brache, authors of *Improving Performance*

Meaningless Change

The media is full of reports that between 65 and 80 percent of change efforts do not achieve the desired results. For instance, a recent poll by consulting firm Arthur D. Little revealed that only 16 percent of executives were "fully satisfied" with their reengineering projects. A similar study by CSC Index discovered that of ninety-nine completed reengineering initiatives, 67 percent were judged as producing "mediocre, marginal, or failed results." In 1997, companies are projected to spend an estimated $52 billion on business process reengineering alone. Two-thirds or more of those projects will fail. That amounts to *$35 billion* in wasted effort—not counting the cost in disrupted business, lost productivity due to low employee morale, or the social cost in human suffering and dislocation.

Companies that downsized to get "lean and mean" generally did not fare any better. *Fast Company* magazine reported the results of a fifteen-year study by Harvard Business School professor Nitin Nohria of the 100 largest public corporations. On average, each company announced fifteen layoffs with each averaging 2,000 people (for a total of 30,000 people per company over the fifteen-year period). So, how did these companies perform financially? Only 8 percent outperformed mutual funds. (*Fast Company* characterized mutual funds as "the most boring stock market investment you could make.") In relation to the opportunity cost of capital, only 30 percent of these companies created any positive value, and the median value added per company was *minus* $5 billion!

Even when businesses do succeed in achieving bottom-line performance improvements, the improvements are often gained by mortgaging the organization's future. This happens in two ways. One way is when managers push through improvements that look good in the short-term, but that hurt the organization in the long-term. Examples include layoffs and downsizing, outsourcing critical functions, delaying maintenance or much-needed investments in infrastructure, eliminating skill-building and learning activities, manipulating the system to overstate results, and seeking economies of scale that cut too deeply.

The second way the long-term is compromised is when managers alienate and demoralize employees by how they handle the change process itself. These practices include heavy-handedness, unilateral top-down dictates, and changes that appear disproportionate, arbitrary, or foolish (all of which are hallmarks of the classical management model). Either way, organizations experience short-term profit improvements only to be faced over time with resurgent problems and the need for even deeper and more extreme measures. Case in point: A five-year study by the American Management Association (AMA) revealed that *multiple* rounds of workforce reductions were required by over *67 percent of downsizing companies.* (Italics added.)

What is the social cost of this "corporate bulimia"? Whether we acknowledge it or not, businesses are living systems embedded within living systems—they are inextricably connected to all aspects of society. When corporations gain at the expense of employees, the communities in which they operate, or the environment, they are pushing their costs out into the social sector. And these costs are enormous. The March 11, 1996 cover of *Business Week* magazine blared out "Economic Anxiety" as its lead story. The article reports that, "ten years of downsizing and widening income inequality have taken an enormous social toll."

Barbara Rheinhold, author of *Toxic Work*, reports that there is more stress in the workforce now than at any time since the Industrial Revolution. High stress and anxiety lead to many ills, including deteriorating health and decreased employee morale and motivation. The largest-selling medicines in America are those for ulcers, anxiety, and depression. The staggering levels of alcohol and illegal drug consumption are further indicators of people trying to cope with stress. Our society is also experiencing breakdowns in cooperation and civility. An international airline reported a 300 percent increase in passengers abusing flight attendants between the years 1992 and 1995. Of the 900 incidents in 1995, 180 were *physical* attacks. A 1993 study by the Society for Human Resource Management indicated that out of 479 human resource managers surveyed, more than one-third responded that one or more violent acts were committed by employees at their companies since 1989, and that 80 percent of these had occurred since 1991.

The not-so-funny joke that has emerged regarding U.S. postal workers really tells the story about the impact of corporate abuses on society: "What do you do when confronted by an angry postal worker? Shoot back!"

I am not implying that corporations should do nothing to improve their performance. On the contrary, if our organizations are to create *significant, long-term* performance improvements and *contribute to a healthier society*, we must challenge our fundamental ideas about business management. Organizations must transform their basic nature—the underlying principles of management and organizational development—and weave a systemic, organic worldview into the very fabric of corporate life.

Classical Management: A Solution for an Era Gone By

"An unexamined life is not worth living," Plato advised. This is far more than just

Prisoners of Our Past Conditioning

some intellectual psychobabble: It holds the key to our freedom . . . our *freedom of mind*. The unconscious beliefs and assumptions that we have absorbed from the classical management model have become, as Deepak Chopra put it, "the prison of our past conditioning." We cannot escape this prison until we understand why we think what we think and do what we do. Reengineering—although deservedly vilified for its many abuses—is based on a valid premise: "Challenge your assumptions." The reason we have trouble managing organizations today is that we have not questioned whether the *fundamental assumptions*

and unconscious beliefs that power our thinking and drive our actions are still valid.

The classical management model emerged in response to problems that could not be solved through existing techniques. What were these problems? What was the environment in which command-and-control management was born? Once we understand the answers to these questions, it will become painfully obvious that the traditional management approach is irrelevant for the majority of the issues we face today. The classical management model was developed for a different world: for a different kind of production environment, for completely different social and competitive conditions, and for a different kind of employee.

At the inception of the American republic, corporations were chartered by the government for a finite period of time to perform public service works. Following the American Civil War in the mid-1800s, legislative changes allowed corporations to shift to their current mode—as machines for producing profit. Technological advances and the advent of industrial era mass production provided a remarkably successful mechanism for achieving this goal. However, in order to sustain this success, the capitalist owners and their professional managers had to address three major challenges over the period between 1865 and today:

1. Organizing and coordinating the efficient work of large numbers of workers

2. Harnessing the productive potential of new technologies

3. Responding effectively to new challenges in a complex and globally interdependent environment

Bureaucracy Is Beautiful

The shift from an agrarian to an industrial economy created the novel situation of placing a large mass of workers together under one roof to produce a common outcome. There were no management practices available at the time that could efficiently organize the efforts of such large groups. Max Weber, one of the founders of social psychology, promoted the idea of *bureaucracy* as the solution. (The fact that bureaucracy was developed as the solution to a problem serves as an exclamation point for the adage, "yesterday's solutions are today's problems.") Weber believed that bureaucracy was "the most efficient method of coordinating and accomplishing large-scale tasks."

All of the budding young social scientists wanted desperately to be taken seriously by the traditional sciences. The best way to make that happen was to base this fledgling science on Newtonian-Cartesian principles and methods. Weber developed a model for bureaucratic organizations that was almost entirely mechanistic. His pride in the technical elegance of his model led him to boast, "The decisive reason for the advancement of bureaucratic organizations has always been its purely technical superiority over any other form of organization."

There were six elements in Weber's model, most of which you will recognize as still active in the vast majority of governmental and private organizations today:

1. A clear-cut division of labor

2. A hierarchy of authority

3. Recruitment of managers based on technical knowledge and expertise

4. An explicit set of rules for making decisions

5. A strict separation of business and personal concerns

6. The establishment of career employment

The fact that bureaucracy was developed as the solution to a problem serves as an exclamation point for the adage, "yesterday's solutions are today's problems."

Bureaucracy was first devised for use in government, but it quickly spread to businesses. Many of the first CEOs were West Point–trained army engineers who brought with them pyramidal structures, orders flowing down "from on high," and unquestioning obedience. "If this system was insensitive to a worker's individuality, or boredom, or the desire to manage his or her own work," economist Jeffrey Madrick wrote, "it was well suited to managing an economy of giant, otherwise unwieldy companies."

Although bureaucracy provided many improvements over the original factory system, it was not up to the challenges of Henry Ford's mass production technologies. Managers at the turn of the twentieth century faced the daunting task of overseeing large-scale tasks in a highly mechanized environment using mostly unskilled laborers. Many of these workers had only recently migrated to America and did not speak English. Turnover among employees ranged as high as 400 percent per year. The management methods imported along with the factory system were proving completely inadequate for improving productivity and efficiency. What were they to do?

Scientific Management

Frederick W. Taylor, along with Frank and Lillian Gilbreth, had the answer. Taylor believed that the principles of classical science should be applied in the business context. *Management science* was the idea "that observation, measurement, classification, and the principles derived from these empirical studies should be applied to all managerial problems; that the methods by which work was accomplished should be determined by management through the same kind of investigation; and that workers should be 'scientifically' selected, trained, and developed."

Taylor wasn't the first to originate many of these ideas, although he was the first to popularize them. Adam Smith, writing in the *Wealth of Nations*, first proposed the idea of "division of labor" and the advantages it had for an efficient production system. The division of labor is a reductionist approach—production is broken down into increments of a few specialized tasks and each worker performs a few narrowly defined tasks. In 1832, Charles Babbage added to Smith's ideas by advocating the use of scientific method in the analysis of business problems and proposing the concept of "time and motion studies" to increase individual productivity on the job. These studies involved timing each task with a stopwatch and then rearranging work stations and the flow of materials through the plant. By 1911, the conditions were right for Taylor to combine these ideas into his Newtonian-Cartesian management model. Madrick described the scientific management approach in *The End of Affluence:*

> So-called scientific management reduced every task in the manufacturing process to its smallest components, with human effort itself as merely one component of a large machine. Work was divided and specialized into simple tasks, and then divided and specialized into even more simple ones. Rarely did any single worker perform all or even more than a few of the functions required to manufacture a product anymore. . . . *The machine became not only a model but a metaphor for human organization . . . and the worker was essentially another cog in the process.* (Italics added.)

With this fragmentation of tasks, how was an organization to put it all together into a coherent and cohesive process? This role fell to "the bosses"—supervisors and managers who could see the bigger picture. These people had "super vision" and each managerial level could "see" farther than the one below it. Authority, information, and access to resources were centralized with management. The boss was virtually omnipotent—he (they were all men in those days) was expected to know more than the employees, to have *all* of the answers, to control the work, and to do the thinking, planning, and strategizing. Workers were given information on a "need-to-know basis" and supervisors (or managers further up the chain) made all of the decisions. Managers were the true representatives of the company, whereas workers were just hired labor. You may recognize many of these attitudes at work in your organization even today. Although timing people with a stopwatch is no longer practiced, many artifacts of Taylorism still linger in our organizations.

> *Workers are adults, but once they walk through the plant gate companies transform them into children, forcing them to . . . ask the foreman for permission to go to the bathroom, bring in a doctor's note when they have been ill, and blindly follow instructions without asking any questions.*
>
> — Ricardo Semlar, CEO of Semco, author of *Maverick*

The Rise of Complexity

Most of the organizational innovation and change prior to 1970 was associated with production improvements and market growth. The implementation and deployment of computer systems brought a new kind of change that broke with a hundred years of management practices. The first computer systems did little more than automate manual procedures, a practice that has been scorned in recent years as "paving the cowpath." Still, these were large projects that required fundamental organizational changes.

Computerization required employees to acquire entirely new skills and to work in radically different ways. Also, computer systems often spanned several departments. This introduced some of the first experiences with systemic complexity. Classical management created an environment of functional specialization in separate departments, also known as "functional towers." Computer systems that crossed these boundaries redefined the connections and relationships between people, departments, and technologies and required a *process* rather than a *functional* orientation.

Large-scale computer system integration is where I received my initial experience in organizational change. I can attest that the traditional management practices proved wholly inadequate for dealing with these complexities. The evidence resides in the vast graveyard of failed technology implementations.

The TQM Movement

Difficulties in implementing computer systems began to illuminate the growing inadequacy of industrial era management practices, but they did not directly challenge them. That distinction belongs to Total Quality Management (TQM) and the continuous improvement movement. As I wrote in *Eating the Chocolate Elephant*, it was the threat of superior Japanese products and Xerox's response that ushered in American industry's mad scramble for quality:

> Because of the low retail prices of Japanese products, Xerox suspected them of dumping copiers in the United States to gain market share. Xerox decided to compare themselves to Japanese manufacturers. . . . the results were startling. They learned that the Japanese were so efficient that the Japanese product *retail* price was equivalent to the Xerox *manufacturing costs!* Compared to Japanese manufacturers, Xerox had nine times as many production suppliers, and seven times as many manufacturing defects; product lead times were twice as long; and it took five times as long to set up a production line.

Xerox's legendary response to this challenge produced huge improvements in quality and earned it the prestigious Malcolm Baldrige National Quality Award. However, few companies were as fortunate in their efforts to implement TQM. Western corporations simply were not prepared to implement the sweeping changes required to fully realize the benefits. The tenets of TQM involve questioning the fundamental ways in which we approach organizational management—a direct challenge to the command-and-control mind-set. In addition, the proposed changes—employee participation, empowerment, teamwork, continuous incremental improvement—required many years to implement, executive commitment, and a large financial investment. These qualifying factors were sure death for TQM in a culture with a decision-making horizon that extends no further than the next quarterly earnings report and that exalts individual contribution and heroic performances.

TQM was originally a call to transform the classical management model. Instead, for many it became a few skills, tools, and policies that were implemented using the very management practices it was intended to change. When Michael Hammer emerged with business process reengineering as an alternative to TQM, business management responded with gusto. Now here was a performance improvement practice that classical managers could embrace. It promised huge savings, took only a few months, and it did not touch the organization from the neck up—that is, it did not require changes of executive management or of the command-and-control mind-set.

New Challenges Require New Approaches

Unfortunately, reengineering rarely delivered the goods. The problem that organizations now face is that after half a decade of reengineering and extreme cost cutting, corporate operating results are not much—if any—better. Worse yet, organizations' ability to respond to new challenges has been seriously damaged. Employees have become cynical, resentful, over-stressed, and physically and emotionally exhausted. And most ominous of all, global competition and technological innovation are still intensifying. The worst is yet to come.

> *This is the end of the industrial age. . . . the institutions that supported this age are dying.*
>
> — Gerald Celente, futurist

Our present-day managerial techniques prepare us perfectly for managing the industrial organization of 1965. Unfortunately, we are most unprepared for the complex, high-tech, and fast-changing world here at the cusp of the twenty-first century. Not only are our traditional approaches ineffective, they are also toxic, both to humans and to the Earth. We desperately need new techniques for operating our organizations—new models of understanding and new skills for managing—that are more balanced, ecological, and better suited for the complex and interdependent world in which we live.

The Quantum Worldview: The World As a Living Web

We can start by looking where we have always looked when we want to make sense of the world—to Nature, which effortlessly creates order out of chaos and manages complexity with ease. How is order maintained without some master plan? How does Nature fend off disintegration without someone in charge to control, plan, and organize everything? How does it create and sustain balanced and healthy ecosystems? How does it manage the tension between competition and cooperation? The answers to these questions, emerging from the sciences of quantum physics, chaos theory, and self-organizing systems offer us much hope. These new sciences present a new and profoundly different view of the world that is far more relevant and immediate to the concerns of managing complexity and change.

When Descartes probed into the workings of Nature, he saw a clock-like machine and built an entire philosophy around this metaphor. The principle tenets of his lifeless mechanistic world—dominance and control, reductionism, determinism, and materialism—provided the foundation from which our modern social institutions have evolved. The result has been the fragmentation and alienation of humans from Nature, from each other, and even from our own bodies and souls. Danah Zohar, writing in *The Quantum Self* emphasized that, "the mechanical worldview successfully gave us a science that explained things, and a technology to exploit them as never before, but the price paid was a kind of alienation at every level of life."

The central metaphor of the new science is that of an organic web—a dynamic and evolving network of relationships. The primary tenets of this life-affirming philosophy are wholeness, balance, connectedness, cooperation, creativity, and open possibilities. If our society had evolved out of these concepts instead of those of the Newtonian-Cartesian machine, what would it look like? If we adopt these organic principles now, what will our society look like for our children and their children? I believe that the human race can change its self-destructive trajectory if we adopt the principles of the quantum worldview and begin to immediately apply them in all that we do.

Business As Driver of Social Change

Although *all* of society must change, this book addresses the business arena because that is where my expertise lies. I believe deeply that if the world is to change, it will be an inside-out process for every single person. However, business will have an important role to play in the greater social transformation. There are two reasons for this. The first is that businesses have the funds and interest to change in ways that benefit them, and the quantum worldview most certainly would do that. Second, businesses are the most powerful social force in the world today. R. Kaku, chairman of Canon, Inc., believes that nations are lead by politicians who must seek the best interest of their countries. It is left to global businesses—which must have a peaceful and stable world in which to operate—to lead the way.

Joseph Campbell, famous historian and philosopher, noted that over the years the largest structures in society always have been associated with the most powerful institution:

> You can tell what's informing a society by what the tallest building is. When you approach a medieval town, the [church] cathedral is the tallest thing in the place. When you approach an eighteenth-century town, it is the political palace that is the tallest thing in the place. And when you approach a modern city, the tallest places are the office buildings, the centers of economic life.

The Edge of Chaos

There is one field of inquiry in the new science of complexity that has particular relevance to business: the workings of *complex adaptive systems* (also referred to as "self-organizing" or "living" systems). Because the study of self-organizing systems grew out of the biological sciences, many of the original concepts are related to biological organisms. As the principles that defined organisms as living systems became known, it became obvious that they possessed applications across a wide spectrum. Today, we are able to apply the concepts of living systems to the Earth, companies, institutions, families, and to the human body and mind.

> Living systems operate in complex environments where centralized control would be a one-way ticket to extinction.

Through the work of such pioneering scientists as Ludwig von Bertalanffy, Ilya Prigogene, Humberto Maturana, Francisco Varela, Gregory Bateson, and others, we know quite a bit about the behavior and characteristics of these living systems. For instance, natural systems are able to achieve a high degree of stability, despite constant environmental challenges and disruptions, with *no visible locus of control*. Can we imagine a universe where, as biologist Stuart Kaufman puts it, we get "order for free"? This is so alien to our experience in business that it may be difficult to even entertain. But that is because natural systems operate in fundamentally different ways. In business we expend huge amounts of energy to force control onto the organization. We know that if we let up even a little, performance will slip, goals will not be met, and heads will roll. Living systems operate in complex environments where centralized control would be a one-way ticket to extinction. Nature *had* to develop a system where central control was not necessary. Instead of control, Nature has *order*, and they are not the same thing.

Complex adaptive systems walk the tightrope between too much structure and too little. With too much structure, organic systems become rigid and unresponsive to the environment. They eventually die. If they are too unstructured, they become too sensitive to environmental disturbances. They can't maintain their organization, and so eventually disintegrate. When natural systems reach critical levels of instability—that is, when they operate sufficiently far from equilibrium, but have not slipped into chaos—they creatively self-organize into higher levels of order that are both more complex and more stable. It is at the boundary between these two conditions—*at the edge of chaos*—that living systems are most flexible and have the greatest potential for novelty and creativity.

Ralph Stacey, writing in *Complexity and Creativity in Organizations*, explains that there are three factors that drive the behavior and complexity of living systems:

1. The rate and volume of information flow in the system

2. The richness of connectivity between agents in the system

3. The level of diversity within and between the agents in the system

Each of these conditions has expanded exponentially in our global social systems during the past two decades, generating an unprecedented degree of complexity and creating an atmosphere where the rules that govern machines are no longer effective, or even relevant. Instead:

The business environment and society as a whole must yield to the rules that govern the behavior of complex adaptive systems.

The realization that organizations are living systems is of profound importance to business management. While we have attempted to control companies through techniques designed for machines, they have operated under a completely different set of rules—those of *living systems*. These systems operate in a distinctive fashion and follow underlying principles very different from those we use in our organizations and institutions today.

The Quantum Organization

Traditional bureaucratic organizations were designed for stability, for creating predictable and certain results. This seemed to work well so long as the environment remained stable, which it generally did for many decades. We can picture these organizations in our minds as immense blocks of stone—solid and immobile. The problem with this design is that bureaucracies cannot easily make large changes. When the need arose, it required the effort of many people to push this immense block of stone until it slid, ever so reluctantly, to a new position. Imagine the sweat and effort demanded of the employees, the yelling and threatening that was required from managers. No wonder people collapsed when the job was done with cries of relief: "Thank goodness *that's* over with!" Then, a long while later, another change became necessary, but the employees were fairly well rested by then and so were up to the task.

The same is not true here at the turn of the twentieth century. Despite all of the changes in recent years, 95 percent of all companies are *still* bureaucratic, and we are being assailed from all sides by the need for change. Now when we muster our forces to shove this massive stone around, we find a workforce that is already exhausted. And workers are cynical: Because the changes take so long, employees never get through with one change before the next one is ordered— often with a dramatic change of direction. Verbal threats no longer work, so managers are now "thinning the ranks" and using the threat of termination to motivate the "survivors." In response, the employees have done the one thing they have control over—they have shifted into a mode of self-preservation. They no longer earnestly try to make the changes happen. Instead, they make it *look* like they are trying. They grunt and sweat like always, but they are not putting any effort into it. They know that before long, they will have to shove the stone in another direction anyway, so why try? Besides, they are angry, bitter, and resentful over their poor treatment and are constantly on the lookout for ways to get revenge. Not a pretty picture!

Now, imagine that managers finally realize they cannot continue in this way. They meet with the employees and agree to partner with them in a "meta-change" effort. Since the need to change is constant and unavoidable, they decide to transform the shape—the fundamental nature—of the organization to make future changes easier. A massive block of stone is disaster to a change effort. What if they rounded its corners so it would roll instead of slide? What if they lessened its weight by making it smaller? Small groups of employees would have no trouble rolling these lighter balls from place to place. Not only that, they would not need managers to force them to do so. Instead, the people in the organization could collectively determine a direction, and then empower the leaders to point the way. Leaders could help teams realize they are off course, and assist them to regain alignment with the whole. If teams crashed together, leaders could work with them to learn how to avoid future crashes. Under this new scheme, front-line employees would be responsible for the movement of the organization, not the managers. Changes would be fairly simple. The challenge for leaders would be to assist in coordinating activities and clarifying the organization's current status and direction, not to carry the burden of responsibility for the whole organization.

I use the term *Quantum Organization* to describe such companies. These organizations, which operate on the principles of living systems, are characterized by openness, flexibility, responsiveness, resilience, creativity, vitality, balance, and caring. The organic principles on which Quantum Organizations are based include an emphasis on indivisible wholeness, dynamic balance,

> Quantum Organizations—which operate based on the principles of living systems—are characterized by openness, flexibility, responsiveness, resilience, creativity, vitality, balance, and caring.

creativity and experimentation, autonomous action in accord with the whole, relationship, openness, purpose and meaning, and flexibility.

The subsequent attributes of the Quantum Organization include personal leadership and responsibility, flexible network structures, democratic participation, openness with information, open interactions between people, diverse people and opinions, connection and belonging, a powerful sense of purpose, teamwork and partnering, focus on creating value for all stakeholders, rational and nonrational knowledge, balanced short-term and long-term goals, and trust, enthusiasm, and confidence. Best-selling author Sally Helgesen, writing in *The Web of Inclusion*, describes the tremendous potential of such organizations:

> The "dynamic connectedness" of the web means that web [quantum] organizations reflect organic rather than mechanical principles; that is, *they work in the same way that life does.* This naturally makes them more congenial environments for human beings to exist in; more nourishing, more favorable for growth. This congeniality is important, for as we move away from the notion of the organization as a great machine—rational, static, compartmentalized and closed—we also move away from perhaps *the* essential aspect of the estrangement of human beings from nature that took root in the Industrial Revolution: the belief that, to be efficient organizations must mimic the design and workings of a machine.

This book is dedicated to realizing the vision of a transformative shift of business, away from the obsolete and destructive bureaucratic organization, toward the life-affirming model of the Quantum Organization. Our future success—the achievement of our collective hopes and dreams—depends on it.

Chapter Two

The Way of Living Systems

I am convinced that the nations and people
who master the new sciences of complexity
will become the economic, cultural, and
political superpowers of the next century.

— *Heinz Pagels, Physicist*

We have a new story to tell about our relationship with Nature, with life. In learning the way of living systems, leading scientists have developed a quantum worldview that offers a whole new way of being that is ecological, systemic, and life-affirming. In this chapter, we will explore the seven organic principles of living systems that we must understand if we are to develop Quantum Organizations.

The concepts that have emerged out of the new science—everything is interconnected, things only seem to be separate because of how we look at them, there are only dynamic processes, living systems self-organize—are difficult for our Cartesian-trained minds to comprehend. Nevertheless, it is how science, the same discipline that gave us the mechanistic worldview, now understands the world. If we hope to operate more effectively in this complex world, we need to learn and apply the principles of the new science as we currently do those of the old.

Self-Organizing Systems

General systems theory was officially introduced by Ludwig von Bertalanffy in the late 1930s. Bertalanffy was the first to use the term *open* to describe the behavior of systems that "feed on a continual flux of matter and energy from the environment to stay alive." Later, these were called "self-organizing" systems. There are several key characteristics of these systems:

- They are "wholes" that are greater than the sum of their parts.

- They are open systems operating far from equilibrium that continually renew themselves through reciprocal interactions with their environment.

- They have the capacity to spontaneously create new forms of order, behavior, and structure.

- They are interconnected in complex, nonlinear ways.

- They are both autonomous from, and merged with, their environments.

Most experts agree that there are two general types of systems. All self-organizing systems qualify as the first, commonly called *dissipative structures*. This simplest form of self-organizing system is pervasive throughout Nature. Snowflakes, whirlpools, and chemical reactions are all examples. The second type, called *complex adaptive systems,* has the characteristics of dissipative structures with the added ability to use its behavior and actions to actively sustain an identity.

There are two other terms that are sometimes used to describe self-organizing systems. They are *autopoietic* and *chaordic*. Humberto Maturana and Francisco Varela, two leaders in the science of living systems, use the term *autopoiesis* to describe the processes of self-organizing systems. Autopoiesis, translated from the Greek root, means "self-making." It is through their ability to "self-make," or "self-organize," that autopoietic systems are able to establish autonomy from their environment—a key characteristic of living systems.

Dee Hock, past president of VISA, coined the word *chaordic* (from "chaos" and "order") to describe the novel organizational arrangement he set up at VISA. Hock encouraged as much initiative as possible throughout the organization (chaos), while building in mechanisms for cooperation (order). The resulting organization—a fully functioning complex adaptive system—was expected to surpass a *trillion dollars* in sales by the end of 1996.

The range of systems that qualify as complex adaptive systems is surprisingly wide. These include all higher organisms such as humans, animals, plants, and many lower organisms. It also includes human cells, certain structures within those cells (like mitochondria), the brain and internal systems (such as the immune system), the mind (which transcends the brain and nervous system), and ideas (those that take the form of coherent models, beliefs, or institutions). All coherent forms of human organization are also complex adaptive systems. This encompasses families, companies, teams, departments, religious organizations, social institutions, and humankind. And finally, through Lynn Margulis and James Lovelock's Gaia theory, we understand the Earth itself to be a living system.

Dissipative Structures

In the 1960s, Belgium chemist Ilya Prigogene provided the first detailed description of how these self-organizing systems operate. Prigogene is the Nobel Prize winner who pioneered the study of one of the simplest forms of self-organizing systems, which he termed "dissipative structures." The second law of thermodynamics (better known as *entropy*), states that all closed systems give off energy that is never recovered, so they "wind down" to a point of complete equilibrium. This equilibrium is not a balanced state, it is a static state where there is no change—just stillness. Equilibrium, in fact, can be equated with death. Classical science saw the universe as a closed system, winding down to its ultimate and unavoidable demise. We can see entropy at work today in isolated and closed

> Classical science saw the universe as a closed system, winding down to its ultimate and unavoidable demise. But there is one small exception to the law of entropy—*living things*.

systems such as automobiles and other machines. (When automobiles run out of gas, they stop; they don't go fill themselves back up again.) Only human intervention staves off the inevitable breakdown—the negative entropy—of our machines. This metaphor has pervaded much of our thinking and has contributed substantially to our desperate need for control, which is so very evident in organizational life. There is one small exception to the law of entropy—*living things*.

Prigogene studied chemicals. Surely there is nothing living about *them*. They just sit in test tubes and do nothing. If he poured red and blue chemicals together they did exactly as entropy would have them do, they turned purple and stayed that way—until he made the environment more complex by creating a disturbance. When he added more of the chemicals, heated the mixture, or added different chemicals, a strange thing happened. The chemical mixture didn't stay purple. When the chemical solution reached a critical level of instability (called the *bifurcation point*) it changed to red and then to blue in an oscillating pattern that continued as long as the disturbances continued.

Well now, this was something altogether new. These chemical reactions, called "chemical clocks" due to their oscillating pattern, consume a lot of energy. But they *renew* themselves by drawing more energy from the environment. Despite constant change and the dissipation of energy (conditions of instability and disequilibrium that organizations generally fear) the chemicals form a very stable structure but only as long as they stay open to the environment. As soon as the disturbances stop, the mixture returns to equilibrium and regains its purple color. These chemical structures display the dynamics of self-organization in its simplest form, "exhibiting most of the phenomena characteristic of life—self-renewal, adaptation, evolution, and even primitive forms of 'mental' processes."

We now understand through the study of these dissipative structures that *disorder*, paradoxically, can be a source of *order*. This is a fundamental shift from how we normally view disturbances in organizations.

How Self-Organizing Systems Work

Interestingly enough, the emergence of the Newtonian-Cartesian worldview in the 1600s illustrates some of the key characteristics of self-organizing systems. When Nicholas Copernicus published his heliocentric view of the universe in the 1500s, he was generating a creative disturbance, called *positive feedback,* in the dominant thought system. For three hundred years prior to that, the Church had used *negative feedback* (via the torturers and executioners of the Inquisition) to crush out all opposition and maintain the status quo. The Church's *purpose* was to remain the dominant force in society, and it demonstrated that it would do anything to protect that position. The Church was rigidly locked into its belief system, which created *stability* for the system but also created a condition of *maladaptive learning* that prevented it from evolving in sync with the larger social system.

In fighting off the threat of new ideas and refusing to change, the Church unwittingly made itself vulnerable to emerging thought systems that were better adapted to the times. New technologies (such as Gutenberg's printing press) were increasing the amount of information available to system agents: Copernicus, Galileo, Kepler, and many others. Diversity of scientific opinion was expanding as scientists asked new questions and got new answers. And the interactions between the agents (scientists and philosophers) in the system increased in frequency. All of these conditions led to the gradual formation of a new system of thought that culminated in the classical Newtonian-Cartesian worldview.

At first the new system was developed in the shadows, far from the repressive action of the Church. Through extensive trial and error, changes and improvements, this "shadow" system gradually grew in strength. Finally, it reached a level of critical mass and emerged to challenge the dominant system. The maladaptive Church system was unable to respond to the "disturbance" in creative ways. When the negative feedback process could no longer contain the change, the Church system was overwhelmed. In very short order the new system overtook and effectively subsumed the old worldview. The dominant belief system self-organized to a higher form of order and stability—a whole new mind-set. Ironically, the same fate is now falling on the mechanistic Newtonian-Cartesian thought system.

The Seven Organic Principles of Living Systems

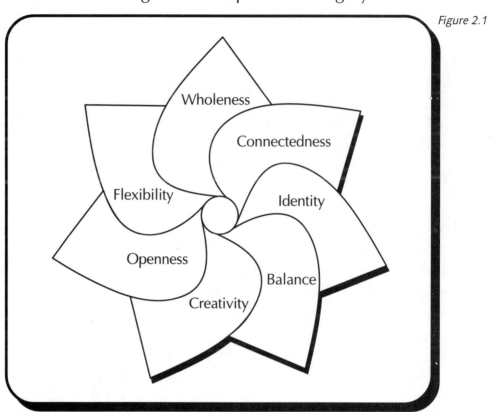

Figure 2.1

The previous example illustrates some of the main concepts in the functioning of living systems. Figure 2.1 illustrates the seven organic principles of self-organizing systems:

1. *Wholeness.* Systems are "wholes" with properties that are emergent, that is, greater than the sum of their parts. Systems cannot be reduced to the operation and characteristics of the individual components.

2. *Connectedness.* Systems are indivisibly interconnected in complex, nonlinear ways. The intricate connectedness of living systems makes it virtually impossible to establish and understand clear causes and effects.

3. *Identity.* A system organizes around a central idea, a strong identity and sense of purpose that transcends its changing structure. Agents in a system have substantial autonomy and act in self-assertive ways, but their actions are integrative and in harmony with the whole. The agents are guided in their actions to maintain the whole by a few key organizing principles.

4. *Balance.* Living systems establish a dynamic balance—a fluctuating stability that is far from equilibrium—among its key parameters. Living systems seek to optimize, not to maximize.

5. *Creativity.* Although most small changes and disturbances are suppressed through negative feedback, certain novel and creative changes are amplified by the system as positive feedback. Feedback systems, then, both maintain the system through self-renewal, and cause it to evolve to whole new levels of order and complexity through self-transcendence. This ability to form whole new levels of order is Nature's true source of creativity.

6. *Openness.* Creativity in systems is increased through three factors: (1) the agents in the system interact extensively both internally and externally, (2) information is rich and diverse and flows freely, and (3) there is tremendous diversity in the system, which is expressed through the agents. Stability is maintained through identity, boundaries, canalization, and maladaptive learning.

7. *Flexibility.* There is tremendous plasticity and flexibility in the system. Processes and flows constantly organize structures to match environmental conditions.

Closed Systems, Closed Minds

When we compare these characteristics of living systems to the design and operation of most of our modern social systems, we see two very different pictures. It is almost as if we have deliberately created *closed* systems that have no choice but to succumb to the law of entropy. The classical management model counts as successful those behaviors that minimize disruptions and unpredictable variations, support rigid structures, restrain the flow of information, control the actions and interactions of the system's agents, and maximize predictability and risk avoidance. Organizations try to ensure their safety and success through planning, predicting and controlling their environment, and they believe with certainty that this is achievable (and failure to do so is a "career-ending mistake"). Given this mind-set, it is inevitable that organizations see variations and disturbances, autonomous action, and creativity as threats.

Rigidity, fear, and equilibrium are the norm in modern organizations. And they are *certain death* for living systems. We can understand rigidity in fixed biological structures. The human body, for instance, cannot just grow another arm because it would make us more efficient. But organizations are not "real" in a physical sense. Corporations, as one example, are only abstractions, hypothetical mental constructs that do not exist anywhere in space-time. The question that has puzzled me in helping companies through large-scale organizational change is, "What makes these companies so rigid and resistant to change?" The rigidity cannot normally be explained by physical limitations. The physical assets of a company—even when they are substantial—are not really limitations, as the retooling of the steel and auto industries have proven. Rather, I have come to understand that it is our *ideas* that are rigid.

It is a humbling realization to discover that we are our own jailers. Few systems are as easily adaptable as our minds, and yet we have somehow managed to make them some of the most rigid in Nature. Throughout human history—but particularly since Descartes—we have deluded ourselves into believing that our mental models of the world were accurate and complete. Joseph Campbell, celebrated scholar and philosopher, warned us of the danger of "concretizing" our beliefs. When we make the mistake of confusing our mental models for reality itself, we are "confusing the map for the territory." This, Campbell maintained, is the equivalent of going into a restaurant, seeing food pictured on the menu, and starting to eat the menu. Worldviews are just mental abstractions of an

> Few systems are as easily adaptable as are our minds, and yet we have somehow managed to make them some of the most rigid in Nature.

unknowable reality. As our experiences change and our knowledge increases, our mental models—whether they are religious doctrines, economic theories, or management models—must change too. Human evolution has for the past 50,000 years been primarily a function of social, not biological change. Before we will be able to create adaptive business systems, we must create adaptive mental systems.

Wholeness: Systems As Indivisible Wholes

Systems are "wholes" that have emergent properties—that is, the whole is greater than, and cannot be reduced to, its parts. This view is sharply divergent from that of the Cartesian "machine." You can buy the chemicals that comprise the human body for a few dollars. However, if you pour them into a bathtub, they don't form themselves into a human. The "whole" of a person is greater than its parts. In systems, the whole organizes the parts, and any sense of order at one level derives from the self-organizing activities at a higher level. This is the functioning of a system's integrative capacity. Your mind is an emergent quality of not just the various neurons in the brain and nervous system, but also the immune and endocrine systems. If you dissect a brain, the integrative qualities are destroyed. You have bits and pieces of protoplasm, but you do not have a human mind.

In business, we commonly engage in activities to "build," "engineer," or "architect" various aspects of our organizations. Our Newtonian-Cartesian belief is that if we can assemble the right parts in just the right way, we will maximize efficiency and profits. In taking this approach, we disregard the integrative aspects of our living systems—the intricate interconnections and relationships that produce the organization. Much of the human trauma experienced during organizational change is related to the violent severing of delicate interconnections between people, their favored activities, their hopes and values, and even their sense of identity. The grief and low morale that accompanies most change efforts are a direct result of the loss associated with these sudden separations.

Developing vs. Building

On America's northwest coastline, there are old-growth forests that have caused substantial political turmoil. Paper companies want the lumber; environmentalists want to retain the integrity of the ancient forests. Corporate interests make the mistaken assertion that new trees can be planted to rebuild the forest. The key word here is "build"—the word *build* means "to put together by assembling parts." A forest cannot be *built*. Like all living systems, forests *develop* in an organic fashion, strand upon strand, from the smallest organisms to the largest, until a complex and diverse network of interdependent relationships emerge. Organizations are living systems too, they also develop; they cannot be built. The truth of this can be seen in countless examples where well-meaning leaders have built a team by gathering the most talented individuals available—only to have them underperform expectations by a considerable margin.

In Quantum Organizations, management is concerned with how an organization develops as it moves toward its goals. The word *develop* means "to unfold gradually, to realize the potentialities of, to grow, to bring into being." An acorn has in it the unrealized potential to be a great oak. As it develops, it increasingly seeks its potential until it finally achieves its full majesty. Do you *build* an oak tree? Do you *build* a skilled employee? Quite obviously we do not. But what about a team, or an entire organization—do we *build* them? The answer is an unequivocal no. If we want high-performing, Quantum Organizations, we need to orient our activities and intentions toward "developing" rather than "building."

Connectedness: Everything is Related

Interdependent nesting is a primary characteristic of self-organizing systems. Fritjof Capra notes that, "the tendency to associate, establish links, live inside one another, and cooperate is an essential characteristic of living organisms." Systems contain other systems and are also a subset of greater systems. When viewing systems as a subsystem, I call them *agents*, and when viewed as the greater system, I call them *hosts,* or simply *systems*. Systems nest in several ways. Some—such as humans in relation to the Earth—are nested within one another like concentric circles. While others—such as the systems of the human body, or such social systems as religions, governments, and businesses—interpenetrate each other like interlocking circles.

When I refer to my body as being mine, there are many organisms that would take exception. The human body is home for many bacteria and other micro-organisms that are also autonomous beings. Some of them are vital to our ability to digest food, and they depend on us for food and shelter. In this symbiotic relationship, I am their host, and they are agents in the system that I call me. Human cells are living systems, as are many of the cells' organelles. Mitochondria, the powerhouse that provides almost all of a cell's energy, is a system that can replicate itself independent of the cell. Humans, of course, are one of many agents who live in a symbiotic relationship with the greatest living system in our direct experience—the Earth. In business, we see nested systems in the interactions of people, teams, departments, divisions, companies, industries, economies, and so on.

> Living systems are inextricably merged with their environment—they produce one another in a cooperative dance of co-evolution.

It might be easy, given our materialistic perspective, to see systems as separate physical objects that interact. That would be a mistake. The nesting of systems is intricate and indivisible. Cells in our bodies can be viewed independently, but they can't *exist* independently. Nor can humans exist without the whole of greater social and environmental systems to provide the integrative flows that sustain us. Living systems are inextricably merged with their environment. These symbiotic interactions are so tightly entwined that systems cannot be considered as separate from their environments—they produce one another in a cooperative dance of co-evolution.

This idea has powerful implications for business. No longer can companies maintain the illusion that the pursuit of their own welfare is separate and independent from the welfare of the greater social environment. The qualities of one will dictate the qualities of the other. They will live or die together.

Power Distribution in Natural Systems

Although there is a hierarchy in the nesting of agents and host systems, it is not related to distribution of power and control as it is in human-created systems. Our belief in hierarchical power originated first in the dominator model that came to us—as philosopher Rianne Eisler outlined in *The Chalice and the Blade*—5,000 years ago as the legacy of invading nomadic tribes. Later we added support to our belief in hierarchy through the image of a machine that has a hierarchical ordering of components and subcomponents. But, as Morris Berman explained in *The Re-enchantment of the World*, "there is no way one can demonstrate that hierarchy [as we think of it in business] is validated by the natural world." Rather, hierarchy (stratified order) in living systems refers to the *organization of complexity.*

Physicist Fritjof Capra deliberately constructs his models of systemic hierarchy as a tree with the highest level located at the roots and the lowest level at the ends of the branches. (The "levels" that we refer to do not really exist separately; they are only a result of the level of the observer's attention.) He notes that, "as a real tree takes its nourishment through its roots and its leaves, so the power in a system's tree flows in both directions, with neither end dominating the other and all levels interacting in interdependent harmony to support the functioning of the whole." Although I have recently seen more corporate organization charts with management at the bottom and front-line workers (or customers) at the top, the reality of the situations does not always agree with such charts. The recognition that power in a healthy system is nonlocal, and is spread throughout the system, will be a challenging shift for many businesses.

Identity: Organizing Independent Action

We have all heard expressions like "keep the big picture in mind," "we can't see the forest for the trees," "remember what we're here for," and "we're losing sight of the goal." We have many such expressions in business that relate to the idea that the "whole" and the "parts" often have different interests and concerns. Our general tendency is to focus on local and parochial concerns and forget the interests of the higher system—the business itself. Often, businesses also forget about the interests of higher systems—society and the environment. In the systems approach, it is essential that we balance the welfare of the larger system with our own. A strong organizational *identity* provides the self-reference that makes this possible.

Integration and Self-Assertion

Nested systems have the opposite but complementary qualities of *integration* and *self-assertion*. Integration is the process of cooperating and acting as part of the whole. Without this tendency, agents would destroy the greater systems through self-maximizing behaviors. Self-assertion, which is the tendency toward autonomy, is also essential for maintaining a system's stratified order. Without this differentiation, life could not have evolved past unicelled organisms. Stratification is one of the characteristics that gives organisms their resilience and flexibility. So in any living system, the agents are both cooperating in sustaining the whole and expressing their unique identity through autonomous action.

It is important to note that self-assertion in living systems is a process of *individuation*, not of *individualism*. There is a significant difference between the two concepts. Self-assertive agents are highly individual—in fact their diversity is essential to the healthy functioning of the whole. At the same time, self-assertive agents demonstrate a high-degree of accountability for the whole. Their actions are not so autonomous as to endanger the whole. "Act Locally— Think Globally" is a fundamental catchphrase for self-organizing systems. The core skill of "personal leadership" addresses the idea that each person must accept responsibility for both autonomous action and the welfare of the whole organization.

Western society, in contrast, has venerated the "rugged individualist" as a high ideal. *Individualism* is the assertion of our own will and personality and would be more appropriately called *egoism*, which is defined as the ethical belief that self-interest is the best motive for all human conduct. The concept of laissez faire and our entire capitalist system is based on individualism, not individuation. Individualism maximizes the welfare of one individual and is destructive for the rest of the system. The maximizing of any

> *Any system that maximizes certain variables, violating the natural steady-state conditions that would optimize these variables, is by definition in runaway, and ultimately, it has no more chance for survival than an alcoholic or a steam engine without a governor.*
>
> — Morris Berman, author of *The Re-enchantment of the World*

variable in a living system leads to a "vicious circle" that inevitably ends in the demise of the runaway system and possibly even the host system.

Living systems require diverse thinking and acting combined with accountability for the whole. But Western society has created the explosive combination of homogenous thinking and self-serving individualism. Empowerment, which is certainly a step in the right direction, is doomed to fail under these circumstances. Corporations are filled with employees who have been programmed their whole lives for compliance and dependency in the presence of authority. These same employees have been trained to "do unto others before they do unto you" and "get while the gettin's good" and have learned that "nice guys finish last" and "you'd better look out for number one!" In many companies, as soon as controlling restraints are removed, employees explode into self-serving behaviors. A few disasters later, the "empowerment program" becomes just another management fad tossed onto the quick-fix garbage heap. In Quantum Organizations, empowerment is not a "thing" that is sought after. Rather, it is an emergent characteristic. Chris

Turner, the "Learning Person" for Xerox Business Services, supported this perspective in a recent *Fast Company* magazine interview:

> The only thing that makes sense to me is to think of empowerment as an outcome of environmental conditions. You create an environment for learning [a Quantum Organization], with empowerment as an outcome. When you start to think like that, you go from an empowerment strategy to a change strategy to where we are now—it's just our business strategy.

The Role of the Big Picture

Systems at every level are interdependent. For instance, we are interdependent with both the bacteria in our intestines (a lower order) and our employers (a higher order). It is normal (in Western society) for people to focus on their own point of view—their issues, needs, and intentions. However, humans are unique in their ability to raise the level of identification—that is, of their ideals and concerns—to a higher order. The degree of pettiness or greatness that pervades organizations is related in large measure to the hierarchical level with which individual agents place their attention. If I identify with only my needs and focus on the system at that level, my behaviors are going to be consistently petty and self-serving. If I am able to *balance* this by also identifying with a higher system order—such as my team, division, or company—my perspective has been raised, and I will behave in a manner that balances the greater system's needs with mine.

Politics, bickering, in-fighting, and selfishness are less an indication of character flaws than they are an absence of a shared vision that transcends individual concerns.

We have within us the capacity to identify with systems much greater than ourselves. In crisis situations, such as earthquakes, people suddenly come together in selfless action. The crisis provides a noble vision and raises people's identification to the level of community. Religions constantly attempt to "raise people's eyes to heaven" in an effort to get them to identify with the highest of all the hierarchical orders—"universal mind" or God. According to Reverend David W. McClure, senior minister of Unity Church in Dallas, Texas, the word *prayer* originally meant "looking at the facts of life from the highest point of view." Achieving identification with God places us in constant accord with the highest expression of human ideals. Likewise, companies that are able to create a compelling vision and strong cultural identity that is shared by all employees are able to consistently keep employees' attention on the big picture and off of petty needs. Businesses must also reframe their big picture to take in systems that are higher than themselves. Politics, bickering, in-fighting, and selfishness are less an indication of character flaws than they are an absence of a shared vision that transcends individual concerns. In the quantum worldview, the processes in which the big picture is established and maintained—that is, how it becomes *shared* by all of the employees—is an integral part of organizational success.

Universal Principles: The Power of Invisible Controls

Theoretically, every human cell is capable of reproducing the entire body. This remarkable capability stems from a microscopic chemical called DNA, which contains the genetic code for the entire body. However, each cell uses only the parts that are relevant to it. In this way, the human body resembles the construction of a holograph in that all of the pieces contain the whole. This is a powerful model for organizing autonomous behavior in organizations.

> Nature creates complexity through a few organizing principles that are shared "holographically" by every agent in the system.

Nature establishes a few organizing principles that are shared by every agent in the system. The agents are then free to interact, experiment, create, and act independently—guided by principles that ensure the welfare and advancement of the overall system. Scientists have been able to recreate rudimentary systems that behave in much the same way. In one such experiment, humorously called "Boids," a computer program simulated the flocking behavior of birds using just three universal rules. Ralph Stacey explains that, "Boids learned to flock, to part around obstacles, and to regroup afterward. No central program determined the flocking strategy and no agent was in charge, instructing the others what to do."

Fractals provide another way to understand the organizing power of universal principles. Benoit Mandelbrot, one of the framers of "chaos theory," coined the term *fractal* to describe patterns in Nature that repeat themselves at different levels of magnification or complexity. Nature uses simple fractal patterns in combination and at increasing levels of complexity to create an astonishing variety of forms. You can see fractals in the patterns of clouds, rivers, leaves, broccoli, and snowflakes. The fractal pattern is self-similar in that it is always recognizable, but never the same.

Not only are fractals *within* a structure similar, but fractal patterns recur *across* different kinds of systems. For instance, the pattern of a river network closely resembles that of tree branches, lightning bolts, human blood vessels and nerve systems, and veins in leaves. Photographer Eliot Porter and author James Gleick collaborated in the creation of a photographic essay called *Nature's Chaos* that dramatically illustrated these remarkable similarities. It includes photos of waves breaking on a beach that look like solidified lava flows, glaciers that look like rivers, and fractal patterns etched in sand that extend to infinity.

Scientists have created fractal patterns on computers through repeated iterations of simple nonlinear mathematical formulas. From these simple beginnings, remarkably intricate and elaborate structures emerge. One example of this, the *Julia set*, demonstrates the self-similarity of the structures formed over *trillions* of iterations. Scientists are using this concept to engineer complex behavior in robots. They establish a few simple rules of behavior and program the devices to combine the rules as needed to meet their objectives. The result is sophisticated behaviors and problem-solving abilities that would have been practically impossible to program on a case-by-case basis. These robots, incidentally, range from human-sized to microscopic devices cut from silicon. The possibilities for molecule-sized machines capable of complex self-directed behavior are simply staggering.

This approach has powerful implications for organizing behavior in human systems as well. Human organizations have always employed a few guiding principles, shared universally, to organize and direct behavior. We call them by many different names, including beliefs, intentions, memories, values, schemas, rules, culture, and mores. Religious institutions have understood the power of this unconscious programming for millennia. Few businesses, however, have taken the power of guiding principles to heart.

Companies that do emphasize the controls inherent in a strong central identity and guiding principles have proven to be both remarkably resilient to change and enormously successful. Collins and Porras, writing in *Built to Last*, reported on eighteen "visionary" companies that had out-performed the stock market average by 1500 percent (15:1) over forty years. They calculated that between 1926 and 1990, "$1 [invested] in the visionary companies stock fund would have grown to $6,356," whereas the same dollar invested in the general market fund would have grown to a paltry $415! Through extensive research, they concluded that these companies shared a few fundamental principles that formed the basis for their success. The principles they uncovered are highly consistent with the tenets of the quantum worldview:

- *Preserve the core/stimulate progress.* A strong core ideology (identity) provides these companies with self-reference that guides them through even the roughest times. Also, they emphasize the need to constantly change and challenge the "old ways" in order to counteract any tendency toward equilibrium.

- *Cult-like cultures.* Individual behavior can be relatively autonomous because these companies have created a powerful shared culture that guides behavior nonlocally.

- *Clock building, not time telling.* Visionary companies tend to focus on building self-renewing and self-transcending processes into the company rather than relying on "hero leadership."

- *Try a lot of stuff and keep what works.* One of the hallmarks of visionary companies is their willingness to engage in "messy" trial and error. They are

concerned with finding something that works—not with getting it perfect the first time.

Dynamic Balance: Optimizing vs. Maximizing Outcomes

Dynamic balance, or what Bertalanffy called "flowing balance," is one of the basic principles of living systems. It is fundamental to virtually all of the system's processes and is an essential element of health. Dynamic balance, also called "homeostasis," is not equilibrium. It is a constantly fluctuating state, far from equilibrium, in which conditions vary widely but within certain tolerance levels.

The idea of living in balance is certainly not new. All of us know the consequences of the "too muches"—too much eating, drinking, working, spending; and the "too littles"—too little sleep, family contact, personal time, intimacy, play, love. In writing this book, for instance, it would be very easy to get caught up in a creative fervor and work two months without a break, ignoring my need to exercise, socialize, and be an active part of my family. This would create an out-of-balance condition that would weaken both the system called "Mark" and my related environmental systems (family, friends, colleagues). Because of the interconnectedness of systems, no part of a larger system goes untouched by changes that occur someplace within it.

Every system has key internal and external parameters that must be kept fluctuating within tolerable limits for all of the nested systems to remain healthy. What constitutes key parameters varies for different organisms. For humans and human systems, the internal parameters are related to body, mind, and spirit. Not only do these need to be balanced among themselves, they must each be balanced within themselves. External parameters for humans and human systems are related to the relationships with stakeholders: interdependent people and systems. These include family, church, employers, coworkers, friends, and the like. For businesses, these are customers, stockholders, employees, employees' families, communities, suppliers, governments, and the environment.

Dynamic balance does not require that an exact balance between all of these parameters be maintained. That would be an equilibrium state which would actually create rigidity and ultimately the death of the system. *Dynamic* means that the parameters vary constantly and cyclically in disequilibrium, but never so widely that they threaten the life of the system. Your heart rate may go as low as 50 beats-per-minute when you are resting, or as high as 200-beats-per minute when exercising. But it will never go to 0, or as high as 500-beats-per minute without killing you. As another example, a company might maximize profit for a short time but, as with maximizing our heartbeat, to do so perpetually would kill the company. A balanced system seeks to *optimize* its key parameters; it does not *maximize* them.

> *The ethics of optima and the ethics of maxima are totally different ethical systems.*
>
> —Gregory Bateson, anthropologist

Balance is one of the characteristics of Collins and Porras's highly successful visionary companies. Such companies are inclined to go beyond maximizing a single variable (profit), and instead balance their needs with that of the greater social system. "Contrary to business school doctrine, *we did not find 'maximizing shareholder wealth' or 'profit maximization' as the dominant driving force or primary objective through the history of most of the visionary companies.*" Collins and Porras go on to say that, "profit is like oxygen, food, water, and blood for the body; they are not the *point* of life, but without them there is no life." Profit, then, is one parameter in the health of a business system—but not the *only* one!

Dynamic balance does not refer to balance only between stakeholder interests, but also to balance in all aspects of life. The ancient Chinese philosophy of the Tao ("the process of the universe," literally "The Way") has flowing balance as one of its principle tenets. This 7,000-year-old system of thought maintains that the natural order of the universe is a cyclic rhythm that flows in a dynamic balance between pairs of opposites. This is symbolized in the familiar Yin-Yang symbol (technically known as "T'ai-Chi T'u" or "Diagram of the Supreme Ultimate"). This symbol illustrates that life is a constant series

of cycles between opposites: good and bad, light and dark, success and failure. It also makes the point that as a variable moves toward its extreme value, it becomes increasingly like its opposite and has the greatest propensity to take on the characteristics of, or suddenly switch over and *become*, its opposite. There are countless examples of this: extreme cold that feels hot, extreme pleasure that becomes painful, pro-life activists who murder abortion doctors, people who strongly resist change and then suddenly become some of the greatest proponents of it, criminals who abruptly become religious fanatics. In organizations, we have seen how efforts to "cure" the company's profitability through extreme cost-cutting measures have crippled the organization as surely as if it had spent money heedlessly.

Yin-Yang Symbol

There are countless examples in our society where we have pushed to maximize particular variables. In addition to the profit motive mentioned above, Western culture maximizes dominance, control, competition, income disparities, analytical analysis, quantitative (numerical) measurement, linear thinking, separateness, and a reductionist emphasis on parts. If we are to heal our social and natural environments, we need to master the concept of dynamic balance.

Creativity: Self-Renewal and Self-Transcendence

The classical management model stresses control of the organization so that risk and surprises are minimized and the company performs as expected. Any variations and disturbances are decidedly unwelcome. The norm under the classical management model is "unvarying predictability." Consider, for instance, the beating that companies take in the stock market when they don't meet expectations—even if their performance was excellent by other standards!

Life, of course, does not cooperate with our expectations. Life varies. It moves in circles and cycles. It does the unexpected: it plays, it creates, and it discovers. One thing that it definitely does *not* do is conform to plans written on a sheet of paper. Managers throughout history have found themselves riding a constantly bucking horse that threatened at any minute to knock them off their targets and goals. This is what "change" means in the classical management model— overcoming variations to ensure the status quo.

> Life does not cooperate with our expectations. Life varies. It moves in circles and cycles. It does the unexpected: it plays, it creates, and it discovers.

Regulatory and maintenance activities that reduce variation and promote self-renewal are called *negative feedback*. These activities include planning, budgeting, measuring, performance reporting, analyzing, and summarizing. Corporate managers are *masters* at negative feedback.

It is creativity—*true* creativity—that baffles most organizations.

Creativity from the classical management viewpoint has to do with inventive approaches to negative feedback, a process better known as *problem solving*. True creativity, in contrast, is an evolutionary leap in which a system transcends itself and attains a higher-level of organization and complexity. This process of self-transcendence, called *positive feedback*, occurs when a small disturbance is amplified by the system until it reaches a critical mass. At this *bifurcation point*, the system pushes past the instability into a novel and more stable structure.

Balancing and reinforcing feedback loops, which figure prominently in Peter Senge's five disciplines of systems thinking, originated in the mid-1940s with the emergence of the science of cybernetics. A feedback loop is a circular arrangement of causally connected elements that ultimately feeds back to the original element (see Figure 2.2 for an example). The looping back of an action to the initiator provides the link by which learning can occur. There are two kinds of feedback loops. The first is a balancing loop. In this scenario, a sequence of events continues until a desired goal is reached. Then, self-

regulating actions keep the system operating at the desired state. A common example is the thermostat in a heating/cooling system. When first turned on, the system will continue to run until the desired temperature is reached. At that point the system will maintain the approximate temperature by cycling a little over that temperature and a little under it.

A Reinforcing Feedback Loop: How Layoffs Create a Vicious Circle

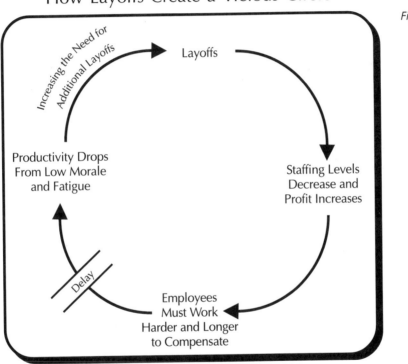

Figure 2.2

In a reinforcing loop, behaviors continue to escalate until the system hits natural limitations or transcends itself to achieve a wholly new and more stable structure. Reinforcing loops are characterized by their runaway effects, which are sometimes called "vicious" or "virtuous" cycles. An example of a reinforcing loop is the ever-increasing consumption of alcohol by alcoholics. The limit to alcoholism comes when the person "crashes" and either gets help or dies. But, not every reinforcing loop must end in tragedy. There is another possible outcome—one that is essential to the advancement of life.

Higher Levels of Order

Life has an innate urge to evolve to ever-higher levels of organization and complexity—toward self-transcendence. In living systems, these evolutionary advances are achieved through positive feedback, without arbitrary goals or directed effort. Human systems, in contrast, have many artificial barriers to creativity and the unfolding of new levels of order. Positive feedback is unpredictable and mostly uncontrollable. It also requires substantial disorder and messiness. These are not popular conditions in most business organizations. In fact, they are normally seen as evidence that the system is breaking down. Nature, by comparison, uses messiness and instability to its advantage. This "mess"—a fluctuating state far from equilibrium—optimizes the system's creative potential for emergent, novel behavior. Where we see trouble, Nature sees opportunity.

In business, we spend an inordinate amount of time trying to prevent fluctuations and disturbances of all kinds, and see it as "good" when the results are what we desire and "bad" if they are not. We could benefit enormously by allowing our organizations to operate far from equilibrium. We could allow and expect profits, stock prices, expenses, and other variables to move cyclically and not continue to waste enormous energy and effort to correct them. We could spend little or no time punishing "bad" outcomes and performance, and just use these as information for learning. We could ignore small fluctuations throughout the organization and focus only on those that seem abnormal and give us the greatest leverage for improvement. This, in fact, is precisely how statistical process control (SPC) works in managing quality in manufacturing processes.

> Life has an innate urge to evolve to ever higher levels of organization and complexity—toward self-transcendence.

SPC is a systemic approach to managing production processes. The key principles behind the approach are relevant for managing in any environment. The underlying concept is to monitor variations from the norm and act only on those that are significant. Small variations, called "common causes," are ignored in the short-term and corrected through long-term

continuous improvement. Large variations, called "special causes," are given urgent attention, whether they are favorable or unfavorable. The large fluctuations are variations and disturbances that have escaped the system's normal self-regulating processes. If left unattended, they are likely to continue to amplify until they overwhelm the system. In machines, this is a terminal situation. In living systems, the amplifying of small variations is how they creatively self-organize to higher-levels of order. Management should view these disturbances with an eye toward their creative possibilities and allow the organization the freedom of movement required to explore their potential. Ironically, most corporations engage in the *opposite* behavior. They are extremely sensitive to minor disturbances, such as the petty complaint from a powerful executive—but remarkably insensitive to major fluctuations, such as declining markets and obsolete management practices.

Creating Space for Novelty

In Nature, creativity requires excess capacities and latent potential. All living systems have within their structures the latent potential for alternative and novel uses. One source of creativity is shifting the function of a part of the system to a new use: Fins become legs; forearms become wings. In fact, some of Nature's greatest innovations emerged from novel uses of existing system features, not from some precise evolutionary response.

Take birds' wings for instance. How did birds evolve to fly as a competitive advantage, when flying requires an entire constellation of changes: wings, feathers, and light bones? What was the evolutionary advantage of 5 percent of a wing? The answer lies in the co-opting of latent potentials. Feathers may have first evolved from scales on early dinosaurs because they offer superior body temperature regulation. Only later did their usefulness for flight begin to manifest. This is one way systems retain flexibility at the same time that they are losing it through increasing evolutionary specialization.

Nature also requires excess capacities and redundancies for evolutionary creativity. If every fiber of an organism's being were dedicated to some productive use, Nature would have no raw materials with which to create novelty. So, it develops redundancy. Early fish breathed through both gills and lungs. This redundancy allowed fish to breathe through their gills while their lungs evolved into air bladders—a vital evolutionary shift that allowed fish to move from bottom crawlers to free-floating swimmers. If early fish had only one device for breathing, such a novel innovation would not have been possible.

> In the effort to maximize efficiency, companies may have eliminated the excess capacities that are essential for creativity and novelty.

The lessons for business organizations are important. First, in their effort to maximize efficiency, companies may have eliminated the excess capacities that are essential for creativity and novelty. Part of the "messiness" that leads to self-transcendence requires excess capacities and inefficiencies in the form of systemic redundancies. The challenge for organizations will be to balance efficiency with creating adequate space for novelty. The second important lesson is that the structure of every living system has latent potential for novel uses. Companies can look to their core competencies, their investments in knowledge or information technology, or to the unused talents of their personnel as sources for strategic differentiation.

Creative-Destruction

It is important to note that the act of creation, which is fundamental to change and self-transcendence, is only possible through the destruction of something else. The terms *creation* and *destruction*, when used by themselves, are actually misleading. It would be more accurate to say "creative-destruction" or "destructive-creation."

Birth and death are central aspects of self-organization. Death is not the *opposite* of life as we seem to think, but *essential* to it. Our Western society, unfortunately, has a deep-seated fear of death and of endings of all kinds. We want new life and creativity but not the death and destruction that precedes it. This is an impossible desire, one that produces an enormous amount of self-imposed suffering. Why do we choose to make transitions so difficult when we could experience them with ease and grace? We need to learn to accept and even honor endings for the important role they play in the natural order. We can learn to cooperate with change in both of its aspects—creation and destruction—instead of resisting and agonizing over it. When we do, we will experience life's transitions in a gentler, more accepting, and peaceful fashion.

> Birth and death are central aspects of self-organization. Death is not the *opposite* of life as we seem to think, but *essential* to it.

Openness: Information, Diversity, and Interactions

Nature relies on a rich soup of potentiality to generate the infinite variety of its forms. There are three critical ingredients in this "soup" that give rise to the process of self-transcendence: information, diversity and interactions. Healthy systems demonstrate a high degree of openness to the free flow of these key parameters. Information is the lifeblood of living systems. Like blood, information must continually flow if it is to keep its vitality and serve the system. In natural systems, information flows virtually unimpeded: "The quality of their communications is dazzling . . .," wrote Margaret Wheatley in *A Simpler Way*. "Nothing we have created in any human organization comes close." Living systems learn as a whole system, so individual agents must be free to mix and mingle in an infinite variety of ways. In the creative process, agents engage in a constant, reciprocal exchange and cross-fertilization of information in a nonlinear and unpredictable fashion. And the agents in the system are highly diverse—the more diversity, the richer the field of creative potential. As Stacey put it, "It is critical levels of diversity that enhance further learning." The greater the degree of interaction, diversity, and information, the greater the system's instability *and* flexibility. It is here, at the edge of chaos, that systems have their greatest potential for novelty and creativity.

> It is the balance point between order and instability—at the *edge of chaos*—that systems have their greatest potential for novelty and creativity.

Information

Before we can engage in a useful discussion about information, we need a better understanding of what it is. From a systems viewpoint, information can be seen to be the very essence of life. What is DNA, for example, if not information made manifest? Mind/Body expert Deepak Chopra, MD, acknowledges that at the quantum level "there is nothing other than information and energy." He goes on to say:

> A flower, a rainbow, a tree, a blade of grass, a human body, when broken down to their essential components are energy and information. The whole universe, in its essential nature, is the *movement* of energy and information. The only difference between you and a tree is the informational and energy content of your respective bodies.

In business, we have developed a rather narrow definition of information. We are caught in the Newtonian-Cartesian web of numerical measurements and quantified assessments that excludes any other forms of information. Our belief in the certainty of our data and analysis strips us of the doubt that is essential for open-minded exploration of additional possibilities. In business, we focus almost exclusively on what we have measured and counted. But we have learned from quantum physics that the act of measuring excludes far more information than it captures. Why aren't we more concerned about the information we are overlooking?

Charles Handy, writing in *The Age of Paradox*, reminds us that in statistics there are two kinds of risk. The first, a Type 1 error, is the risk of reaching an erroneous conclusion based on the facts at hand. This is the kind of risk that businesses are usually concerned with. But the second kind of risk, a Type 2 error, has far more potential influence on our organization's health and longevity. This is the risk associated with missed opportunities that result from "the path not taken"—errors of omission, rather than commission. With regard to Type 2 risk, we should take a closer look at our analytical and information gathering methods. What legitimate information are we excluding from our

thought processes? If an observation can't be quantified, does that necessarily mean that it isn't relevant and useful? Are we sensitive to seemingly irrelevant sources of information such as emotions, intuitions, poetry, metaphor, unrelated industries, and different social contexts?

Our attempts to reduce everything to numbers, strips the life and vitality out of information. Asked to describe a painting by Rembrandt, scientists might respond that it weighs a certain amount and that it has 21 percent red, 13 percent yellow, 28 percent blue, and 38 percent white pigments. Business people would probably respond with its market value, insured value, and carrying cost. Neither of these descriptions really tells us anything meaningful about the painting. We could ask very different questions that would yield far more information: How do people respond to the painting? What emotions, thoughts, and questions does it evoke? What is its history? What was the artist thinking when he painted it? Where do our minds lead us when we look at the painting? What tangential references are brought to mind, and what new insights do they offer?

> *Western managers . . . need to get out of the old mode of thinking that knowledge can be acquired, taught, and trained through manuals, books, or lectures. Instead, they need to pay more attention to the less formal and systemic side of knowledge and start focusing on highly subjective insights, intuitions, and hunches that are gained through the use of metaphors, pictures or experiences.*
>
> — Ikujiro Nonaka and Hirotaka Takeuchi, authors of *The Knowledge-Creating Company*

Customer satisfaction is like a Rembrandt painting. When we try to reduce customer satisfaction—an unquantifiable quality if there ever was one—to a number, what information are we missing? What does it really mean that we scored 4.7 on a 5.0 scale, instead of 4.6 or even 3.5? What erroneous conclusions will we reach because of how we have distorted the information to fit our analytical microscope? What if we were to give up on quantifying everything and focused more on the subjective *qualities* of our business experiences? What new possibilities would emerge? What if we described customer satisfaction through a word picture, or a dramatic re-enactment, or purely through videotaped comments from customers? What images and understandings could we evoke through metaphor, or the use of poetry, or by painting word pictures? There is a vast tapestry of information available to us if we would only choose to acknowledge it.

Information is literally the stuff of life, as vital to living systems as blood is to the human body. So how do we treat information in a business context? In my experience assisting companies through large-scale change, I have seen firsthand the stinginess with which information is shared throughout organizations. The classical organization actively distorts information and impedes its flow, precisely *opposite* of what is required from a systems perspective. "Information chastity belts," Wheatley quipped, "are a central management function." What are we so afraid of?

Losing control, that's what.

Information under the classical management model is a tool for establishing and maintaining control. The bureaucratic "need to know" policy toward the dissemination of information is alive and well in many corporations. Managers fear what would happen if employees gained access to meaningful information. They have a desperate need to maintain control and so fret over concerns such as: How would we control employees' reactions? What might they think or do that we can't predict? How might they misinterpret the information or use it against us? How can we make this bad news sound like good news?

The real irony is that this is also what employees do with the information they have that management needs. They are equally afraid to share unadulterated information. They worry: How can we control the boss's reaction? How can we skew the information so that management does what we want? How can we make things look better than they really are? How can we put a spin on the information so that we can take credit (or avoid blame)? It is evident from

these examples that our attitudes about control and access to information are very deeply intertwined. Changing such fiercely held beliefs will not be easy.

Nevertheless, organizations that hope to survive in this complex world need to liberate information to flow where it will. For instance, Ford Motor Corporation broadcasts 30 minutes of news throughout the company (approximately 200,000 viewers) every morning over the Ford Communications Network. The company has concluded that there are few real secrets in business, "so why pretend a company should (or can) keep its people in the dark?" The policy of sharing information on a "need to know" basis needs to be reversed—it is the *recipient* of the information rather that the *holder* who should determine whether there is a need to know. The trend toward "open-book management" is a solid movement in this direction. Jack Stack, CEO of Springfield Remanufacturing Corporation and author of *The Great Game of Business,* is one of the founders of this approach. He believes that "a business should be run like an aquarium, where everybody can see what's going on—what's going in, what's moving around, what's coming out." Stack even attributes his company's success to its openness with information, "We never would have made so much money, or generated so much wealth, if we hadn't been open with our information, ideas, and numbers."

> *The more people know about a company, the better that company will perform. This is an iron clad rule.*
>
> — Jack Stack, CEO of Springfield Remanufacturing Corp., author of *The Great Game of Business*

Diversity and Interactions

At the quantum level, we know that there really aren't any particles, only interactions—a universe of interconnections connecting to other interconnections. The same is true at the macro level. Connections between agents and the exchange of information are the fundamental structures of the universe. Systems thrive when there are large numbers of interactions between agents both within and outside of the system. Information is discovered, created, and spread through these interactions in unpredictable and nonlinear ways. Differences in the information, spawned through the diversity of the individual agents, enrich the exchanges, and increase the creative potential of the overall system.

> Information is the lifeblood of systems and high-quality, diverse interactions are the beating heart.

If information is the lifeblood of systems, then high-quality, diverse interactions are the beating heart. Systems deprived of adequate interactions and information flow are headed toward cardiac arrest. The classical management model was deliberately designed to limit the interactions between employees. This was an essential element in the scientific management practice of segmenting work and coordinating activities through supervisory direction. Managers had the most (or only) education and so problems had to be escalated to the appropriate level. Uncoordinated actions between employees who saw only a tiny piece of the whole picture and who were uneducated in fundamental production concepts could—in the early days of the industrial era—have caused enormous mischief. But these very practices, when applied in twenty-first century organizations, are a primary source of our performance difficulties.

Most companies have elaborate rules for who can interact with whom and under what circumstances. For instance, the fact that companies have practices called "open-door policies" points to the underlying belief that employee interactions must be codified. Informal, ad hoc interactions are frowned on and even actively discouraged.

One situation that happened to me illustrates this point. I was a vice president in a high-tech firm and was managing a very large reengineering project. One day as I was getting coffee, I encountered an employee from one of the affected departments. I was preoccupied with an idea for certain organizational changes and seized the opportunity to explore my thoughts with someone who had direct experience with the subject matter. I asked a

few questions to clarify how things currently worked, and then asked the employee's opinion on the suitability of the ideas that I had in mind. (It is important to note that this was *not* a manager.)

Within an hour, I received a call from the senior vice president of this department, and he was furious! I had broken the unofficial protocols that required inquiries to go through the

> *I realized that if I can give everybody complete access to information about the company, then I don't have to tell them what to do all the time. The organization starts moving forward on its own initiative.*
>
> — Bob Buckman, CEO of Buckman Laboratories

proper channels. Managers in the department were terrified that they would not be able to control what information I received or how I would use it. This is a classic example of how controlling behaviors cannot be reconciled with systems' principles that require a high-degree of diverse interactions and the continuous flow of information.

Interactions and the quality of information flow are further limited by our communication practices. In business, most two-way communications take the form of a debate in which adversaries try to find the weaknesses in the other's arguments in order to "win" the discussion. In meetings, people interrupt and talk over each other with no intention of really understanding each other. Extroverted personalities dominate and introverts, who often have valuable insights, rarely speak. Agendas are generally not open for modification and facilitators are often used to prevent "extraneous and irrelevant information" from entering into consideration. Emotions (another form of information) and intuitions (nonlinear, right-brain perceptions) are explicitly taboo. Participants are often limited to a few people with remarkably uniform outlooks, and rarely include people from different hierarchical levels. In fact, people from different hierarchical levels rarely have *meaningful* interactions of any kind. A client of mine once lamented that executives in her organization never mixed with front-line workers in a "management-by-walking-around" manner. One of her colleagues responded with the cynical observation: "That's because they can't get the golf carts into the elevator."

Interactions that are homogenous in content and outlook are the equivalent of "empty calories"—lots of sugar and no nutritional value. Systems thrive on diversity. Consider, for instance, the importance of the exchange of diverse DNA materials to the health of a species. In-breeding of ideas has the same potential for "genetic" deformity as does in-breeding in physical species. Although many organizations have initiated diversity programs, these are generally oriented toward cultivating social tolerances between different ethnic and gender groups. Although this is an essential first step, true diversity involves surfacing and valuing different perspectives and thought processes. A meeting that contains people of different ethnic origins does not guarantee that the ideas put forward will demonstrate a high-level of diversity. The issue for most companies is one of truly valuing, rather than fearing different viewpoints, and using the cross-fertilization of opinion as the catalyst for generating novel ideas and approaches.

> Interactions that are homogenous in content and outlook are the equivalent of "empty calories"—lots of sugar and no nutritional value.

Freedom Within Limits. When I first immersed myself in the principles of self-organizing systems, I quickly came to a point where my Cartesian-trained mind revolted. "If we encourage all of this disorder and mess," I wondered, "what is to keep the organization from becoming so chaotic that nothing can get accomplished?" The answer, of course, is right in front of us. Stability in systems operating far from equilibrium comes from the very controls that we use to choke the life out of our organizations. The key difference lies in how we apply these controls.

Beyond the organizing power of purpose and principles we discussed earlier, there are three sources of stability in living systems: general boundaries, canalization, and maladaptive learning. *Boundaries* take the form of rules, authorization levels, and limits that define the edges of the organization. *Canalization* means "channeled in a specific direction." Routines, habits, procedures, cultural norms, and policies are all mechanisms that channel behavior in organizations. These first two sources of stability are important—when applied appropriately—to the healthy functioning of living systems.

Maladaptive learning is a destructive source of stability that increases the rigidity of the first two types of controls. It results from a system obstructing feedback from its environment through defective sensing mechanisms or by actively distorting or blocking the information.

Under the classical management model, we have become pathological "control-aholics." Dee Hock, speaking at a recent conference, joked that he had to resist falling back into old habits—that it was very easy for him to reach for a bottle of "Old Command-and-Control." I think all of us who are trying to shift to the quantum worldview have felt the same way. Our culture has emphasized control to such a degree that breaking the "habit" requires enormous determination and commitment. Nevertheless, businesses must dramatically loosen controls if they are to survive and prosper in today's fast-changing environment.

> Under the classical management model, we have become pathological "control-aholics."

Flexibility: Substance Over Form

Ask a manager to describe a company and he or she will typically hand you an organization chart, describe the product line, or explain the company's market share and strategic positioning. This emphasis on structure and parts is indicative of our managerial indoctrination. For instance, the flow of decision authority up and down the hierarchy is carefully spelled out, while the flow of activities across the organization is practically ignored. The tasks required to construct a machine component are thoroughly documented, but how the tasks link together across and beyond the organization to create value are not. Profit is known but the organizational dynamics that produce it are not.

Industrial era management practices emphasize reporting (power) relationships and control mechanisms as the critical tools for managing organizational performance. They are the "load-bearing structures" that hold the company together. Something of this importance must remain stable so steps were taken to ensure their permanence. Although this design is rigid and inflexible, it is very stable when moderate winds of change blow. But when the winds of change reach the intensity of a gale—as they have today—these structures get knocked over and destroyed (the epitome of instability). Meanwhile, Quantum Organizations, although more sensitive to moderate disturbances, are extremely resilient in times of tremendous change. No matter how strong the winds of change blow, these organizations just "bend and sway."

Quantum Organizations display a lot of internal plasticity, forming and dissolving structures as needed for a given time and context. They emphasize flow and patterns of interactions over the structural specifics (such as job definitions, reporting lines, and work groupings). When I was learning the basics of accounting, I was taught that one of the fundamental principles was "substance over form"—the essence of the information was more important than adhering to set reporting standards. Similarly, in living systems, "form and function engage in a fluid process where the system may maintain itself in its present form or evolve to a new order."

> Quantum Organizations display a lot of internal plasticity, forming and dissolving structures as needed for a given time and context.

This is a difficult concept for many of us, trained as we are in traditional notions of structure and control. We are used to structures determining the information that they need. We do not easily accept the opposite—the power of information to organize the structures that *it* needs. Information, as odd as it sounds, is far more permanent than the physical matter that we normally experience as real, tangible, and permanent. Physicist David Bohm states that, "all matter, including ourselves, is determined by 'information.' 'Information' is what determines time and space."

Flexibility and Flow

Matter is constantly changing, flowing through physical structures in an orderly manner that ensures the continuity of the form. Our bodies are renewing our cells and tissues at every moment. At the atomic level, particles and photons are continually being exchanged with the surrounding environment. Rivers are constantly dispersing water into the soil, the air, and other bodies of water. Companies experience frequent turnover in personnel, products, and services. And yet all of these structures maintain a consistent identity despite all of the changes. It is information—the only constant in each of these cases—that is organizing the matter into structures.

When we consider a whirlpool, it is easy to see that the water is flowing through a structure that remains uninterrupted despite its changing elements. A whirlpool is merely energy and information that organizes the water and maintains a pattern. Humans, companies and all other structures are similar in this way to whirlpools. We are fields of energy and information—patterns that organize matter into structures. Continually changing matter flows through the information field like water flows through a whirlpool. This realization can guide us to a new respect for the role that information plays in creating order and for the importance of allowing structures to change and evolve to support the life of our organizations.

Flow is the principle mechanism by which self-organizing systems overcome energy and matter dissipation and renew themselves. Information flow also provides the feedback essential for organisms to adapt to environmental changes. When flow is blocked, the demise of the system is inevitable. The Chinese have recognized the flowing nature of the universe for thousands of years. To be in harmony with the Tao is to put yourself into accord with the flow of life. Chí (Ki in Japanese) is life essence (vital energy) that must be kept flowing if a person is to remain healthy. The practice of acupuncture is intended to open blockages in "energy meridians" so that chí can flow through the body and restore its natural balance. T'ai Chi exercises are also

> *Everything flows;*
> *only process is real.*
>
> — Heraclitus, philosopher
> 540-480 B.C.

designed to stimulate the flow of chí through the body. The ancient Chinese practice of Feng Shui (pronounced "fung schway") is the design of building layouts to maximize the flow of chí through the structure. All of these practices believe that to block the flow of chí creates stagnation, the build-up of toxins, and poor health.

The importance of flow to the health of living systems cannot be overstated. The river Jordan in the mid-east provides a wonderful allegory for the importance of flow. The Jordan flows over 350 km through Israel and Jordan and feeds into two different seas. The first, the Sea of Galilee, is vibrantly alive—a source of water for irrigation and an important fishing ground and tourist attraction. The second, the Dead Sea, is just that—*dead*. It is seven times more saline than an ocean and cannot support any form of life beyond simple micro-organisms.

Although Jesus is purported to have walked on water at the Sea of Galilee, today—because of its salinity—*anybody* can walk (float without effort) on the water in the Dead Sea. Since the Jordan River supplies both seas, why is one dynamically alive and the other completely dead? The difference comes down to this: The Dead Sea *has no outlet,* and the Sea of Galilee does. Because its flow is blocked, the Dead Sea has no way of renewing itself. As a closed system, its water cannot escape except through evaporation. This results in toxins that cannot be flushed out of the system—accumulating to levels where most organisms can no longer survive.

> Human organizations often resemble closed systems because people have so completely blocked the system's natural flows.

Human organizations often resemble closed systems because people have so completely blocked the system's natural flows. Closed systems are subject to the law of entropy—the inevitable breakdown and demise of the system. The tendency of our organizations to break down has justified our belief in the need for control and external interventions. Without these actions, we believe that our organizations will self-destruct—and as long as they are closed systems, they probably will. However, it is *our controlling behaviors* that have closed off our organizations' natural flows in the first place! A key to creating

Quantum Organizations is to restore the system's natural flows in all aspects, including information, power, personnel, money, and technology.

Business and the Way of Living Systems

Over the past twenty years, as I have assisted organizations through large-scale transformational change, I have become increasingly concerned about our traditional management methods. I have seen management fads come and go, I have seen a widespread and consistent pattern of failed organizational change efforts, and I have seen increasingly frenzied—and ineffective—efforts by businesses to improve profitability. I have also witnessed the increasing destructiveness that these patterns of behavior have had on both people and the larger social system. I was puzzled by these developments, and I wondered, "Why are organizations struggling so?" and "Why is it that no matter what changes companies try, they never seem to improve performance over the long run?"

I have come to understand a simple truth about organizations:

Organizations are <u>perfectly designed</u> to produce
the results that they are getting.

No matter what results our businesses and social institutions are creating, they are perfectly designed to create them. The corollary to this simple truth is this: If you want different results, change the organization's design.

The obvious questions become: How are our organizations designed? Why are they creating the conditions described earlier in this chapter? The answer is that they are designed to operate like *machines*. But organizations aren't machines—they're living systems, and they operate under a different set of rules. The tools that we traditionally use to understand the performance of our businesses—organization charts, financial statements, budgets—are inadequate for understanding their systemic nature. We need a new model that describes organizations as they really are. The next chapter introduces the Organizational EcoSystem Model. Through this model, we can answer the questions: Now that we understand the way of living systems, how are we to apply this knowledge in our everyday business activities? What changes does this information imply for our organizations? Once we understand the elements of the Organizational EcoSystem Model, we can apply the seven organic principles of living systems to change our businesses into Quantum Organizations—flexible, responsive, high-performing systems operating at the edge of chaos.

PART TWO

POWERFUL NEW WAYS
OF WORKING

The choice is no longer for or against transformation. Transformation has already been initiated by a changed environment. The choice is rather, evolve to a new way of doing business, or go out of business.
> — Harrison Owen, author of
> *The Millenium Organization*

Chapter Three
The Quantum Organization

The study of complexity asks us in effect to open a window and let in fresh air to the organization, to bring a little of the wilderness into the domesticity of the workplace and free us for greater things.

— David Whyte, Poet, author of *The Heart Aroused*

Ever since Michael Hammer published his first article on business process reengineering (BPR) in the *Harvard Business Review* in 1990, reengineering has raged like wildfire through organizations—scouring everything in its path. All manner of abuses have been justified under the auspices of reengineering. In the words of one disgruntled manager, "Reengineering is so hot that the label is being slapped on everything from requests for new chairs to across-the-board layoffs." Before we go any further, though, I must confess to being a *reformed* reengineering advocate. I still believe in transformative organizational change, but not in the way that it has been carried out through reengineering.

As a management consultant in a Big-6 professional services firm, I was involved in leading some of the first forays into reengineering. However, the more BPR projects I conducted, the more dissatisfied I became. It was clear to me early on that something was terribly wrong with the way organizations were approaching these transformative change efforts. I knew that the Total Quality Management (TQM) movement had not fared well in many corporations, and now I was seeing the same fate for reengineering. I began to research why a few change efforts succeeded while most did not. I discovered a wide range of reasons that organizations failed at change and noticed a single underlying theme: Managers were implementing change as if their organizations were machines, and they were employing the same command-and-control management techniques they used in everyday operating conditions.

As we saw in the previous chapter, organizations are living systems. Yet, we do not generally understand them in that way. Normally, we view organizations as machines with parts that we can disassemble and reconstruct in any fashion we wish. Organizational change is frequently an exercise in moving parts around until we achieve the magic formula that produces the performance results we desire. We expect to be able to predict the outcomes of these changes and to control them completely. But it never works out that way. And it never will. We keep trying the same ineffective approaches and are surprised when we keep getting the same disappointing results. When we adopt a quantum worldview, and begin to treat organizations as complex adaptive systems, our approach to organizational change is transformed. Happily, it becomes possible to end our futile game of "change program roulette."

In Zen, the masters speak of their teachings as "a finger pointing at the moon," not the destination but what points to the destination. Likewise, the ideas presented in this chapter are intended to point the reader to the endless possibilities available to them as they engage in creating Quantum Organizations.

The Organizational EcoSystem Model

An *ecosystem* is defined as "a community of organisms *and* their environment." Organizations participate in a host ecosystem that includes: the natural environment, society at large, customers, shareholders/owners, governments, regulatory agencies, suppliers, lenders, and competitors. Organizations are also ecosystems. The primary agents in organizations are, of course, people. These people join together in groups to form larger systems such as departments, teams, tribes, castes, plants, divisions, and subsidiaries. These larger systems interpenetrate each other to form a complex web of interrelationships.

The Organizational EcoSystem Model

Figure 3.1

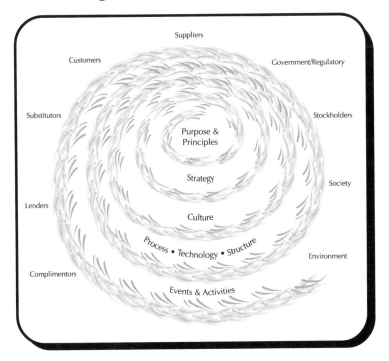

The Organizational EcoSystem Model (shown in Figure 3.1) depicts not only some of the other agents in the host environment but also the internal elements that comprise the organization. It is important to note at the outset that this model is inaccurate, just as all models are by their very nature, inaccurate. Models are "maps" of the territory, not the territory itself. It is impossible for them to be accurate. But like street maps, they are useful as *approximations*, just as long as they change when the territory changes, and we remember that they are limited.

The seven internal aspects of organizations are purpose, principles, strategy, culture, structure, process, and technology. It is important to understand what I mean by the word *aspect*. For example, my cat, Yoda, has short white hair, green eyes, a mischievous disposition, and a long tail. Although I can describe these characteristics separately, they are not in any way "separate" from the "whole" that I know as Yoda. Rather, they are inseparable *aspects* of Yoda. *Aspects* then, are characteristics with unique properties that can be described separately but do not exist independent of either the whole or each other.

When I describe the Organizational EcoSystem Model as having process, structure, culture, and so on, I am describing aspects of the whole. I often illustrate this relationship with a set of interlocking circles that show the connectedness of the elements (shown in Fig. 3.2). This idea is a radical departure from our usual conception of organizations which more closely resembles players on a game board.

Connectedness of the Organizational EcoSystem Elements

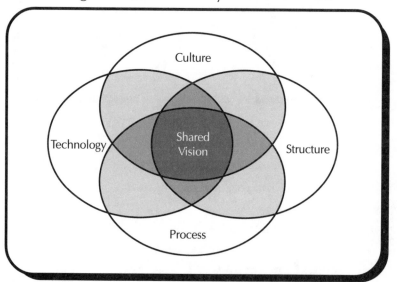

Figure 3.2

A Viking Metaphor

Let me use the metaphor of a Viking ship on a great voyage—such as Eric the Red's venture across the Atlantic Ocean—to briefly explain the Organizational EcoSystem Model. The ship (Eric the Red's "Company") has all of the elements of our model. The Vikings' *purpose* was adventure (discovering, conquering, looting, pillaging, and so on)—that is, the journey itself. *Principles* were the deep beliefs and values that guided the Vikings' decisions and behavior. Some of these would have included domination, ferocity, risk-taking, courage, teamwork, and other such beliefs. Their *strategy* was the unique way in which they intended to fulfill their purpose. They chose a destination: the new world; a particular kind of vehicle to get them there: a boat; and a particular approach: violent conquest.

The crew had a distinct *culture*—the way of sailors, their own language, tribes, castes, and social norms. The *structure* included a hierarchical command-and-control management style, clear authority levels, separate roles and responsibilities, performance feedback (the lash . . . hmmm there's an idea!), training systems ("Here's an oar, now stroke!"), and compensation (all the "booty" you can carry). The ship's processes included sailing, feeding the crew, maintaining the ship, navigating, managing, leading, fighting, and pillaging. Their technology included navigation and charting tools, rigging, sails, and winches.

A Dynamic, Open System

The spiral shape of the Organizational EcoSystem Model depicts the dynamic nature of organizations—a ceaseless whirl of activity where nothing stays the same for long. Humankind has a long affinity for spirals; this pattern shows up in art and sculptures from 5,000 years ago. Spirals are a very organic pattern—they are a common motif in nature, as seen in galaxies, hurricanes, and the shape of shells. Most recently, scientists have noted the spiral pattern even at the atomic level. When cosmic rays collide with atomic particles in huge "accelerators," they form spiral tracks on the photographic plates used to record the experiment.

Another important design characteristic is that the model is open to the environment. It isn't an enclosed box like most other models that we have seen. The Organizational EcoSystem Model illustrates that organizations are simultaneously bounded (have a fixed identity) and they are unbounded (open to and interact constantly with the greater social and natural environment). Also, if you follow the spiral in the ecosystem from the center outward, you will notice that there are no barriers between the seven elements. One flows seamlessly into another. Although a hierarchy is implied by the order of the elements, they mutually influence each other. For instance, strategy will influence the technologies that are deployed, but an emerging technology may also influence strategy.

At first, some people may be uncomfortable applying this spiral pattern to organizations. Organizations have been drawn as hierarchical trees or pyramids for so long that seeing them depicted as an unusual shape can be disorienting. Do not be concerned if you feel uncomfortable; this model will become more familiar and comfortable as time passes. It may help to imagine it as a three-dimensional figure: a conical seashell or a party hat. Now imagine a line drawn on the shape starting at the top and spiraling down to the bottom. When looked at from the side, the lines would be pyramidal, with purpose and principals at the top, followed by strategy at the next level, then culture. Structure, process, and technology would all be on the next level, and events and activities would be at the very bottom. When you turn this shape and look straight down on it, you can see the original spiral pattern. It is important while learning a new way of thinking to create new symbols that connote the beliefs of the new worldview. It would not do to promote an organic view of organizations and then represent them with old hierarchical models that were developed using the command-and-control mind-set. The spiral is a new symbol, intended to remind us to think about our organizations differently—as living systems—not machines.

> The spiral is a new symbol, intended to remind us to think about our organizations differently—as living systems—not as machines.

Organizational Alignment

Top-performing organizations are those that create a clear sense of shared purpose and principles and then develop alignment among all of the ecosystem elements. Few companies, however, achieve this. In most cases, cultural norms are working in opposition to strategy, which is inconsistent with technology, which doesn't support the processes, which are broken up into parts by the organization's structure. In addition, there is no clear consensus as to the company's purpose, direction, and principles of behavior. Everyone is operating out of limited understanding of what is "right" and "best" for the organization. The lack of integration around a common purpose results in self-imposed anarchy (which, in turn, justifies the need for a command-and-control management style). If we use a wagon as a metaphor for our organization, the lack of alignment is the equivalent of hitching horses to each of the four sides of the wagon and expecting it to go somewhere. No matter how much we whip the horses, our wagon isn't going to move. We will only get lots of activity—sounds and fury, but no movement. Now doesn't that sound like many of the bureaucratic organizations that we know?

The answer is to create alignment throughout the organization around a strong sense of purpose. A highly aligned organization has the focus and power of a laser beam. Lasers are little more than normal light in which the light rays are aligned in the same direction. Similarly, the difference between a magnet and an inert hunk of iron is that the electrons in a magnet are all aligned. In organizations, coherence occurs when people and organizational design align around a globally shared vision, purpose, and guiding principles. In Quantum Organizations, this is one of the most important roles that management has.

In Search of The Quantum Organization

The remainder of this chapter is dedicated to discussing what the Organizational EcoSystem Model would look like for a Quantum Organization. There aren't many examples of organizations that would currently qualify. Dee Hock contends that there are only two: VISA and the Internet. But this understates the progress that companies are making. There are countless groups that are experimenting with the principles of Quantum Organizations around the world today. Many of these are entrepreneurial start-ups, small groups within larger companies, high-tech and women-owned companies, professional services firms, and companies that have fully implemented the true spirit of Total Quality Management. Visionary businesses such as Semco, W.L. Gore and Associates, IDEO, Southwest Airlines, Springfield ReManufacturing Corp., Whole Foods Market, Levi Strauss, Starbucks Coffee, Nickelodeon, and Tom's of Maine have many of the characteristics of Quantum Organizations. But few if any could be looked upon as an absolute model. It is from companies such as these, however, that I draw examples for illustrating the ideal Quantum Organization.

Quantum Organizations have a strong shared vision that is both inspirational and challenging. Balance is maintained among the needs of each of the major stakeholders. Everyone is subject to shared "rights and responsibilities" in the form of core principles and beliefs. Power, authority, and accountabilities are bottom-up. Employees are self-reliant and accept responsibility for the organization's overall success. Information flows freely based on who needs it (rather than who has it). Openness is the norm—anything kept secret is highly suspect. People are free to interact with whomever they think is necessary to achieve a goal. Structures are fluid and are formed based on a goal to be accomplished. They may disappear quickly when the goal is met.

Work is defined based on the skills required—not on formal job definitions—and people flow freely between tasks. Compensation is based on the performance of the company. Employees share in both the downside risks and the upside rewards. Although differences in pay still exist (and some may be substantial), there is no place for remuneration abuses as in some current top-executive compensation schemes. Performance feedback, which is disassociated from compensation, is constant and can be derived from anyone with whom the employee interacts. Employees and the organization as a whole are intent on learning and see knowledge creation as an essential part of life. Change is constant and results both from environmental challenges and creative innovations that originate internally. Relationships are revered.

> Quantum Organizations are about humans, and as so, strive constantly to fulfill the full range of human needs for purpose, meaning, significance, and connection.

Quantum Organizations are about humans, and as so, strive constantly to fulfill the full range of human needs for purpose, meaning, significance, and connection.

Every company that I have encountered has plenty of room for improvement toward becoming Quantum Organizations—even the best of them. VISA, for instance,

has mastered the integration of autonomous member organizations without centralized control or authority. However, the member companies are themselves extreme examples of industrial-era management and organizational design. No one company has "done it right"—nor would I expect them to. After all, the chief characteristic of Quantum Organizations is that they are constantly in a state of "becoming."

Core Ideology: The Changeless Center

At the center of every organization, there is a core ideology—a statement of the beliefs and aspirations of the people in the organization. I use the terms *purpose* and *principles* to describe two key aspects of a core ideology. However, there are many other terms that companies use. For instance, many companies have *vision* and *values*, but *mission* and *objectives* are also popular terms. AT&T has a "common bond," Saturn has a "philosophy," Johnson & Johnson and Ritz-Carlton have "credos," J. C. Penney has "The Penney Idea," Levi Strauss uses the phrase "Aspiration Statement," Reader's Digest has "Words to Live By," and Gannett has a "Game Plan." Regardless of what they are called, all of these serve as core ideologies. So, if you and your organization happen to use different words for purpose and principles, recognize that I am talking about the same thing.

By now, many companies have defined their core ideologies. They will have committed a lot of time, resources, and money to carefully crafting every word in their statements. A company's ideology will be printed, framed, and hung in offices and hallways throughout the organization. Miniature versions will lie tucked away in wallets and desk drawers. But ask any employee what the company's mission statement is, and how it affects his or her everyday job, and 99 out of 100 won't be able to tell you—and this includes the executives!

There are probably no areas other than change projects that are the source of as much cynicism and derision as "mission and values" statements. For most people, these statements are worse than useless—they are seen as boring and irrelevant platitudes dreamed up by some consultant or out-of-touch management team and imposed on the organization. Few people know them, nobody seems to live by them, and rarely does anyone—including management—seem to care either way.

This must change.

A strong, well-understood core ideology is *vital* to a Quantum Organization. It is through shared beliefs and intentions that people are able to act autonomously and remain

> *You know you have a rockin' Vision Statement when it inspires the employees to think of themselves as being involved in something much more important than their pathetic little underpaid jobs . . .*
>
> — Scott Adams, author of
> *The Dilbert Principle*

in accord with the whole—thus drastically reducing the need for external controls. A strong core ideology fulfills the organic principle of *identity*, and makes it possible for the organization to remain stable despite extreme environmental changes. I have dedicated a substantial portion of this chapter to core ideology and its two major components (purpose and principles) because they are so important in the effective operation of Quantum Organizations.

This is an area that bureaucratic organizations typically ignore. Bureaucracies establish order through external controls and rigid structures, so they perceive little need for—and have little interest in—the organizing power of shared purpose and principles. Quantum Organizations, in contrast, rely heavily on core ideology and shared vision for creating order and make little use of external controls.

A Bill of Rights and Responsibilities

A core ideology is the organization's Bill of Rights and Responsibilities that spells out the ideas and beliefs that every member of the organization needs to subscribe to. It grants protections and privileges to all of the organization's stakeholders. This means that if an organization aspires to the principle of "openness," for instance, no one will be penalized for speaking the truth. If such a situation does emerge, then the person needs to have a recourse that guarantees fair treatment. Without such a system, a core ideology is not worth

the paper it is written on. Ray & Berndtson (a leading international executive search firm) is faced with just such a situation regarding a significant cultural shift it is undertaking. To ensure that its new principles are applied equally to all of their firm's members, it has established a board of appeals. This is a temporary group that will last only until their new culture of openness makes it possible for any employee—regardless of position or power—to address issues directly with any other employee.

Rights and privileges must be accompanied by responsible stewardship. A core ideology explicitly states the shared commitments to all of the organization's key stakeholders. Tom Chappell, CEO of Tom's of Maine, provided an example of what such a commitment to principle means. His organization has a Statement of Beliefs that includes: "We believe that we have a responsibility to cultivate the best relationships possible with our co-workers, customers, owners, agents, suppliers, and our community." Recently this belief was put to the test. After Tom's of Maine changed the ingredients in one of their deodorant products, customers complained that the deodorant was "conking out halfway through the day." Chappell was faced with a dilemma. To recall the product would cost $400,000 and 30 percent of their projected annual profits. To not do so would make a sham of the company's guiding ideals. Chappell explained his thinking during this crisis:

> The Mission had left us no choice. Leaving a weak product on the shelves would have risked the faith and trust of customers and employees alike. How could we expect our employees to live by the Mission if the company itself threw it aside? Our values and beliefs as a company helped put the crisis in perspective.

Tom's of Maine recalled the product. Other companies have set similar examples. Odwalla, a fresh juice bottler on the U.S. West Coast, voluntarily recalled all of its apple juice-based products after an E. Coli outbreak that was traced to the fresh apple juice used in some of its blends. The entire company became involved in the effort, and within 48 hours of learning of the problem, the recall was complete. Throughout the ordeal, Odwalla kept the public informed through full-page newspaper ads and frequent press conferences. Afterward, Odwalla took the further step of founding the Nourishment and Food Safety Council in case similar situations occur in the future. Odwalla's values provided the company with clear guidance during the crisis, and although painful financially, the decision itself was quite simple.

As demonstrated in the examples above, an effective core ideology not only provides guidance for decisions, it also provides a changeless center that holds the company together during times of change and hardship. People can come and go; the company can expand into new markets or products and withdraw from others; it can have good years and bad years; and it can undergo gradual change or dramatic change. And through it all, the core ideology remains changeless. Like the roots of a tree in a windstorm, the core ideas and guiding beliefs of the company keep it standing firm and allow it to withstand the change. Many people credit IBM's principles—respect for the individual, excellence, and service—with pulling them through their financial crisis in the 1980s. In my work helping organizations achieve transformative change, I have noticed that it is invariably the ones with the strongest "center" that fare the best.

> *It's not hard to make a decision when you know what your values are.*
>
> — Roy Disney

Although "changelessness" is one of the virtues of the core ideology, it is equally important to recognize that the organic principle of *flexibility* applies even here. Change to the core ideology is something that happens much more slowly and less frequently than all of the other elements of the Organizational EcoSystem Model. However, it too must be open for challenge and change. Part of the reason that IBM had troubles in the first place is that the shared interpretation of their basic beliefs became rigid and inflexible. The commitment to "respect for the individual" had, over the years, been distorted into a belief in employee entitlement. As a result, complacency and resistance to change increased. As external competition heated up in the early 1980s, IBM was unable to shift this belief in accord with the changing environment, and it paid a painful price. The principle itself wasn't inappropriate, it was the distorted *application* of the principle that was inappropriate. Part of IBM's performance improvement

resulted from rescripting the meaning of this principle throughout the organization—keeping the best of the original intent and discarding the destructive component. Strengthening and clarifying the organization's core ideology is an important responsibility for leaders in Quantum Organizations.

Purpose

An organization's purpose should answer the question: "What is it that we are gathered together to do?" In answering this question, companies must walk the fine line between being too general and being too specific. Quantum Organizations have a purpose that is broad enough to remain relevant despite dramatic changes in the marketplace.

The Trammel Crow company found this out the hard way. Their original vision was "to be the premier customer-driven real estate company in the U.S." This vision served them well for years, but it had a hidden deficiency that did not surface until the real estate recession in the 1980s. Suddenly, the limitation to "real estate" did not leave the company with a large enough pool of opportunities to sustain them. So, the company added one word—"services." Expanding into real estate services broadened the company's market substantially. However, making a change like this is not easy. Trammell Crow estimates that it reduced its workforce by 35 percent as a result of the changes required by adding that one word.

In a related situation, Ray & Berndtson found it necessary to change its corporate mission in response to new competitive pressures in the executive search industry. Its new purpose broadens the company's potential services from just finding and placing the "right" executive (as is common in this industry), to providing "superior people and organizational solutions worldwide." This focus on *organizational solutions* is based on the awareness that it isn't just the executives who must perform—it is the executives and his or her environment which must perform *collectively*. Ray & Berndtson recognized that this may involve its client organizations in making many systemic changes that are unrelated to the search for a new employee, and it needed to be prepared to provide these services. Although the revised purpose statement will require sweeping changes throughout all of the elements of the company's organizational ecosystem, it is convinced there will be tremendous benefit over the long term.

> Organizations are about *people*. They are the gardens in which the collective hopes, aspirations, and beliefs of the people within them are planted, grown, and harvested.

An organization's purpose must answer a second question: "What are our intentions toward and commitments to each stakeholder?" This question challenges head-on the pervasive notion that businesses are machines for producing profit for the stockholders. Organizations are about *people*. They are the gardens in which the collective hopes, aspirations, and beliefs of the people within them are planted, grown, and harvested. It is people who breathe life into organizations through their commitment and positive energy. What is it that inspires people to commit to an organization's purpose? Well, the surprise for most companies is that it isn't *money*. Anita Roddick, CEO of the Body Shop, explained that "money is not the most important thing to people. What most people *really* want from their work is the feeling that they are part of something *important*." Dee Hock believes that "money motivates neither the best people nor the best in people. It can move the body and influence the mind, but it cannot touch the heart or move the spirit."

People are attracted to meaningful purpose. Consider this statement from Merck's Declaration of Strategic Intent:

> We are in the business of preserving and improving human life. All of our actions must be measured by our success in achieving this goal.

Now compare it to the first sentence in Southland's Corporate mission statement:

> The Southland Corporation exists to maximize the long-term value of shareholder equity.

Which of these two statements do you suppose would be more inspiring to the average employee? If you were an employee at one of these companies and

were asked to "go the extra mile," which purpose would you feel better serving? We will discuss this need for meaning in more detail when we address shared vision in the next chapter, but it is important to understand that inspiration begins with an organization's purpose.

Balancing Stakeholder Interests. As living systems interdependent with the greater social and natural ecosystems, organizations must seek dynamic balance between *all* of their stakeholders. This means that they need to have a conscious purpose not only for customers and stockholders, but also for employees, the communities in which they operate, the natural environment, suppliers, national and global society, and governments. Businesses have clear intentions toward their stockholders (make money for them), and in the last decade many companies have added intentions toward their customers (make them happy). From a systems perspective, unless companies have comparable intentions toward their other major stakeholders, they have created an *out-of-balance* condition. Without this balance, the organization will inevitably bias its actions toward highly valued stakeholders (stockholders and customers) at the expense of less-valued stakeholders. And this "expense" is literal—the transfer is not a reciprocal exchange. Value is taken from employees, society, and the ecology and transferred to the stockholders.

For instance, in recent years, many companies have established aggressive deadlines and goals (through reengineering and similar efforts) that were intended to produce significant profitability improvements. These efforts have required employees to make substantial personal sacrifices—working extremely long hours and committing enormous amounts of personal energy. Most companies revere this sort of dedication. What companies do not acknowledge is that these sacrifices take employees' time and energy away from their families and friends, their social organizations (churches, charities, and community), and their physical fitness. All of these other systems are put under stress so that one—the business—might have disproportionate benefits. As a result, the health of the overall system declines.

The scary fact is that virtually every company does this. In *The Fifth Discipline*, Peter Senge describes a type of system feedback loop called "The Tragedy of the Commons." This model shows what happens when one agent takes more than an equitable share of the system's common resources. In the original story, a sheep rancher allowed his sheep to eat more of the grass from the village commons than was his equitable share—the rancher was transferring an excess of the village's value (the grass) to himself (fatter sheep). The trouble with this behavior was that soon all the other agents in the system (other ranchers) caught on and everyone started to overuse the commons. Eventually the common resources were consumed or damaged beyond further use. The principle of *dynamic balance* makes it clear that such behavior is unsustainable in the long term. Out-of-balance behavior creates a "reinforcing feedback loop" that will eventually reach natural limits and crash—bringing the system down with it. Conversely, a balanced system creates equitable value for all of its stakeholders. The vibrant, healthy ecosystem that results, co-evolves to *everyone's* benefit. Although Quantum Organizations are inevitably egalitarian, this is not based on what some people would cynically describe as "altruistic bleeding-heart liberalism." This principle is based on our scientific understanding of how living systems work most effectively.

> *The most enlightened companies view all their employees as freelancers who are independent entrepreneurs. They just happen to be inside your boundaries and on your payroll, but in fact they can choose to live and work anywhere. So the quality and vitality of the community matters a great deal—it affects employee's ideas, what they bring to the job, and their staying power with your company.*
>
> — Ed McCracken,
> Chairman and CEO, Silicon Graphics

The organic principle of *flexibility* requires that living systems have the ability to make a "big push" periodically as the environment requires, in the way that an antelope must be able to flee a lion. However, an organization cannot sustain this energy beyond certain limits any more than an antelope can run at full speed indefinitely. Dynamic balance requires that such explosive expenditures be

matched *in kind* with recuperative periods. The "in kind" requirement is essential. When people have sacrificed excessive time at the expense of themselves and the greater social system, their balance cannot be restored through *money*. It was *time* that was "overdrawn," and only *time* can restore the balance. This is a key point that our society misses, and one that is a primary contributor to our society's overall distress.

Fortunately, we have evidence to show that it *does pay* to value all of the stakeholders equally. Terrence Deal and Allan Kennedy, authors of *Corporate Culture and Performance,* studied the cultures of twenty-two top companies in ten different industries. One of their key conclusions was that "valuing all key constituencies differentiates the better performers from the others." Said another way, companies that valued all of their stakeholders were more adaptive in the face of dramatic change and outperformed the organizations that put stockholders first. Also, Collins and Porras reported that the high-performing visionary companies in *Built to Last* did not have a driving force to maximize profit. Rather, they saw profit as a natural consequence of service to customers, employees, and society. Recall that over the past forty years, these companies outperformed the stock market by an average of 15:1. George Merck II (of the pharmaceutical company) captured this sentiment when he said:

> We try never to forget that medicine is for the people. It is not for the profits. The profits follow, and if we have remembered that, they have never failed to appear. The better we have remembered it, the larger we have been.

Decisions everywhere in the organization need to take into account the need to balance the commitments to all of the stakeholders. Measures, comparable to those established for profitability and stock value, must be developed for all of the major stakeholders. This is the true sense of a "balanced scorecard." Ralph Estes, writing in *Tyranny of the Bottom Line,* proposed a "scorecard" where businesses would have explicit accountabilities to customers, workers, communities, and society. Holding senior executives accountable for balancing the needs of all of the key stakeholders would change the face of business virtually overnight. Layoffs would all but disappear because there would be no net advantage to the executives—any benefits from increased profitability would be more than offset by decreases in the measures for employee satisfaction. Pollution would be sharply curtailed for similar reasons. Decreases in environmental quality would outweigh any cost savings from not cleaning up the company's polluted discharge. In such cases, the company would have to find new and creative solutions to balance the needs of the stakeholders, rather than maximizing the benefit to one of them.

> Holding senior executives accountable for balancing the needs of all of the key stakeholders would change the face of business virtually overnight.

Major decisions, where possible, should include an advocate for each stakeholder's position. If that is not possible, then the roles should be assigned to those involved. The medicine wheel council—an American Indian tribal decision-making approach—demonstrates how this can be done. In this practice, each of the attending chiefs takes one of eight different perspectives that corresponds with the points of a compass. Each role represents a point of view. One must speak for the future, another for emotion, and others for strategy, the health of the tribe, and so on. In a business context, this can be applied by assigning one person to adopt the perspective of each of the major stakeholders. Through dialogue, each point of view would be heard and factored into final decisions.

Guiding Principles

Principles define the qualities that are most important to the unique identity of an organization. These principles shape (and are shaped by) people's individual and collective behaviors, as well as the operation of the company. Most companies explicitly declare their guiding principles as part of their core ideology. These are called the *espoused* principles because they are documented and actively communicated. The espoused principles are the characteristics for which the company wants to be known: what the company believes will make a difference in the marketplace. In many cases, these principles derive from the personal principles of a company's founders. In companies with strong cultures, one or two of the core principles tend to become associated with the company. Some

examples include enthusiasm at Mary Kay Cosmetics, reverence for employees at Southwest Airlines, ethics at Levi Strauss, customer service at Nordstrom's, quality at Motorola, and innovation at 3M.

As you likely know from personal experience, there is often a substantial gap between the espoused principles and those that are practiced on a daily basis. These latter principles are called *principles-in-action*. It is the principles-in-action that are *really* shaping employee behavior, and this is where many companies run into trouble. Often the principles-in-action bear little, if any, relation to the organization's espoused principles. When the guiding principles are absent or not clearly understood, different groups inevitably develop their own. Left to chance, principles are almost always related to local interests. This contributes to conflict and the feeling of disarray that is pervasive in many businesses. Not only are there many different principles-in-action in different groups, but they are also often in direct conflict with the organization's stated goals. For example, in many large bureaucratic organizations, efforts to increase efficiency through innovation have run headlong into a principle-in-action of "avoid risk." Principles are powerful forces in shaping behavior. They can either work for the organization or against it. Companies that ignore them are guaranteed to pay a high price.

Most principles are stated as a single word: quality, service, integrity, openness. How are employees to understand what they mean? What, for instance, is meant by "openness"? Does that mean that everyone should share everything, and wouldn't that result in a deluge of data? Are decision makers to share their initial thinking about a decision, even though it may change by the time it is finalized? Are employees to be open about salaries? Are the details of employee firings and misconduct to be spread throughout the company? How open should employees be with customers, and on what topics? These are the kinds of issues that employees run into in applying the core principles in their everyday activities.

In Quantum Organizations, leaders have a primary role in communicating and clarifying the organization's espoused principles. Unless employees gain clarity about the meaning of the guiding principles, they have no way to implement them in a consistent manner. This is by no means an easy task. It requires the ability to listen, empathize, and dialogue—skills that few traditional managers have. When Ray & Berndtson embarked on its journey of corporate transformation, it identified four principles that will be critical to its future: integrity, client focus, teamwork, and innovation. The first step in creating broad-based understanding of these new principles was to define several clarifying points for each. For example, the points that describe integrity are:

- Creating a safe environment where people interact openly and honestly
- Respecting everyone
- Owning our integrity 24 hours a day
- Neither practicing duplicity nor condoning gossip
- Acting with integrity, even when profits are at stake

The leaders of the transformation effort at Ray & Berndtson knew that this was only the start. The process for employees to fully understand and internalize the principles would require many months or even years of ongoing dialogue.

Strategy: The Difference That Makes a Difference

An organization's *strategy* is its unique approach for fulfilling its purpose. Purpose is *what* a company intends to do; strategy is *how* it intends to do it. It is essential to the survival of any company to select an approach at which it can excel, one that customers will value. The determination of an organization's strategic positioning has a profound impact on the design of the remaining elements of the organization's ecosystem. They must be configured to achieve the chosen approach, which makes it difficult or impossible for the organizational ecosystem to support a dissimilar strategy, even if it relates to the same purpose. This is a key point that many companies do not grasp.

We can return to our allegory of Eric the Red and his Viking adventurers to gain a better understanding of this point. The Vikings chose to achieve their goal by boat. The decision of a strategic "vehicle" is not easily changed—it is a deep

commitment to a particular approach. A boat for instance, does not easily convert to a wagon train, nor would the crew have the skills for over-land travel.

While working for a software company, I had the opportunity to launch a consulting division to support our customers' use of the software. Consulting was a new strategy. It was a unique way of fulfilling the company's purpose, and I soon learned that it was completely incompatible with the organization's processes, technologies, and structures. Worst of all, it clashed with the company's culture. Consulting required different credit policies, and billing and collection processes. The compensation scheme could not be adapted to consultants who made more money on average than the other employees and were rewarded based on different criteria. There were no processes for organizing and conducting training seminars. The information systems could not capture the information that was needed. The organization's culture led people to resent dedicating any time to what they considered blasphemy: non-software activities. Before long, the venture was ended—despite an extremely positive response from customers.

This is not an isolated experience. It is what any company can expect that creates new strategies (lines of business, changes in distribution channels, new customer markets). The rule of thumb is this: Changes to any ecosystem element require changes to every element further out in the model. When a company buys an unrelated subsidiary or creates a new division or product line, it cannot assume that the existing organization can support the new venture. Most likely, the company will require either major changes or entirely new cultures, processes, technologies, and structures. For my business unit to have been a success, it would have required branching off completely and forming an entirely new organizational ecosystem. It was this experience that solidified my understanding of the interdependency that strategy has with the other ecosystem elements.

BHAGs and Stretch Goals

For an organization to embark on its "journey," it needs a destination, a goal to work toward. In Eric the Red's case, this was a new land, what we now call North America. This was a "stretch goal," if there ever was one. It held tremendous promise, but *nobody* had ever done it before. In *Built to Last*, Collins and Porras called these "Big Hairy Audacious Goals," (abbreviated BHAGs). In change management terminology, these are called "super-ordinate goals." BHAGs are important for stimulating progress in organizations and can be powerful motivators during times of organizational transformation. Examples of BHAGs are: NASA's 1962 goal to "put a man on the moon and return him home safely by the end of the decade," Motorola's goal of six sigma quality, and Chrysler's goal to reduce its new car development cycle from sixty to thirty-nine months. Effective BHAGs have three characteristics: they are audacious, inspiring, and unifying.

Audacious. The word *audacious* means "unrestrained by convention or propriety." An audacious goal elicits responses like: "You are going to try to do what?!!!" In order for a goal to be audacious, it must stretch the imagination. In 1962, when President John F. Kennedy laid his challenge before NASA, the space program was in its infancy. At the time, the idea of putting a man on the moon by 1970 was preposterous. And yet, NASA accepted the challenge and its glory is now etched in the annals of time. Some people balk at first when exposed to this concept. They voice concerns that if a goal isn't reasonable enough, it may backfire and demoralize employees. This is where the next part comes in.

Inspiring. The second aspect of a BHAG is that it is inspiring. The best way to think about this is with a question: "What if we *could* achieve this BHAG somehow; what would it mean for us?" Imagine what the scientists at NASA would have thought in regard to this question: they would make history; they would shatter the limits of human potential; they would do what humans had only dreamed about for tens of thousands of years. "This," they must have thought, "is something that I *must* be a part of." Most effective BHAGs are not about money or stock prices. It wouldn't do well, for instance, to have a BHAG of

increasing the stock price by 30 percent in two years. People are inspired by meaningful contribution—doing something significant in the world. BHAGs will always have the indirect effect of dramatically improving profitability. Don't try to make "profit" the BHAG itself.

Unifying. One of the real benefits of a BHAG is that it unifies the efforts of the entire organization toward a common goal. The way it accomplishes this is that the goal *cannot be achieved otherwise*. NASA could not have put a man on the moon without every individual doing their part. The same for Motorola: How does a company achieve such extreme levels of quality without a tremendous amount of teamwork and cooperation? When engineers at Chrysler first heard of the thirty-nine month goal for new product development, they were sure that it could not be done. When they finally achieved it, they realized it took the participation and support of every single department.

New Thinking About How to Develop Strategy

I believe it is important to demystify the concept of creating corporate strategy. Consultants have probably charged a gazillion dollars over the years while helping companies determine new strategies. In addition, there must have been a thousand books published on the subject. Through all of this, strategy has been made into something mysterious and elusive—something that only the "high-priests" of consulting could divine. But it does not have to be this way. Strategy is this simple: You have a strategy when you have given customers a reason to substitute your product or service for another.

Pundit Tom Peters reminds us that tomorrow's sales are only as secure as our ability to convince customers that we have something special to offer. He calls this "the power of WOW." Fortunately, the possibilities are literally endless, with the only limitation being our imaginations. The fast-changing world in which we live requires that organizations develop innovative strategies and then constantly challenge them. Following are some guidelines to consider:

✠ *Take off your cultural blindfolds.* Learn the industry's rules and beliefs—then break them. The examples set by Outback Steakhouse and Charles Schwab Corp. illustrate how effective this can be. (See page 99 for more information.)

✠ *Democratize the process.* As with everything else in Quantum Organizations, it is essential to engage the collective wisdom and creativity of the employees in all aspects of running the company, including developing strategy. There is no way in this quantum environment for centrally located planners and executives to know what their organizations of hundreds, thousands, or even tens of thousands of employees know. This is a rich field of potential that the successful organization has learned to tap.

✠ *Develop scenarios of possible futures.* The process of developing scenarios requires that an organization look at alternatives. Companies use this information to pose the question, "What would happen to us if this or that scenario were to unfold instead of the one that most people expect?" Royal Dutch Shell did this to prepare for a possible drop in oil prices—which nobody else believed possible—but which eventually *did* occur in the early 1970s. Foresight enabled the company to respond faster and more effectively than any others in the industry, and led to its rise to the top of the field. (Peter Schwartz describes the scenario process in detail in *The Art of the Long View.*)

✠ *Consider every aspect of your organization's internal ecosystem as a potential source for differentiation.* Nature uses latent potential in systems as a potent source for evolutionary creativity. Every aspect of your organization that is unique—whether it be an eccentric culture, world-class processes such as distribution, cutting-edge technologies, novel organization structures, or core competencies—is a potential source of strategic advantage. Southwest Airline's fun-loving culture adds to its attractiveness to many travelers. Texas Instruments used the reengineering skills that they developed internally to offer a new service externally. The Charles Schwab Corporation leveraged its technological advantage to offer services no other brokerage company could match.

✠ *Join with other agents in the greater social ecosystem to co-evolve new market innovations.* Through their practice of "Keiretsu," the Japanese have for years taken advantage of the interrelated destinies of an entire web of companies.

This practice has given the participating companies tremendous stability (although their rigidity in applying the concept is beginning to put them at a disadvantage globally). Western companies are beginning to see the wisdom of an ecosystem approach and even traditional enemies are beginning to cooperate. IBM and arch-rival Apple Computer's recent collaboration on new product developments is one such example. Many companies have leveraged close relationships with suppliers to improve product design, speed up development, and reduce costs.

✳ *Obsolete your own products before the market does, and accept that valid and valuable products and services may have a very short life.* Companies will increasingly be forced to shorten the life spans of their own products as the speed of innovation continues to increase. (See page 102 for more information.)

✳ *Add new competencies.* A company's flexibility can, in part, be equated to the number of competencies that it has. Western companies have been busily shedding potential competencies in the name of efficiency for years. Through the practice of outsourcing, companies have gradually stripped themselves of new channels for competitive advantage. As a general rule, Japanese companies do not make this mistake. Master strategists C. K. Prahalad and Gary Hamel point out that Japanese firms enter into alliances with other companies with the intention of eventually learning and bringing in-house a new competency. They quote one Japanese executive as saying, "Collaboration is second best. But I will feel worse if after four years we do not know how to do what our partner knows how to do. We must digest their skills." If you have the skills, you can choose not to deploy them—but if you never develop them in the first place, you do not have that choice at all.

Break the Rules. When the founders of Outback Steakhouse launched their new chain of restaurants, industry experts said they were crazy. They broke many rules that—based on conventional wisdom—should have guaranteed their failure. They opened for dinner only, ignoring the additional sales available from the lunch crowd. They paid more than the industry average for their meat, choosing to buy only the best meat available. They allowed store managers to participate in a significant way in the restaurant's earnings, and they avoided creating layers of middle management. They also made the kitchens in the restaurants much larger than the norm. All of these ideas break with convention, however, they were consistent with the company's strategy: create a company of owners, decentralize control, and provide first-rate food and service. The results? Outback Steakhouse grew from nothing to $544 million in sales in just seven years. In 1994, the company won *Inc.* magazine's *Entrepreneur of the Year Award*.

Discount brokerage firm Charles Schwab has had a similar experience. In the late 1980s, Schwab broke with the industry practice of using commissioned sales personnel to schmooze and advise clients, a practice which often came at substantial expense to the client. Instead, they offered a no-pressure, low-cost approach that was backed up by innovative use of technology. Between 1991 and 1993, Schwab's assets swelled by 150 percent.

Substitutors and Complementors. If you look closely at the Organizational EcoSystem Model, you will notice two unfamiliar terms, Substitutors and Complementors, both of which have important strategic significance. *Substitutor* is the term that I use instead of "competitor." The mental image that we hold of competitors is of companies or people who are out to destroy us. This concentrates our attention on other companies rather than on our customers. For instance, one high-tech firm found itself falling behind a competitor in the marketplace. Because it was competitor-focused, the organization spent its time and efforts to match the other company's product innovations. This was a game of catch-up that they could never hope to win.

The word *competition* often has a fear-filled connotation. Companies regularly use the threat of "relentless and cutthroat" competition to instill fear in their employees, with the idea that this will somehow motivate them. What it does, instead, is create a tremendous amount of counterproductive behavior.

The word Substitutors carries no negative connotation. Its use helps companies to focus on their customers and realize that those customers have the choice of substituting someone else's product and still have their needs met. Such a focus is a powerful source of creativity and the only real security any organization ever

has. Another advantage of the concept of Substitutors is that it broadens our horizon—we begin to see products, services, and innovations outside of our "competitive radar" that are legitimate Substitutors.

Ray & Berndtson had this experience when it began its strategic transformation. The companies that it had historically concerned itself with were a small field of large, well-known executive recruiting firms. As it began to investigate the Substitutors for executive job placement, the firm made several surprising discoveries. The first was that the Internet was quickly becoming a viable source for job postings and search—one web site already had some 20,000 job postings. Despite the fact that the jobs were largely below the compensation level that Ray & Berndtson was usually interested in, the listings held powerful implications for the future of the search industry. Another revelation was how similar the top-tier executives were becoming to sports and entertainment stars. Ray & Berndtson realized it was probably just a matter of time before these executives began to retain professional agents, a possibility that has already been realized in the high-tech field. Both of these findings paint a new environmental scenario, and this has helped Ray & Berndtson establish a much wider range of strategic choices.

Complementors, on the other hand, are companies that sell products that your customers can combine with your products to create greater value. A prime example of this is computer software and hardware. One without the other is useless, and each can be enhanced by the quality of the other. What products are Complementors to your company's products? For the auto industry, the Complementors include oil companies and road construction companies. However, it also includes some less obvious sources: radio stations, audio tapes, and compact disc makers—each of which can make the driving experience more enjoyable. At Ray & Berndtson, the Complementors included teamwork trainers, executive coaches, organizational development consultants, and universities, to name a few. As with Substitutors, organizations can use information about Complementors to broaden their strategic focus. How could you partner with your Complementors as computer manufacturers do when they bundle software with their hardware? Your customers are almost always Complementors in that they transform your product in the process of integrating it into their uses. What complementary activities could you take over for them? General Electric recently announced a major expansion to offer services for many of its customers' activities that complement not just GE hardware, but also hardware from other manufacturers. How could you increase the attractiveness of your own products by working with Complementors to modify their products in regard to yours?

Obsolete Your Own Products. This almost heretical notion will soon become the norm. Certain companies are already seeing the wisdom of this, particularly in the high-tech arena. A recent example was IBM's decision to replace its award-winning fold-out laptop computer keyboard design. Rather than retain the innovation until the marketplace rendered it obsolete, IBM chose to obsolete it. Why? IBM already had a better product in the labs and knew that to sit still was equivalent to falling behind.

Another trend is toward new products and services that come and go in a relatively short time. Many companies today ignore any innovation that won't have a very long life. The problem is that there will be very few of these in the future, as we are seeing in the software industry. We need to learn to view these, not as failures like we do today, but as products whose time has come and gone. This practice, I believe, will be the model for sustained corporate growth in the future. The concept of "growth," rather than meaning "continually getting bigger," will soon evolve to mean *renewal*: constantly innovating and changing, but not necessarily increasing the revenue base. (Many professional services firms already do this and have done so successfully for years.)

> The concept of "growth," rather than meaning "continually getting bigger," will soon evolve to mean *renewal*: constantly innovating and changing, but not necessarily increasing the revenue base.

Even innovations that companies choose not to pursue can be used to advantage. *Wired* magazine (October 1996) chronicled the (mis)fortunes of Atari, which went from startup in 1972 to sales of $512 million in just eight years, only to be bought out in 1993 with sales of a paltry $30 million. During this time, Atari experienced defections of a large number of what *Wired* called "the sharpest scientists and programmers in the business," many of whom went on to found or lead a wide range of successful new companies. What

did it cost Atari to not support and fund the success of these bright inventors? Its existence. Rather than killing new product innovations or forcing their creators to leave the firm to achieve their personal visions, companies should spin products off as stand-alone start-ups.

Springfield Remanufacturing Corporation (SRC) has taken exactly this approach. SRC has spun off seventeen new ventures over fifteen years. During that period, it has increased in size 1000 percent, and has not laid off a single employee. At the same time that SRC has been strengthening its own revenue base; it has been promoting the spread of wealth, increasing the diversity of the marketplace, creating new jobs, and increasing the health of the overall social ecosystem.

Culture: Believing is Seeing

Beliefs are deeply-held ideas both about how the world *does* work and how it *should* work. Taken collectively, beliefs form our "mental maps," or what I have been calling a "worldview." People hold worldviews that consist of several layers: beliefs rising out of their personal experiences, beliefs they have adopted through the society in which they live, and beliefs of the organizations to which they belong.

The Quantum Culture

The differences between people who were raised in China, Japan, America, Russia, and Saudi Arabia are principally due to the social worldview that these countries espouse. I call these deep beliefs *meta-principles* in order to emphasize the power they have over our lives. Although there are many ways to play "reductionist" and categorize the various differences between cultures, I will focus on an East/West dichotomy. The Eastern philosophies—Taoism, Buddhism, Hinduism, (and the mystical traditions of Western religions)—as well as those of indigenous peoples, are intrinsically organic. They all speak of a single universal god, of "all is one," of everything being interconnected, of the need for balance and flow, of inner wisdom, and of Nature being alive and revered. The Western worldview, in contrast, is almost entirely dominated by the Newtonian-Cartesian philosophy of the world-machine. It is at the level of these meta-principles that traditional organizations must change if they are to function effectively in this increasingly quantum world.

When we talk about cultural change in organizations, we normally refer to changes in the beliefs at the organizational level, such as customer service and quality. In order to become a Quantum Organization, companies must instill principles at the organizational level for integrity, honesty, trust, empathy, learning (or some other reference to change such as "continuous improvement"), risk taking, equity, dialogue, inclusion, participation, and personal responsibility.

Quantum Organizations base their design and operations on the principles of the quantum worldview, but they do not simply reject the principles of the classical worldview. Rather, the organic principle of *dynamic balance* requires that they be included as an important element in our complete repertoire of responses. The principles of the mechanistic model are still appropriate in those situations that have machine-like qualities, such as when people engineer the design and operation of machines. However, they are no longer appropriate for *every* situation in the way that they are applied today.

How Culture Is Created

It is important to understand how culture is developed. This will explain in part why we find culture so difficult to change. When an organization is formed, the culture derives almost entirely from the founders. As time goes on, the organization receives feedback from the environment as to what works and what doesn't work. Through organizational memory, these lessons are institutionalized. The "things that work" become beliefs about what to *do* in the future to succeed. The "things that don't work" become beliefs about what *not* to do in the future in order to succeed. When these beliefs are applied over a long period of time and continue to produce success, they keep getting stronger until they reach the status of core beliefs.

Once a mind-set is established, the organization uses it to filter information and interpret events. Because an organization has a particular belief, it looks for evidence that supports it and excludes what does not. The organization also

unconsciously creates situations where its beliefs can be validated—it manipulates situations so the belief *has* to be validated. At this point, beliefs become unchallengable—they become "sacred cows" that must be taken as given assumptions. As soon as something becomes rigid and can no longer change, the organization's flexibility and ability to adapt are compromised and it has started down the road to obsolescence. For instance, in the late 1970s, IBM believed that the mainframe computer would remain supreme

> *There's an old expression, "Seeing is believing." But it's more accurate to say that "Believing is seeing." That is, you tend to see what you believe you're going to see. You bring to a situation what you expect you are going to experience"*
>
> — Dr. Carl Sorensen, Professor at Stanford University

and that personal computers would never catch on. It believed this because mainframe computing was its core competence; to believe anything else would require drastic changes. So, in the process of researching the viability of PCs, IBM filtered and denied the results so that the answer had to come up in favor of mainframes. Of course, we all know how this story ended: IBM fell drastically behind in this huge business segment.

Deeply held convictions make beliefs difficult to change. When management introduces the need to change a cultural belief, people's first reaction is to defend the belief and show how it is still valid; it is simply being implemented incorrectly. This is the "just try harder" defense. People are understandably fearful of new ideas. The question becomes, "How do we know this new idea will work any better?" People are normally convinced that it *won't* work any better, but few voice this concern. (Of course, the real issue is, "What happens to *me* after these changes are in place?") The only way that any new belief ever catches on is that it *produces success.* This is one reason why it is so vital for change efforts to demonstrate "quick wins." The sooner the organization begins to see that a new idea or approach works, the sooner the rescripting of the cultural beliefs can occur.

> A healthy organization remains aware of its core beliefs and encourages people to continually question them.

A healthy organization remains aware of its core beliefs and encourages people to continually question them. When it is clear that a belief is no longer viable or healthy, the organization must begin to experiment and learn so that it can modify or replace the outdated belief. In the quantum worldview, all solutions and structures—including beliefs, which are mental structures—are understood to be temporary. Quantum Organizations look forward, not back.

The Organizing Power of Beliefs and Principles

The organizing action of beliefs can be compared to the way fractals work. In Nature, fractal patterns combine repeatedly until they form magnificent structures with ever-increasing levels of complexity and order. The result is a highly interrelated organic entity. In human organizations, principles form the basis—the fractal pattern—for decisions at every level. Over time, layer upon layer of harmonized decisions produce a coherent and consistent pattern of behavior and organization. The resulting structures and behaviors are elegant complexes of interrelationships that would have been impossible to engineer in the manner of an architectural design. This is the self-organizing behavior of living systems.

We have fooled ourselves for years into thinking that organizations were inanimate objects that we could design and construct to precise engineering specifications. We have identified the parts and prescribed how the parts should fit together, but no one has ever designed the way the system comes together in an integrated whole. The best we can do is lay out the basic pattern. The details—the intricate connective tissue—have to be left up to the organization to develop for itself. When a major organizational change is proposed, the common practice is to design it on paper and then hand it off to a team to implement. The front-line employees who must execute this design are seen as inert "lumps" that have to be prodded into executing the change as it was designed. The problem that occurs

> Core beliefs are like fractal patterns in Nature; they combine repeatedly until they form magnificent structures with ever-increasing levels of complexity and order.

is that no plan could ever be complete enough to anticipate every contingency. And when these contingencies surface, the project team gets exhausted trying to race from "fire" to "fire" in an effort to keep things going.

In a Quantum Organization, it is the front-line people who assume responsibility for changes. Because the "design" principles for how the organization will operate are shared with everyone, the people who surface contingencies are in position to make independent decisions about what to do. Part of Ray & Berndtson's new strategy is to complete their searches 60 percent faster than the industry average. There were several principles (which the firm called "key success factors") that provided the theoretical underpinnings of the strategy. One of them was "process in parallel" (that is, do many things simultaneously). As the new process design was being implemented, countless situations arose that were exceptions to the rule. Individual consultants were able to adapt these exceptions to the organizational design without top-down direction because they already knew "process in parallel" and the other design principles. There was little for the implementation team to add. This behavior represents the organic principles of *identity* and *creativity* in action—individual agents acting autonomously to promote the welfare of the whole, using new information and interactions with other people to devise creative and novel responses to environmental challenges.

Structure: People and Governance

There are three aspects to structure: governance, people and physical layout. Structure is an element of the Organizational EcoSystem Model that has been heavily influenced by the Newtonian-Cartesian worldview, and that has significant opportunity for improvements.

Governance: Distribution of Power and Authority

Few (if any) of the popular change programs have seriously challenged the power structure in organizations. *Fortune* magazine (February 21, 1994), described corporate chiefs who supposedly embraced the "post-heroic" distributed leadership concepts: "What they didn't do—deep down inside—was actually give up much control or abandon their fundamental beliefs about leadership." When organizations removed layers of middle management and "flattened" (there is more than one way to interpret that word . . .) the organization, they had really changed very little. They now

> *Everything I thought I knew about leadership is wrong. . . . What is the new definition of leadership? I can't offer absolute answers. . . . But I do know from my own experience that the leadership techniques that applied 20 years ago don't apply anymore.*
>
> — Mort Meyerson, CEO, Perot Systems

had a command-and-control style that was merely spread across fewer people. The issue was the distribution of authority—and that was not touched. There is ample evidence that the command-and-control approach to governance is inadequate for the speed and complexity of today's environment. And no amount of "tweaking"—such as reducing managerial layers, delegating authority, and implementing teams—will suffice. "Whips and chains are no longer an alternative," says leadership guru Warren Bennis. "Leaders must learn to change the nature of power and how it's employed." Only fundamental transformation of our governance practices will create the flexible, adaptive, and creative organization required to succeed in the twenty-first century.

Governance is an extremely sensitive, but nonetheless important, topic in regard to the creation of Quantum Organizations. Governance gets to the heart of society's beliefs about power and control. I cannot imagine any two subjects with more emotional attachment than these. Beliefs gain their power over us when they have been successful for a long time. Dominance and control, then, must be the "father of all meta-principles" in Western society because they date back more than 5,000 years. As Rianne Eisler explained in her thought-provoking book *The Chalice and the Blade*, the belief in dominance and control became central to Western society between 5000 and 3000 B.C., when warrior tribes overran the peaceful "partnership" civilizations that originally settled Europe. The invading tribes brought with them their male warrior gods (Zeus, Yahweh) and patriarchal

power structures that emphasized male values (strength, forcefulness, aggressiveness), autocratic hierarchy, enforced compliance, hero leaders, wealth redistribution to those with power, and a conquest mentality. These characteristics of patriarchal warrior societies are readily apparent in today's command-and-control organizations.

Autocracy and Powerlessness. In bureaucratic organizations, 100 percent of the power is resident in the CEO. The board of directors grants this power on behalf of the stockholders, but short of extreme malfeasance by the CEO, the board is often essentially impotent regarding corporate policy. The CEO then delegates his (they are practically all men) power to the next level and they to the next level and so on down the line. Eventually, authority to perform certain tasks is delegated to some front-line worker. The key point in this is that no one in this organization owns his or her work (has power over it) except for the CEO— who doesn't do any of it.

> *Your life is so structured that you really become insulated. When you're a CEO, you never rub shoulders with the people who make your cars, or buy them, or service them. . . . It was worse at Ford; they really treated you like a king, because Henry Ford II wanted it that way.*
>
> — Lee Iacocca, retired CEO of Chrysler Corporation

The CEO and his lieutenants can give commands to anyone in the organization—whether or not they know anything about a situation—that *must* be carried out. The primary survival tactic of employees in bureaucratic organizations is *compliance*, what we call "politics" and justify with the cynical observation that "it is just human nature, and no one can ever change that." This is the power of an autocratic dictatorship. Even if it is benevolent, it is still a structure of unilateral power, and wise and equitable governance is contingent completely on the personality and disposition of the leader. Abuse and exploitation—natural and unavoidable characteristics of this sort of system—make for a toxic environment for the healthy functioning of human beings.

What we have, at their essence, are *powerless* organizations. The CEO—who has all of the power—cannot do the work. The people—who do the work—do not have any power. Powerless people struggle relentlessly to regain control of their life and circumstances, usually by taking it from someone else through psychological or physical abuse, domination and repression, or manipulation and exploitation. People also gain power by hoarding information, knowledge, and access to people or other resources. In the language of addiction, these are "one-up" or "one-down" actions; they are intended to make one person feel superior at another person's expense. These exchanges, which self-help expert Stephen Covey calls "win-lose" and "lose-win," are indicative of an unhealthy, abusive, and even *addictive* psychology. "Ruthlessness, rigidity, and dishonesty," Anne Wilson Schaef and Diane Fassel observe in *The Addictive Organization*, "are exactly the ways that an active drunk would respond to a crisis." Each of these behaviors, which are inherently counter-productive and destructive, can be seen throughout bureaucratic organizations. Regretfully, they do not remain there. Due to the indivisible connectedness of systems, these abuses are carried over and passed on to other people throughout the social system, creating an epidemic of fear, powerlessness, and abuse.

The Illusion of Control. The "power positions" in such companies may not be such great places to be either. Recently, there has been a growing exodus of top executives from these roles because they have simply burned out and, as with Jeffrey Stiegler who resigned as president of American Express in 1995, they "want a life." Command-and-control structures put the responsibility for results squarely on the shoulders of the CEO and the top management team. This is an impossible responsibility. Control, and the attendant belief in certainty and predictability, is an

> *Maybe the country's entire leadership elite is on the verge of a nervous breakdown. Some of these men sound so frail and lost that I have to remind myself that they steer major corporations. If they were driving Amtrak trains, somebody would say to them: Time to come in for a little testing.*
>
> — Harriet Rubin, founder, Currency/Doubleday

illusion—particularly in large organizations. It is futile to think that people can ever control the myriad factors that influence performance to such an extent that they can achieve their goals through force of will. The efforts to do so are not only exhausting, but also fruitless. "Just ask the fired ex-heads of such companies as GM, IBM, Kodak, Digital Equipment, Westinghouse, and American Express," suggests author John Huey, writing in *Fortune* magazine, "where the time-honored method of ordering up transformation—maybe even stamping your foot for emphasis—proved laughably ineffective."

Imagine sitting on a hillside slope with a small ball on the ground in front of you. As the ball starts to roll down the hill (the equivalent of having problems emerge) you will have no difficulty stopping it and returning it to the top of the hill. This would also be true if there were two, three, or maybe even six balls. But, how would you fare if the complexity of the environment was increased to ten balls, or a hundred, or even a thousand? The prospects of being able to control all these balls would be utterly hopeless. This is the situation of leaders in bureaucratic organizations. The only way out of this miserable gerbil-wheel of frantic activity is to shift to the democratic power structure of the Quantum Organization. The responsibility, authority, and accountability for performance then transfers to the organization (where performance actually occurs) and the leaders *assist* the organization in achieving its goals—a much more fulfilling and manageable responsibility.

Personal Leadership. In Quantum Organizations, the goal is to restore power to the individual employees. Being "powerful" means that people are *full of power*—isn't that the kind of person that every organization needs? Who really thinks an organization can survive for long with fearful, powerless people who are more intent on keeping the boss happy than in doing what is right for the marketplace? Living systems thrive when their agents are powerful, when they are able to operate independently and creatively. Dee Hock describes one of the rules of quantum organizations (which he calls "chaordic organizations") as: All decision-making authority and all power must be held at the closest possible point to where the work is being done. With such power comes responsibility and accountability for its use and an end to the traditional caretaking activity of managers and leaders. People learn to stand on their own—to accept the risk of personal accountability and to become a whole person.

> *There's considerable evidence that eliminating the employee mentality and creating companies of businesspeople, of owners, has become a kind of "Hidden Secret of Success in the American marketplace."*
>
> — John Case, business writer, *Inc. Magazine*

Personal power and responsibility are, in fact, the essential elements of "personal leadership." Power in any form, whether it is personal or positional, is an awesome responsibility that requires wisdom if it is to be used for good. There are four important elements in the wise use of power:

1. *Responsibility*. The commitment to take action.

2. *Accountability*. The willingness to own the results of an action.

3. *Humility*. The awareness that one's actions may profoundly effect others and so is a great honor.

4. *Caring*. The intention to act in the best and highest interest of everyone affected by an action.

For each measure of power that a person takes, he or she should take two of responsibility, three of accountability, four of humility, and five of caring. These are the essential ingredients for the wise use of power.

In Quantum Organizations, leadership is not a position, it is a process. It isn't limited to a few people; it is something in which everyone participates. Through personal leadership, each person in the group accepts responsibility for the group's results. The leader of the group is an equal who happens to have the responsibility—agreed to by the group—for certain activities. The leader is often selected through a process such as that at W. L. Gore where the leader "evolves from within" and must be approved "in a consensus reached through discussion—not a vote." "The community creates the opportunity for a person to

be in a position of power," says Peter Block in *Stewardship*. He emphasizes this point by saying, "Power is bestowed upon us by those we 'lead.' " Leading a group is often not a fixed role, but one that is determined by the circumstances. When I participate in transformation projects, members of the project teams each lead different parts of the projects. At any point in time, each person is both participating as a supporting team member and leading some aspect of the project.

> *Leadership is a verb, not a noun.*
>
> — Wilbert "Bill" Gore,
> founder of W. L. Gore and Associates

Individual employees are accountable for bringing real value to the group. Someone who cannot contribute in a substantive way simply is not needed in the team. Teams at Whole Foods Market, for instance, hire and fire not only team members, but the team leaders as well. This places the responsibility for maintaining expertise and high performance where it has always belonged—on the *individual*. Ray & Berndtson has adopted just such an approach in their organizational transformation. As a professional services firm, their concern is in knowing what expertise they need to have on hand and in being able to keep their consultants working productively on client assignments. One of the first things they noticed when the new approach was implemented was that individual performance was put under a spotlight. When information about performance began to flow freely, poor performers suddenly had nowhere to hide. Consequently, consultants now actively seek out learning and knowledge development because their careers depend on it.

Another outcome is that the organization's structure has become remarkably fluid. Not only do consultants participate on multiple teams, but they also now perform a wide range of roles on those teams. Their ability to contribute is not restricted by a title—only by expertise. Here again we see employees taking responsibility for themselves. They are very active in increasing their knowledge and staying productive because no one will look out for them if they do not look out for themselves.

The New Leaders. So, do Quantum Organizations have hierarchies? Well, yes. There is a hierarchy but, as with natural systems, the hierarchy is associated with increasing levels of complexity and not with power and control. People who hold what we would traditionally call "leadership positions" are vitally important to Quantum Organizations. However, the skill requirements and responsibilities are radically different from that of traditional management. Creativity and self-organization in living systems is contingent on having a clear identity (shared vision), a high degree of autonomy among the systems agents (personal leadership), and openness (the free flow of information, interactions between agents, and diverse viewpoints). The new leaders understand that the organization does not need to be controlled, that it will generate its own order and respond creatively to the environment once these conditions are met. The new leaders' responsibility is to assist the organization in creating these conditions. The operating style of many women leaders, which Sally Helgesen describes in *The Web of Inclusion,* is highly aligned with that required for Quantum Organizations:

> In the process of devising ways of leading that made sense to *them,* the women [Helgesen] studied had built profoundly integrated and organic organizations, in which the focus was on nurturing good relationships; in which the niceties of rank and distinction played little part; and in which the lines of communication were multiplicitous, open, and diffuse. [Helgesen] noted that the women tended to put themselves at the centers of their organizations rather than at the top, thus emphasizing both accessibility and equality, and that they labored constantly to include people in their decision making. This had the effect of undermining the boundaries so characteristic of mainstream organizations, with their strict job definitions, categorizing of people according to rank, and restrictions on the flow of information.

Leaders in the Quantum Organization are active in *connecting* the organization to itself and to the environment, in *creating meaning* out of a bewildering array of information, and in *disturbing* the system so that it can grow and change. Some specific responsibilities include:

✵ *Creating and maintaining a strong culture and shared vision.* The new leaders bring into focus the shared vision that the organization is trying to manifest, and connect the people in the organization to it through active participation and extensive dialogue. Employees are encouraged to develop and maintain "20/20 vision"; that is, a focus on both the long-term and short-term organizational goals. The new leaders actively nurture and expand the organization's culture, becoming living examples of the desired behaviors.

✵ *Creating alignment.* Even the best-intentioned employees cannot create organizational performance if the elements of the organizational ecosystem are not aligned. The new leaders use their global perspective to promote alignment around the shared vision.

✵ *Creating meaning.* The new leaders assist the organization in understanding and interpreting information and events in the context of the organization's shared vision. The data that people are inundated with is often ambiguous, contradictory, and confusing. The new leaders help clarify this "noise" and transform it into *information*. People in organizations work in many different contexts, and leaders need to find the language that speaks to people where they are, both physically and psychologically. The message to engineers cannot be delivered in the same manner as the message to manufacturing plant workers. Their realities, cares, and concerns are totally different.

✵ *Nurturing relationships.* The new leaders look for opportunities to help people and groups connect with each other. They reinforce the vital importance of the long-term health of relationships, actively promoting high-quality relationships that are characterized by collaboration, cooperation, and mutual enrichment.

✵ *Ensuring the rich flow of information.* The new leaders are essential in helping the organization to obtain accurate and useful information and feedback from the ecosystem in which they are operating. They reflect the performance of the organization, so individuals and groups can self-correct to bring their efforts into accord with the company's goals. In particular, the new leaders help the organization see important information that it is being ignored, denied, or distorted.

✠ *Disturbing the organization.* The new leaders play a vital role in disturbing the organization so it will constantly learn and evolve. They engage the organization in establishing stretch goals, by challenging "sacred cows" and stimulating thinking through new ideas and approaches, and by holding up an unforgiving mirror that accurately reflects the organization to itself and makes clear the need for change.

✠ *Promoting learning.* The new leaders promote the diffusion of learning within the company. They seek out innovations throughout the firm and introduce them to others who might benefit. They advise the organization on skills and competencies that may need to be added to its repertoire. The new leaders recognize that learning is a process of trial and error, and promote risk-taking and tolerance for failures and mistakes. Learning is also a process of expanding people's awareness, and of broadening their worldview. The new leaders encourage diverse ideas and viewpoints.

> *America is used to killers, familiar with the species.*
> *But failures? Ahh, failures get special, unique attention.*
> *Screwups and mistakes aren't the American way.*
> *We tolerate murder, but not defeat.*
>
> — John Katezenbach, author of *Just Cause*

✠ *Promoting ownership and self-reliance.* The new leaders are constantly promoting employees' ownership of the company's success, as well as employees' self-reliance in doing whatever is necessary to achieve the goals. They communicate the importance of commitment and self-reliance and strive to create the conditions where people can feel ownership for both their work and the company.

✠ *Holding anxiety.* Change and disturbance evokes anxiety in people. Being able to hold this anxiety and still function effectively is the mark of both mature people and mature organizations. Leaders in Quantum Organizations help people to hold and use this anxiety by putting it into its proper perspective as the energizing spark for creative action.

Staff Functions. Leadership, as we have traditionally approached it, is a staff function. Staff functions in bureaucratic organizations have traditionally controlled people and in many ways promoted dependency on the company. In these cases, staff functions are another manifestation of the control ethic of the classical worldview. Accountants control people's spending of money, human resource personnel control the hiring and compensation of people, information services personnel control people's use of computers, and managers control people's performance.

Quantum Organizations make use of controls too. However, these controls define the outer limits of behavior, what is sometimes called "below the waterline risks" (a hole in a boat above the waterline won't sink it, but one below it will). The role of staff functions in a Quantum Organization is to promote self-sufficiency and learning. (This is also the role that third-party consultants should play in Quantum Organizations.) An accountant, for instance, would not peruse financial statements and expense reports from a "policing" or "watch-dog" role. Rather, the accountant would teach personnel how to read and understand their own financial statements and would encourage people to be accountable for their own expenses by helping them understand the consequences of their actions. Making *all* information available to everyone in the company helps with self-regulation. If anyone can witness fiscal and behavioral abuses, they are less likely to occur. There is no pressure like peer-pressure.

The current practice of making staff functions into profit centers with internal "customers" is a step in the right direction. This approach suffers, though, from the illusion of separateness. The system is a whole, and all of the parts are intrinsically interconnected. The staff functions and their internal customers are not separate parts that are interacting. They are integral aspects—partners—in the production of a common result. Staff functions need to be shifted to the value-added activities of promoting independence and learning, and they should be seen as an integral part of the organization's success—not ancillary to it.

People

Our discussion of the people portion of structure will address compensation and benefits, performance assessment, job definition, and career progression.

Compensation. The materialistic influence of the traditional worldview has created a tremendous emphasis on compensation. We have come to equate our income level with our worth as a person and believe that happiness lies at the end of a large paycheck. Neither are true. Nonetheless, these beliefs make it difficult to discuss compensation without invoking vigorous resistance. Modern compensation schemes are based on the principles of individualism, linear cause-and-effects, measurability, and objective assessment. We know from the new science, however, that nothing is separate; the whole system cannot be reduced to the functioning of the individuals in it. We know that causes and effects are not linear; they are systemic and non-local. We know that the act of measuring excludes far more information than it captures. Measuring performance requires an abstraction of a part from the whole that says more about the measurement method than what is being measured. We also know that there is no such thing as objective detachment; the observer influences what is being observed. These new understandings invalidate the old assumptions about pay-and-performance assessment and highlight the need for new approaches.

Most corporate compensation schemes seek to maximize the pay of the executive leadership and minimize the pay of all of the other employees. "Worker" pay is for all intents and purposes limited to salary and wages; there is little risk (other than not getting a raise) and very little upside potential. In the Quantum Organization, individual employees assume responsibility for their own actions and for the collective outcomes of the company. This is no longer the purview of just the senior management team. Compensation, then, should reflect the risk and reward that comes with personal accountability. Much more of each employee's total cash compensation needs to be put at risk—say anywhere from 10 to 50 percent, depending on circumstances.

> In the Quantum Organization, individual employees assume responsibility for their own actions and for the collective outcomes of the company.

Earnings should be based on results achieved. The amount to be paid should not have an artificial upside based on the idea that you shouldn't pay people too much. Authors who sell a million books do not limit themselves to a small salary—they reap the entire rewards of their effort. Likewise, the amount paid out to employees in a corporate setting should only be limited by the need to reinvest and pay a *fair* return to corporate investors. The profit produced then becomes the fruit of everybody's labor and is not seen as "pay" so much as return on value created. Recent experiments in gainsharing are an example of how this can happen. Microsoft has an effective approach; it keeps salaries low, but makes extravagant use of stock grants. Through this practice, Microsoft has helped more than two thousand people become millionaires.

Western society is a culture of heroes. The image of the "rugged individualist" still holds in the minds of many people. We have translated this belief into the need to compensate certain individuals far in excess of the norm. In the case of executive pay, these excesses have often become obscene. Organizations are whole systems; it is impossible to ever segregate and quantifiably measure any one person's contribution. Such an effort relies entirely on subjective abstractions that have little basis in reality. Besides, it defies common sense: No one is irreplaceable. With that said, common sense also affirms that different people do contribute at different levels. Not only are there differences in expertise and ability, certain activities in organizations are substantially more important to the success of the organization than others.

But how does one measure the relative differences, without being subjective and arbitrary? Compensation schemes should focus on the value of the results produced and the expertise required for the tasks. These differences should then be recognized through differences in compensation. However, the pay abuses in effect today do not acknowledge the contribution that the "whole" makes to the individual's performance. Companies succeed or fail as a whole. The organic principle of *wholeness* guides us to base individual compensation mostly on *group* outcomes, with the smallest portion related to individual contribution. Author and leadership expert Peter Block, writing in *Stewardship*, advised companies to form a single compensation scheme for the company—based on the way executives are paid—that acknowledges absolute differences in pay, but calculates it in the same way.

Trust is vital to the healthy functioning of a Quantum Organization. Secrecy conceals abuse and destroys trust. Look at any abusive system in the history of humankind, and you will find secrecy and isolation at its root. Even when there is no abuse behind the secrecy, the suspicion that naturally arises

> *If you are trying to build a high-trust organization, where people are all-for-one and one-for-all, you can't have secrets.*
>
> — John Mackey, co-founder and CEO, Whole Foods Market

creates an imagined abuse with effects that are just as real. Individual pay has historically been an area of so much secrecy that to discuss salaries often was grounds for termination. This is another practice that must change: The principle of openness needs to be brought to bear in regard to compensation. For many people, revealing pay is a horrifying concept that conjures all manner of apocalyptic images. These people may be surprised to learn that companies are already doing this without incident —Whole Foods and Semco, to name two. John Mackey, CEO of Whole Foods, explains that after the novelty wears off and people realize that the system is fair, they focus on what is important: team goals and job satisfaction. And he adds, "the trust-building payoff is substantial."

Performance Assessment. The idea behind our current assessment system is that money can be used to motivate and control behavior. This entire system is based on an approach to behavioral reinforcement called "operant conditioning." B. F. Skinner, the leading proponent of the behaviorist school of psychology, developed this "carrot and stick" model that uses rewards and recognition (carrots) or threat and punishment (sticks) to modify behavior. Skinner is a Newtonian scientist par excellence who believed that humans are soulless machines subject to strict rules of behavioral modification. People must be pushed to do what is wanted (rewards or positive reinforcement) and pulled back from doing what is not wanted (punishment or negative rewards). People do not have their own will or internal motivations according to Skinner's model because they are controlled exclusively by conditioned responses to external stimuli.

Kohlberg's Six Stages of Moral Reasoning

Figure 3.3

STAGE	PRIMARY BEHAVIOR	DESCRIPTION
Preconventional morality (Ages 1-10)	Decisions based on external rewards and punishments	Morality is almost entirely external
1. Punishment and Obedience	Avoid punishment	Children obey because adults tell them to obey
2. Individualism and Purpose	Seek rewards	Children act in self interest— they obey when they think it is in their best interest to obey
Conventional Reasoning (Ages 10-20)	Decisions based on a combination of internal guidance and social rules	Morality is partly internalized, but still largely based on social norms.
3. Interpersonal Norms	Gain approval/avoid disapproval	Trust, caring, and loyalty to others shapes reasoning
4. Social System Morality	Conform to social *rules*	Social order, law, justice, and duty influence moral reasoning
Postconventional Reasoning (Ages Over 20)	Decisions based on personal moral code	Morality is completely internalized and not based on other's standards
5. Community vs. Individual Rights	Apply society's *principles*	Values and laws are understood to be relative and can be changed. Some values are understood to be more important than society's laws
6. Universal Ethical Principles	Apply *universal principles*	Moral standards are based on universal human rights. People follow their conscience even though it may involve personal risk.

Psychologists have known for years that these concepts are useful for only limited applications, and yet their use still pervades modern organizations. According to psychologist Lawrence Kohlberg, people operate at six different stages of moral reasoning (see Fig. 3.3). Rewards and recognition operate only at levels two and three, both of which are juvenile levels. Fully functioning adults operate at levels five and six, "principles of conscience," where they follow internal guidance from moral guidelines and principles of universal justice and empathy for others. It is ineffective to motivate emotionally mature people as if they were juveniles.

For example, a chief financial officer (CFO) that I know was baffled by a key employee who left the company even though he had been offered *twice* the other company's salary offer to stay. The CFO was a habitual "carrot and stick" manager and simply could not conceive that a person would turn down so much money (reward) just to do work that was more interesting.

> . . . .*The day-to-day reality is that we do not have enough money to actually purchase behavior from people inside an organization.*
>
> — Peter Block, author of *Stewardship*

People at levels five and six operate out of their own centers—their own internal guidance systems—and are motivated by the results they achieve when they do so. These people may say, "Quit patronizing me with promises of rewards and let me share in the wealth that I am creating."

Quantum Organizations rely on responsible, autonomous behavior (Kohlberg's levels five and six) on the part of all employees. This requires people to develop and orient their behavior based on a strong inner compass. They need to "do what is right" even when the "boss" is not looking (mainly because there *are* no bosses). External rewards and recognition do the opposite. They reward compliance (desired behaviors) and punish deviations from the norm. This places the locus of control outside of people, leaving them with a greatly impaired ability to operate without explicit direction. If there is one thing no one has time for today, it is to watch over other people and constantly tell them what to do. It is clear that our current performance assessment system is an anachronism of the control-oriented, industrial-era management that must be completely overhauled. Compensation should be based on what is *accomplished*—performance feedback should be an entirely separate consideration.

Most assessment systems rely on a supervisor providing "objective" feedback on an employee's performance. We know from the new science, however, that there is no such thing as an independent observer. The observer always influences what is observed. In the case of a performance review, the supervisor's assessment is really a statement about how the supervisor sees the world and, in particular, the person being reviewed. Peter Block noted that "everyone likes the idea of pay for performance, but most of us have rarely experienced it. We most often get paid on the basis of how our boss evaluates us. This is more accurately called 'pay for compliance.' " This assessment process is made worse by trying to reduce an entire year of performance down to a single number of somewhere between one and five. I have received these kinds of reviews and I have given them, and to this day I defy anyone to tell me how anybody can objectively and rationally select one number that represents the totality of a person's performance for an entire year. Then, to add to the absurdity, managers provide a year's worth of feedback to employees in a single hour or less.

> *One of the most frightening and degrading experiences in every employee's life is the annual Performance Review.*
>
> — Scott, Adams, author of *The Dilbert Principle*

In addition, performance ratings often must be force-ranked to fit a bell curve that places the majority of the employees at "average" or lower. This forced ranking is intended to reward the top 20 percent of the employees who shine as performance "stars." An unintended side-effect is that it demoralizes the other 80 percent of the workforce and pits team members against one another. Jay Cober, an executive who recently left the oil industry, saw this practiced for fifteen years at his former company. "The consequences," he points out, "are that the talents and creative energy of the majority of the workforce go unused. Companies would be vastly better off if they devised a system that allowed all employees to seek their maximum potential."

The purpose of performance assessment should be to provide feedback to help an individual learn and evolve. This feedback should come from everyone who has significant interactions with a person, and it should be given on a just-in-time basis—not a year later (which may as well be a lifetime in today's environment). The responsibility for learning and performance improvement should fall to the only people who can do anything about it—the employees. Ray & Berndtson has devised a skills inventory system that helps each employee track his or her personal and professional growth. From this, employees can seek training and assignments that will enable them to enhance the skill areas they need to develop. In addition, every employee receives "360 degree" evaluations on each assignment. The idea is to provide maximum feedback to support learning and performance improvement.

Benefits. The management-labor polarization over the years has lead to a system that requires companies to provide a wide range of benefits to employees. These benefits are seen by all parties as equivalents to compensation, and many companies issue a benefits statement that calculates company insurance statements and ESOP contributions as a dollar figure. The result has been to further the dependency of employees on the company and to provide another lever for ensuring employee compliance. Individuals in Quantum Organizations are fully responsible adults. This level of maturity is difficult to reach in a company that takes care of employees through their benefits.

In organizations that shift to compensation plans where employees share in profits in a meaningful way (as executives do today), the benefit system should be drastically reduced. Employees should be responsible for their own insurance and investments; however, to eliminate benefits and keep the current pay schemes would be a gross injustice that would only serve to reduce net compensation for employees. Obviously, laws that require employers to provide certain benefits would have to be amended. With the termination of most benefit requirements, everyone, ultimately, would be better off. Employees would have more money and more control over their lives, companies could turn more of their attention to achieving their shared vision, and the government would have one less thing to regulate.

Job Definition. The organic principle of *flexibility* has a great deal of bearing on how we define jobs. Historically, job definitions have meticulously spelled out distinct duties, going as far as to specify what percentage of a person's time would be spent on each duty. Perhaps the most extreme manifestation of this was in the definition of union jobs; for example, a carpenter could refuse to plug in an office machine because that was the work of an electrician. In the past, job definitions helped people understand clearly what was expected of them. They provided stability and made it possible to control the work of each employee. In the Quantum Organization, expectations are determined by the group's goals and by the immediate work context. In a fast-moving and complex environment, the work that someone does has to be determined by the context—what needs to be done and who has the time and expertise to do it. It is for this reason that some companies are defining the basic unit of work as a "project," instead of a "job."

Here again, we see how important it is to base compensation on group outcomes with individual contribution being the smallest component. Members of a team belong because they have something unique to contribute. People will naturally gravitate to the tasks for which they are uniquely experienced or skilled. However, in Quantum Organizations, everybody is called to do whatever it takes to produce the desired results. When compensation is tied to the group's results, people are far less inclined to focus on who was "supposed" to do what. Producing the end result takes precedence. Employees focus on outcomes: shifting between tasks, helping out teammates, seeking out

> *When people are free to define their own goals and roles at work, their commitment intensifies, and the job becomes more personally meaningful. You don't feel as if you are leaving your real self in the parking lot before you come in to work. Your contribution can be richer. You're energized at the end of the day, instead of feeling "I'm dead, give me a drink."*
>
> — Mei-Lin Cheng, Project Manager, Hewlett-Packard

what needs to be done next. At Ray & Berndtson, project teams are developed based on the skills required to complete the assignment. Individual consultant assignments are based on knowledge, experience, availability, and learning objectives. Once on the team, people with more expertise will perform the more complex tasks. However, they will also perform even the most menial task if necessary to get the job done. Likewise, employees are expected to continually learn and grow. As a result, they are often thrust into responsibilities that stretch them to the limits of their ability.

The traditional job definition approach hinders people from achieving their full potential. Bureaucratic organizations seek to prevent people from stretching beyond the narrow confines of their jobs. People are not allowed to assume responsibility until they have "paid their dues" or proven that they can "handle it" (a control-orientation). Similarly, people are not allowed to branch into activities outside of their traditional areas of expertise. An accountant, for instance, would not be considered for a position in manufacturing. In Quantum Organizations, the opposite is true. People are encouraged to learn, to take on responsibilities that will stretch them. This cross-fertilization of expertise has the added advantage of bringing new perspectives and creativity to the job at hand.

It is surprising how often we underestimate what people can do. Given the opportunity and a reasonable amount of support, people can perform beyond our wildest imaginings. I started my career working for a Fortune 50 bureaucracy. I quit when I got tired of hitting my head on the artificial ceilings that management had built to keep people down. Several years later, I joined a Big-6 consulting firm where I saw first-hand how delusional and arbitrary we can be about each other's capabilities. But this time, I was the culprit—I was trying to keep an inexperienced consultant from taking on a project manager role that I thought was beyond him. The partner-in-charge had more wisdom and gave him the role. The consultant stumbled a bit, but soon had the project firmly in hand. The amazing thing for me was the transformation in the person—he quit seeing himself as a person with limited abilities and stepped fully into his personal power. Normally, he would have had to wait another two years for such a role. After this project he walked, talked, and made decisions as any manager would.

> Unleashing the full potential of every employee is the explicit goal of Quantum Organizations. Until this is done, companies haven't the slightest idea what *real* productivity is.

From this and similar experiences, I now understand that the only limitations most people have are the *assumptions* that they and other people have about those limitations. Unleashing the full potential of every employee is the explicit goal of Quantum Organizations. Until this is done, companies haven't the slightest idea what *real* productivity is.

In the "old days," it was a fairly simple matter to define jobs. People worked from 8:00 A.M. to 5:00 P.M., five days per week. Vacation became a benefit intended to promote workers' long-term employment. Attire (like everything else) had to be controlled. The labels "white-collar" and "blue-collar" came to characterize the difference between professionals and labor. Professionals were expected to wear suits—a uniform intended to mark the distinction of the jobs.

> *Nothing seems more medieval than dress codes. Office personnel are supposed to stroll around in suits and ties or dresses, but who remembers why? . . . Dress codes are all about conformity.*
>
> — Ricardo Semler, CEO of Semco, author of *Maverick*

Conditions are different today. The focus in Quantum Organizations is on *producing results*. Working hours flex based on what needs to be done. Employees make such decisions in conjunction with their teams—not based on the desires of some control-minded manager. Companies have many schemes for employment that include variations for both full- and part-time work. Attire, beyond certain standards of decency, is up to the employee. The exception, of course, is when customer considerations dictate a particular style of dress. The idea of a "casual day" in the Quantum Organization is laughable. "What is it about a *Friday*," the quantum employee might ask, "that is different from any other day of the week?" "Casual day" is nothing other than a patriarchal, control-oriented, external reward system that should be abolished and replaced by letting employees determine their own attire.

Vacation in the Quantum Organization takes on a completely different intention. Rather than promoting long-term employment, paid time off is seen as an important way for employees to maintain a balanced life. Today's high-stress environment also dictates that people need more recovery time—two weeks per year is simply not enough. Some professional services organizations, for instance, provide four weeks for all employees. Where employees are participating in profits, vacation does not need to be paid by the company. Employees could take as much time off as they wanted based on how much money they wanted to earn. Many companies, such as the insurance company USAA, have four-day work weeks (ten hours per day) for the majority of their employees. The three-day weekends not only help employees fully recover their energy and enthusiasm, but they also give people a weekday in which to schedule routine activities such as doctor appointments, shopping, and home repairs. It also frees up time for people to volunteer more in their communities, schools, and charitable organizations, which helps in balancing the needs of the greater social system.

Career Progression. In traditional organizations, the only way to increase responsibility and compensation is to move up the management ladder. This results in limiting the potential and contribution of many people who are denied management roles. Likewise, it puts people in management roles who are wholly unqualified. In particular, many technical experts move into management only to demonstrate that "as managers they make great engineers." In Quantum Organizations, hierarchy and functional towers as we know them do not exist. Compensation is based on expertise and responsibility. As such, careers as we traditionally think of them—a ladder of jobs with ever-increasing responsibility and compensation—cease to have much meaning.

Over the course of their life, a person will work with many different companies. Within a company, a person will not likely hold a "job"; rather he or she will hold one or more "roles" in various different projects of varying lengths. People will seek roles that build on their previous experiences and stretch their capabilities, creating opportunities to learn. Compensation will not follow an increasing staircase pattern as has been expected in the past. It will likely fluctuate substantially over time, varying with the fortunes of the company and with the person's own contribution to the overall effort. Career tracks in the future are

much more likely to "wander up and down, over and around." They will offer variety, require personal responsibility and accountability, and produce substantial personal satisfaction.

Physical Layout of Facilities

The third aspect of structure is the physical layout of facilities. The use of space is highly symbolic. In the command-and-control company, offices are assigned based on hierarchy. The higher a person has climbed, the more office space he or she will receive and the better the view becomes. This scheme has led to the creation of a "mahogany row and cubicle-alley" design. The top executives work on a separate floor (often with secured access) that features opulent decorations and massive allocations of floor space. They are far removed—physically and psychologically—from the workplace. Meanwhile, workers are confined to cubicles that are as small as is practical for them to work productively. People are grouped based on functional towers, not on how the work gets done.

> *Depending on your status in the company, your furniture sends one of two messages: "Ignore the worthless object sitting in this chair." Or . . . "Worship me!! Kneel before the mahogany shrine!"*
>
> — Scott Adams, author of *The Dilbert Principle*

In the Quantum Organization, flexibility is the key. People work where and how they are best able to produce the desired results. People may telecommute from home part of the week and go to the office for the rest. In some companies, no one has an office; people simply "check-in" when they arrive—like at a hotel. Others have done away with desks; scattering couches, coffee tables, and phone connections about a room in the manner of an airport lounge. Teams often share large open areas and reserve walled offices for confidential meetings or for times when someone just needs to "get away." Multidisciplinary teams work together at the same location, returning periodically to "centers of expertise" as needed to research more complex topics. Office allocation and space do not correlate to hierarchy; they correlate to need. Andrew Grove, CEO of Intel, exemplifies this: His office is a cubicle that is only slightly bigger than average.

The fast-paced environment that characterizes the modern organization takes a high physical and psychological toll. Companies are learning that they need to create an environment where people can defuse the stress that results from high-pressure work activities. Some common approaches have included providing facilities for physical exercise and offering ten-minute shoulder and back massages from health professionals. However, few companies as yet offer employees a place to escape from *noise* itself. The office of the future will set places aside for "quiet" or "meditation" time, where employees can go to refresh and center themselves. The benefit for the employee is improved health and peace of mind. For the company, the benefit is higher productivity from employees who are more balanced internally—an important factor in promoting resilience, determination, and effective interpersonal relations.

Process: The Fabric of Organizational Life

Process is the flow of activities and interactions that sustain an organization. These flows are vital to the healthy functioning of a living system. The emphasis during the past few years on improving processes is a critical step in shifting to a Quantum Organization. However, there are two practices that have reduced the effectiveness of these efforts. First, when companies organized around processes and became "horizontal organizations," many kept the command-and-control mind-set (a prime example of changes that do not take the *entire* ecosystem into consideration). What they ended up with was a hierarchical organization centered on processes—a step in the right direction, but not by much. Second, many companies have attempted to diagram and standardize processes. In the case of highly mechanical processes, such as those on the manufacturing floor, this makes some sense. But for the vast majority of processes, this is a study in futility.

Most of the processes in a company are either nonrepetitive or have a multitude of variations. These I call *virtual processes*. For these, companies need to develop a process "template," an "archetype" of the process, from which employees can create a wide range of variations. Organizational change is one such process. When a team is formed to conduct a change project, team members review the template from the context of the change that needs to be made and construct a novel version of the process that is best suited for the effort at hand. This promotes quality by ensuring that the team has reviewed all of the possible process steps to make sure that they have "covered all of the important bases." It also allows the flexibility required for the process to be adapted to the particular use.

> When companies organized around processes, many kept the command-and- control mind-set. What they ended up with was a hierarchical organization centered on processes—a step in the right direction, but not by much.

Processes or Skills? One of the ideas behind TQM is that quality is contingent on the processes being executed so that all of the necessary steps are conducted appropriately. When we think of a manufacturing environment, it is fairly easy to see that it includes processes with certain standard activities. This is also true for back-office activities, such as paying an invoice or processing a payroll change. It is less easy to recognize that changing organizational flows and structures, making decisions, communicating, and visioning are also processes. When people treat these as "skills" instead of processes, they do not adequately think through the factors that should be considered for the process to be executed with quality. Take organizational change as just one example. Change is frequently handled as an order: "Improve customer delivery time by 20 percent!" People then scurry off to their functional towers to do their part with no thought of the process of the change. In the end, the attempt to change fails. I have seen executive decision-making handled with the same disregard for process. Executive teams will articulate a problem and begin immediately to debate the "one right answer." In the end, the best or most powerful debater wins, but the problem does not get solved. These are processes, and in the Quantum Organization that need to be treated as such.

Flows. I developed the Organizational EcoSystem Model several years ago. As I prepared to write this book, I considered changing the names of several of the elements to reflect the true nature of living systems. In particular, I wanted to change *process* to *flow*. I decided to stay with my original terminology because I felt people were not yet familiar with these concepts and needed to see familiar words.

The word *process* is commonly understood to focus on activities. It does not usually lead us to consider the flow of information, knowledge, interactions, people, cash, equipment, and authority. Flows are vital to the healthy functioning of living systems. Ray & Berndtson recognized that in order to achieve its vision, it would have to radically improve the flow of information, knowledge, and human resources. Prior to the new organizational design, it operated as most of the executive search industry did: Partners sold their own individual assignments and used their own consulting and research personnel. Very little information, knowledge or resources was shared. The new design called for "radical" openness: Everything was expected to flow freely to the place where it was needed. Technology made it possible to begin to capture and share the stored knowledge of all employees, as well as the lessons learned on each assignment. The organizational structure was changed to allow for the free flow of personnel to projects based on the human resources and expertise required (new technologies assisted with this as well). The end result is the free flow of information, ideas, and resources as needed based on the environment. This has not only dramatically improved productivity, but the organization is much more effective as well. Ray & Berndtson can quickly bring the combined intelligence of the organization to bear on any problem anywhere in the world.

Organizational Learning
Organizational learning is such an important process that it needs to be discussed separately. Bureaucratic organizations—particularly in the West—seek to maximize efficiency. They have succeeded but at a tremendous cost to adaptability. Continuing education is one of the first areas to be cut in companies

headed down the path of "corporate anorexia." From the perspective of living systems, this is suicide. It is the equivalent of farmers who, having a bad year, resort to eating the next year's seed-stock. What happens when the nourishing rains come the following year and there is no seed to put in the ground? Learning is the "seed-stock" for next year's organizational crop.

> Continuing education is one of the first areas to be cut in companies headed down the path of "corporate anorexia." From the perspective of living systems, this is suicide.

The Quantum Organization attends to the short-term, but focuses consistently on the long-term. Learning is a core competence that is essential to the long-term health of the organization. It is a process that is so vital that it cannot be left to happenstance. Instead, it is consciously developed and nurtured. It is one of the quantum organization's core principles and an important part of the shared vision. If business people were to develop budgets for *learning* instead of for *training*, it would make a significant difference in its relative importance. Reducing or eliminating training does not usually cause second thoughts. But how does an executive's thinking change when he or she realizes that the organization intends to eliminate *learning* for the next couple of years? This is not something most people would do without very careful consideration.

Peter Senge, author of *The Fifth Discipline*, is galvanizing interest in what he calls "the learning organization." This approach is explicitly systemic. In it, he promotes shared vision, personal mastery, mental models, team learning, and systems thinking. However, few companies have really caught on to these concepts. I believe that the central reason for this is that organizations must first value learning before they will invest in it; as of yet, they don't. Businesses are too interested in *doing* to worry much about learning.

Quantum Learning. What exactly is learning? Well, for one thing, it is *not* training. Training is a mechanistic approach that imposes a teacher's choice of lessons and teaching style on students who are supposed to absorb information like sponges. This is not sufficient. Peter Vaill provides a scathing critique of traditional teaching techniques in *Learning As a Way of Being*. Russell Ackoff does the same regarding university education in *The Democratic Corporation*. The point of education is *learning*—not teaching. People are not students, they are *learners*. The desired outcome is that they have expanded their understanding of the world and they become more capable. As with all else in Quantum Organizations, learning is something that people must do for themselves.

Focusing on people's need to learn for themselves has profound implications for our approach to education at every level in our society. As Vaill points out, learning is not something someone does, it is something someone *is*—it is a *way of being*. Learning is an integral aspect of living and cannot be separated out. It is contextual in that it has to relate to something relevant to the learner. What, then, does learning look like in a Quantum Organization? Here are a few thoughts:

⌗ Learning is a natural outcome of everything people do.

⌗ Learning is the gaining of new insights—the shifting of perspective to take in an ever-larger view of the "truth" of a matter. People are intent on listening and gathering knowledge rather than simply being viewed as having it (as is so common in business today).

⌗ Diversity is a key to learning. People of both genders, with diverse cultural backgrounds, diverse viewpoints, and diverse courses of action are essential to learning. Conflict, which is a natural outcome of diversity, is seen as an opportunity for enriching the understanding of an issue.

⌗ Learning is self-motivated and self-directed. People learn only when they want to learn, not when someone else wants them to learn. In the language of TQM, learning is on a "demand-pull" rather than a "supply-push" basis. People recognize the importance of knowing as much as possible. Instead of resisting new ideas and innovations, learners seek out and embrace them.

⌗ Formal teaching environments engage the learners in the experience. Learners have an active role in shaping the content and delivery of the experience.

✠ Tacit learning is an integral part of the learning environment. It acknowledges that we know much more than can ever be said. Tacit learning involves learning by observing others and picking up nonverbal physical and contextual clues.

✠ The outcome of learning is not measured from an absolute sense of the content (in the form of facts and figures) that can be recited. Rather, it is rated on people's abilities to relate the learning to their lives.

Traditional education, both as it is realized in institutions and as the "idea" of how education should be, bears little resemblance to this image of quantum learning. In many ways, our educational institutions are proving to be bureaucracies that are themselves "learning-impaired." They have known for years that their methods are ineffective and actually discourage people from wanting to learn. They seem to be more effective in teaching compliance and resentment than in promoting learning. Vaill thinks that it is our distaste for learning itself—spawned through our repressive educational system—that makes it difficult for people to embrace continuing education. He points out that in schools, "There is no mission to produce *learners*. The mission is to produce graduates, as measured by some fixed amount of information correctly regurgitated on examinations and term papers."

Fortunately, there are signs that innovations are starting to take hold and are gradually gaining more influence. Consider the description below of the philosophy of a Montessori school. How would you compare this to traditional notions on education?

A Montessori education allows each child to follow his or her own curiosity and supports a natural desire for learning. Children within a three-year age span are grouped together to serve as models for one another. Each child is allowed to develop to the fullest of his or her own potential, often exceeding the bounds associated with traditional methods of education. [The student] has the opportunity to achieve a deep understanding of all academic basics and other subjects in an interrelated manner. He or she develops a love for learning, a self-assurance, and self motivation which serve as a preparation not only for secondary and higher education, but also for all of life.

Technology: A Powerful Enabler

There are countless technologies that have emerged over the past few years that make it possible to achieve incredible improvements in organizational performance. I will focus on those that support the development of a Quantum Organization. Certain technologies are particularly important in relation to the principles of autonomy and integration, flexibility and flow, and openness.

One of these is "groupware." This is software (such as Lotus Notes) that makes it possible for geographically separate people to collaborate in developing common work products. Groupware also serves as a powerful tool for capturing and disseminating organizational learning. Many of the leading professional services firms, including McKinsey and Company, Price Waterhouse, and Ray & Berndtson, use these systems to leverage the knowledge of their consulting staff. International companies use it to allow the parallel development of products around the globe. And there are many other uses.

Intranets are another potentially useful technology for Quantum Organizations. These are the equivalent of miniature Internets that are established for use within a company. The advantage that intranets have over traditional systems is that they assume neither *who* will use the information nor *how* it will be used. Instead, information is available to anyone in the organization based on interest. This solves one of the biggest drawbacks that traditional information systems have, which is how to "push" information out to everyone who might need it in a cost-effective and productive way. The structure of the intranet allows for employee-driven searches for information.

Chapter Four
The Power of
Shared Vision

Where there is no vision, the people perish.
> *— Proverbs 29:18, The Bible*

Purpose, principles, and strategy come together in a company's *shared vision*. *Vision* refers to a detailed mental image of some hoped-for state that is created either by a single person or a group of people. Visioning has helped countless individuals in psychological and medical healing. Doctors like Bernie Siegal, MD, author of *Love, Medicine and Miracles*, have documented many cases where the use of creative visualization resulted in unexplainable disappearances of inoperable cancer and other such "miracle" recoveries. Athletes and artists have long used visioning to prepare for their performances. One study of a group of Olympic athletes showed that those athletes who spent 75 percent of their time visualizing and the remainder practicing, showed more improvement in performance than did those who spent the *entire* time practicing. Visualization works and can be applied to the business environment.

Creating Organizational Alignment

In organizations, a shared vision is the mental image that all the people in an organization have of a desired future state. The company's purpose, guiding principles, strategy, and BHAG (if there is one) are woven together into a single tapestry. It is vital that this mental picture be shared throughout the organization because ultimately it is the source of integrative behavior among diverse individuals and groups of people. In traditional organizations, order is maintained through external controls. In Quantum Organizations, external controls form absolute boundaries, but it is the shared vision that brings individual activities into harmony.

By "harmony," I do not mean that there is no conflict. People will not be sitting around in a circle holding hands and singing "Kumbayah." Rather, harmony is "a pleasing combination of the elements forming a whole." The beauty in a symphony is in the harmony of the various elements. It is the *differences* in the musical notes and instruments and their combination in ways that complement each other that produce the sound that we enjoy. Harmony emerges from the *individual expressions* of the instruments when they are in *accord with the whole*. If these same instruments were to express their individuality by branching off into different songs, the discord that would result would be pretty horrible. Shared vision in organizations makes harmony possible; individual employees act autonomously but in accord with the whole to produce coherent and powerful results. This is the self-organizing action of the organic principles of *identity* and *creativity*.

When everyone in the organization has internalized the big picture—really understand it and live it every day—there is very little need for external controls. When people elevate their attention to a purpose that transcends their own concerns, they are able to achieve unified action and remarkable results. Unfortunately, very few companies today have a strong shared vision. Without it, employees engage in fulfilling smaller

> I've learned that the most effective way to forge a winning team is to call on the player's need to connect with something larger than themselves.
>
> — Phil Jackson, coach of the Chicago Bulls basketball team, winners of three consecutive NBA championships

purposes—their own or that of their "tribe"—with little regard to the impact on the overall organization. This is evidenced by pettiness, in-fighting, politics, and a lack of cooperation. "In the presence of greatness, pettiness disappears,"

Robert Fritz, author of *Corporate Tides*, explained. "In the absence of a great dream, pettiness prevails."

Most of the CEOs I know complain that their executive "team" doesn't bear even a distant resemblance to a team—the executives just can't work together. CEOs are also frustrated that departments and divisions can't get along and constantly seem to be operating at cross-purposes. Meetings consistently break down into bickering, fault-finding, and airing petty concerns. The lack of a shared vision is also evidenced in bottom-line profitability, but this can be deceiving. Sometimes profits in "traditional" companies

> *In the absence of a great dream, pettiness prevails.*
>
> — Robert Fritz, author of *Corporate Tides*

are acceptable based on industry averages. These averages, though, are of other traditional companies—not Quantum Organizations. The real question is: How much better could profits—and other non-monetary measures of organizational health—be if the company had a strong shared vision?

The Importance of a Worthy Cause

A shared vision should carry a sense of destiny, of hopes and dreams, of the organization's unique place in the world. People are inspired by participating in something important, something from which they can derive personal meaning and satisfaction. Chester Barnard, past CEO of New Jersey Bell captured this thought perfectly:

> *People want to be bound to some cause bigger than they,*
> *commanding, yet worthy of them,*
> *summoning them to significance in living.*

"People want to be bound . . ." One of the key words in this passage is "bound." People are bound to a cause when they fully commit themselves to it. Commitment is *voluntary*. This is a key point for which bureaucratic organizations have little or no respect. In command-and-control organizations, executives are used to giving orders and expecting them to be carried out. There was a time, many years ago, when this approach was effective. Modern employees, though, do not respond well to orders. They are well educated, know as much or more than their bosses, and want more from a job than a paycheck. Their commitment must be *earned*.

What executives get when they give orders is not commitment but *compliance*. With compliance, people will do the work, but their hearts are not in it. They may do what they have been asked to do (more or less) but they probably will not *own* the effort. With commitment, people take ownership for the success of the effort; this is a vital distinction. In the process of co-creating a shared vision, Quantum Organizations create the conditions in which employees can voluntarily commit themselves to the vision. The company's success becomes owned by all employees, and polarization evaporates.

> Commitment is *voluntary*. This is a key point for which bureaucratic organizations have little or no respect.

When people fully commit, they will do whatever it takes to succeed. If "the old way" of doing things is a barrier, they find a way around. If there is no way around, they will get "the old ways" changed. They listen for the *essence* of what is being asked of them and, rather than blindly following orders, they interpret what is needed and do what is right. Committed people are emboldened to take risks and to experiment. They are comfortable doing so because they have a way to assess for themselves the results they are creating in relation to the vision. If they start to get off-track, they can move immediately to correct the situation and try something else. This willingness to improvise, to do what it takes, is critical to the success of any effort—and it can only be gained through voluntary commitment.

" . . . to some cause bigger than they . . ." People have an innate desire to belong, to participate in social settings with other people in pursuit of common goals. People want to love their companies. Much of the anger and resentment evident in the workplace today comes from the pain and shock of a perceived betrayal by the company. In the past, many people entered into a co-dependent, parent-child relationship with their companies as part of the

employment-for-life agreement. People need to learn to create boundaries where they are free to love their companies without any attendant dependency or excessive attachment. This is a far cry, though, from recommending that people adopt a mercenary attitude toward employment such that their commitment is only as strong as their paychecks. In the Quantum Organization, people commit to a shared vision that is a "cause bigger than they" because they believe in it and want to belong. There is a genuine love for the organization and for the people involved. These very same people recognize their responsibility for managing their own lives and for pursuing employment elsewhere when it is appropriate—but this does not diminish their full-hearted commitment to their current companies.

" . . . **commanding, yet worthy of them . . .**" Many executive teams exhort their organizations to increase profitability (often at the employees' expense) so that some remote and unknown group of stockholders (and the executives themselves) can become wealthier. The company is viewed as a machine for making profit, and employees are seen as "things" with no purposes of their own; they are cogs that make the corporate wheels turn. This has violated the dignity and spirit of people from the beginning of the Industrial Revolution. People are not machines; they have their own purposes, their own hopes and dreams, and they resent their companies for ignoring them.

Through the years, there has been a growing clamor for companies to provide more fulfilling work—employment consistent with employees' sense of destiny. People know that they will spend the majority of their waking life working, and they want their effort to add up to something great, to something meaningful. They don't want to look up after forty years, as many of their parents did, and say: "Is this all that I have to show for an entire lifetime of effort?" For this reason, a shared vision must appeal to the human spirit. It needs to be a dignified and worthwhile cause—something that people will be proud of, and that is worthy of their time, their energy, their love, their life.

> People are not machines; they have their own purposes, their own hopes and dreams, and they resent their companies for ignoring them.

" . . . summoning them to significance in living." Many people in bureaucratic organizations are lost in meaningless jobs, performing some small task with no awareness of their place in the big scheme of things. This experience is demoralizing, devaluing, and deadening. It reduces even the most loyal employees to what C. Wright Mills calls "cheerful robots." Robert Blauner described four ways in which workers were alienated in the context of their work: workers (1) felt powerless, (2) felt the work to be meaningless, (3) felt isolated from other workers, or (4) regarded the work as just a means to an end. Although this description was written in 1964, it depicts conditions that can be found in almost every organization in America today.

A Quantum Organization is essential for people to experience "significance in living." In Quantum Organizations, the work is challenging, allows for a high degree of autonomy and interaction with other people, and relates people to the purpose of

> *Most men would feel insulted if it were proposed to employ them in throwing stones over a wall, and then throwing them back, merely that they might earn their wages. But many are no more worthily employed now.*
>
> — Henry David Thoreau

the overall organization. It is to this latter point that shared vision plays a role. The way in which a shared vision modifies behavior is that people understand it and how their particular job fits in. People gain an appreciation for the importance of their piece—no matter how small—to the success of the whole.

Co-Creating Shared Vision

How a vision is created is a key aspect of its effectiveness. Many CEOs feel that it is their responsibility to create a vision for the organization. This stems, in part, from Western society's deification of the "hero leader." In some cases, the vision

springs from the breast of a company's founder, as with Bill Gates and Microsoft. In others, the CEO and executive team huddle for a few days at some off-site retreat and return with a carefully crafted and polished vision.

However, in a Quantum Organization, shared vision is co-created through an ongoing process that involves the entire organization. It really does not matter

> *It's been my experience that people will support that which they help create . . .*
>
> — Mary Kay Ash, founder of Mary Kay Cosmetics

where the original idea comes from. What matters is how the organization participates in shaping its final form. In order for a vision to be "shared," people need a say in creating it.

Originally, Ray & Berndtson chartered a traditional reengineering project with the purpose of dramatically improving the core search processes. However, the CEO had an intuition that something more was needed. When I described the workings of the Organizational EcoSystem Model to him, it crystallized his thinking about the changes that his firm needed to make. He realized that the company's mission, values, and strategy were too traditional. They had served Ray & Berndtson well in the past, but would not be adequate for the environmental changes that lurked just over the horizon. So the project scope was expanded from a process reengineering effort to a complete corporate transformation based on a new strategic vision.

Shifting Responsibility to the Organization

CEO Paul Ray, Jr. was known and respected in the company for his strategic insights, and the partners and other employees looked to him for direction in this regard. However, the company had a track record of starting out strong on change efforts but never fully realizing the expected benefits. The core project team—which consisted of CEO Ray, CFO Reece Pettigrew, and Director of Change Management Carrie Ham—used a systemic problem-solving approach to isolate the reasons. The process was:

1. Identify the discrete events

2. Establish the long-term patterns of behavior and underlying systemic structures (such as shifting the burden)

3. Isolate the beliefs (the mental models) that give rise to the behaviors

Ray & Berndtson learned that the organization's reliance on Ray and the corporate staff shifted the burden away from the front-line personnel. The core team's mental model was, "If the change is to succeed, then we have to make it happen." The front-line employees' mental model was, "We are responsible for conducting searches—if others want to implement changes, it will be up to them." This was a classic case of co-dependent behavior; the "parent" (the core team) was responsible and the "child" depended on being told exactly what to do without accepting accountability for the outcome.

> *Our efforts to do a better job of living our values will undoubtedly come with flaws. But if we meet those flaws and occasional failures with both persistence and patience, we can unlock a fortune.*
>
> — Eric Harvey and Alexander Lucia, authors of *Walk the Talk*

The way to break the pattern was to make the management team responsible for the success of the entire change project—not just the part that they were assigned. The managers, in turn, made it clear to the front-line employees that they, too, were responsible for the success of the change effort. This shift in responsibility was both welcomed and resisted. Most people saw immediately that it was the correct thing to do. However, the mantle of responsibility is uncomfortable the first few times a person wears it. In addition, the required behaviors—principally teamwork and dialogue—were new and unfamiliar to the organization. Training, behavior modeling by the organization's leaders, and ongoing communication were essential elements in the learning process.

Co-Creating Purpose and Principles

Although Ray had strong opinions about the purpose and principles that the firm needed to adopt, he recognized that for them to be shared, the employees had to have a voice in creating them. There are many ways to generate employee participation in creating the shared vision, but the approach Ray & Berndtson chose was to involve employees in half-day meetings. After a brief introduction to the concepts of purpose and principles, cross-functional and multilevel groups of employees shared their ideas about the firm's purpose in regard to customers, employees, shareholders, and the community. They also brainstormed the core principles they thought would be critical to the success of the firm over the long term. The detailed results of these meetings were immediately documented and relayed back to the participants (an essential step anytime people are asked to give their ideas and opinions). The participants had to accept that participation did not mean that every person's input would end up in the final design. Rather, every employee had an opportunity to voice a point of view with the understanding that it would be considered with due seriousness. Most of

> *Tell me and I'll forget, show me and I may remember;*
> *involve me and I'll understand.*
>
> — *Chinese proverb*

the participants were enthused by the visioning sessions. Others were more cynical; in their previous experience, these exercises were simply wastes of time. The future challenge for Ray & Berndtson will be to overcome this legacy of cynicism toward "vision and values" and make the vision a viable force.

After the office meetings, a core team refined the employees' input and developed a draft of the firm's new purpose and principles. This draft was distributed throughout the organization for feedback and was eventually submitted to the board of directors for final approval. The purpose (in relation to customers) became: "We provide superior people and organizational solutions worldwide." This was an important expansion of the possible scope of services that the firm would provide in the future. Ray & Berndtson intends for traditional executive search to become, over the long term, the core element in a much broader service offering. The core principles became Integrity, Client Focus, Innovation, and Teamwork.

Strategy and BHAG

The market research and one-on-one customer interviews conducted by Ray & Berndtson revealed that customers wanted much more value than they were getting. Many of the firm's clients had conducted their own reengineering projects and knew the importance of fast cycle-times in core processes. This experience increased client intolerance to the six-month average timeframe to complete a search. In addition, internal analysis indicated that the firm was not able to leverage its learning. Too many of their assignments were unrelated in any meaningful way. As a result, "speed" and "focus" became the key elements of the new strategy.

Ray & Berndtson recognized the need for a BHAG that would inspire and motivate the workforce to achieve the new strategy. Ray realized that to achieve this, the BHAG had to be something that people could connect with. An objective that was meaningful at a personal level would have to emerge from the organization's "center," or "spirit." The core team approached this objective by developing several possible BHAGs. Over the course of two months, as I conducted interviews and facilitated meetings, I tested several possible BHAGs for their appeal.

> *Without a pull toward some goal which people truly want to achieve, the forces in support of the status quo can be overwhelming. Vision establishes an overarching goal. The loftiness of the target compels new ways of thinking and acting.*
>
> — Peter Senge, author of *The Fifth Discipline*

The BHAG relating to the speed of conducting searches caught fire in most people's imaginations. Selected clients who were asked to comment also responded favorably. The goal eventually selected was to achieve an average

sixty-day search while maintaining the highest standards of quality. This goal was coupled with the firm's emphasis on fewer clients using a more focused strategy to form the full BHAG referred to as "60-70-80 by 1998." The "70-80" portion means that 70 percent of the firm's business will derive from targeted accounts while obtaining 80 percent of the desired business. This met the three criteria for BHAGs:

✠ *Audacious.* The goal of sixty days was chosen because it was possible—but just barely. Although the industry average is 160 days, many search firms routinely market to prospective clients that they can complete a search in ninety days. If a lesser goal had been selected, the firm would not have appeared to its clients to be creating a differentiated service.

✠ *Inspiring.* Employees quickly realized that a sixty-day average search would set an enormous precedent in the industry and create a huge strategic advantage. Typical comments were, "If we can achieve a goal like that, we will own this industry."

✠ *Unifying.* This ambitious goal requires the combined efforts of every person and function in the firm. From secretaries to partners, researchers to accountants—each must contribute his or her part if the goal is to be achieved. And, in validation of the ecosystem concept, clients need to do their part in the process as well.

The creation of the elements of the shared vision is just the start of a long-term effort to get every employee to internalize the company's vision. Ray & Berndtson has combined multiple forums and media approaches to getting the message out, and after a year-and-a-half, they are beginning to see their first tangible results. In the words of CFO Pettigrew:

> I think people were receptive to the vision until we realized that each
> one of us really had to do things differently—each person was
> receptive to the idea of everybody *else* changing. When our firm got
> to the point where the "rubber meets the road," we realized that it
> was going to take a lot of time and effort to fully understand and

internalize the vision. We are just now—a year-and-a-half-later—beginning to understand why we're going through all of this and actually what it's going to look like. We are seeing the "lights go on" more often. People are finally starting to understand. Not to say that it's still not difficult to get participation in some respects, but it's much easier.

Chapter Five
Transforming Corporate Culture

*As you go the way of life you will see a
great chasm. Jump. It is not as wide as
you think.*

> *— Advice given to a young Native
> American at the time of initiation.*

Do you know how a caterpillar becomes a butterfly? The answer may surprise
you. Once a caterpillar finishes spinning its cocoon, it *completely dissolves*. This
"caterpillar soup" then follows the principles of organization hidden in its genetic
code to create an entirely new and higher form. From the cocoon emerges an
incredible, free-flying creature that mesmerizes us with its beauty and elegance.
Although not quite this dramatic, the transformative change that bureaucratic
companies must embrace to become Quantum Organizations is similar. Many
will ask: How does a bureaucratic organization achieve such dramatic change? In
1992, I developed a holistic methodology for large-scale organizational change
called Total Process Management (TPM). Since I first published the TPM
methodology in my book *Eating the Chocolate Elephant*, it has evolved and
grown—as all healthy models should.

TPM has gradually evolved into the Integrated Change Methodology. This model
includes all of the elements that a particular change effort may require.

Remember that a methodology can only serve as a template for change; it has to be customized for every single change effort. As a result, your organization will need to modify certain aspects of the material presented in this chapter to fit the context of your change effort.

Types of Organizational Change

When bureaucratic organizations experience a problem, the tendency is to focus on the individual event. The resulting "fire-fighting" activities usually solve the immediate symptoms of the problem. However, the "solutions" often cause new and unexpected problems or provide only temporary relief. It is common practice to couple fire fighting with a "search for the guilty." These "witch-hunts" are completely useless—they only lead to finger pointing, political infighting, and risk avoidance—pure poison for a living organization. When problems reach intolerable levels, companies initiate deeper changes. At this point, the three most common performance improvement approaches are to implement new technologies, downsize, and reorganize. Although each of these actions has the potential for positive long-term effects, they rarely achieve them.

> *We tend to meet any new situation by reorganizing, and a wonderful method it can be for creating the illusion of progress while producing confusion, inefficiency and demoralization.*
>
> — Petronius Arbitor, Greek Philosopher, 210 B.C.

Business Week magazine (June 14, 1993) reported that corporations had spent more than a trillion dollars on information technology in the previous decade that businesses have not come close to recouping through productivity improvements. In addition, downsizing—despite its wide-spread popularity—practically never pays off. The final alternative, reorganization, is usually a sort of shell game that causes endless cynicism among employees. In the early 1980s, for instance, employees at Atlantic Richfield would roll their eyes when a reorganization was announced and joke that ARCO stood for Another Reorganization Coming On.

Outside-In Change

In relation to the Organizational EcoSystem Model, traditional approaches to change are *outside-in*. The first changes are usually at the level of events, followed by changes in structure and technology, and then process. Culture is practically never touched, and purpose and principles are rarely more than words on some neglected corridor wall. Executives are under tremendous pressure to deliver short-term stock performance, and practically all of their energy is directed toward that goal. One reason that management favors superficial changes is that they are relatively *easy*. Compared to shifting the corporate culture from a victim mentality to self-responsibility, a structural reorganization is a "no-brainer." Another reason is that these changes tend to be more *visible*. A new computer system or people sitting in different offices can be seen—we can tell something is happening—creating a shared vision is a different matter altogether. External changes are also *immediate*. There are few things as anxiety-filled for senior executives as having to wait long periods for the benefits of deep organizational changes to manifest. Finally, superficial changes tend to be *local*. They generally don't require broad coordination across the entire organization. It is no coincidence that these four reasons—easy, visible, immediate, and local—form the acronym EVIL.

Actually, short-term, outside-in change is only "evil" when it is the *only* action that is taken. Ultimately, Quantum Organizations create a dynamic balance between short-term (outside-in) change and long-term (inside-out) transformative change. Neither can be neglected for long. If you run out of cash before the long-term improvements are in place—they become irrelevant. Likewise, if you sacrifice your future for today, there will be no tomorrow.

Inside-Out Change

Implementing change from the *inside-out* is the only way to consistently deliver significant and sustainable long-term performance improvements. Part of the nature of living systems is that they reach a balanced state and then self-regulate to stay that way. The organization automatically counteracts superficial changes through its natural "immune" system. This is called *compensating feedback*, and we see it constantly in our organizations. Social Scientist Kurt Lewin used a diagram called "Force Field Analysis" (see panel 1 of Fig. 5.1) to describe this phenomenon. In this diagram, balance is achieved in organizations between the forces that are driving change and those that are restraining it. If we merely increase the driving forces, we will achieve short-term improvements. However, since the energy of the restraining forces has not changed, it is as if they have become coiled springs (as shown in panel 2 of Fig. 5.1). As soon as the pressure from driving forces is lessened, the restraining forces push back to the original equilibrium. This is the action of *compensating feedback*. Deep organizational changes—those that start from the center of the Organizational EcoSystem Model and work outward—change the whole system so compensations are eliminated. The immune system is reprogrammed to remove the restraining forces rather than just repress them.

Compensating Feedback
Illustrated Through Lewin's Force-Field Analysis

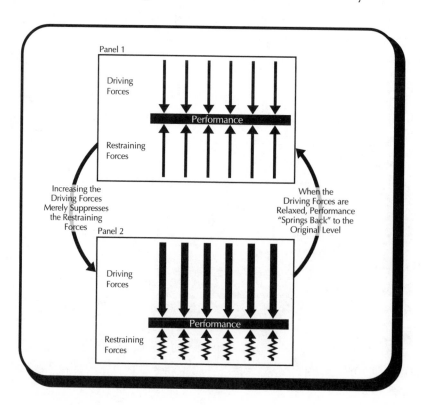

Figure 5.1

It is interesting to note that if we reverse the acronym "EVIL"—in the same way that I am recommending reversing the order of our change efforts—it spells LIVE. Inside-out changes are the only sure way to ensure the health and vitality of any organization over the long-term.

Types of Change Projects

Most organizations will have many change projects in progress at once. These range in size from very small incremental changes at the task level to complete transformations such as that required to make the shift to a Quantum Organization. The sections of the pyramid in Figure 5.2 illustrate the four primary types of change: reactive, operational, fundamental, and transformational.

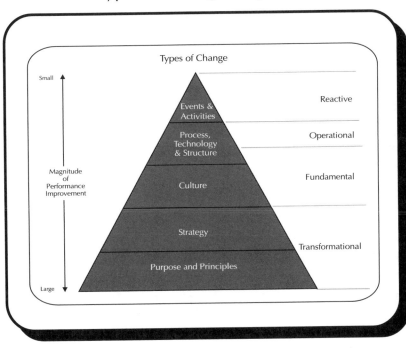

Figure 5.2

1. *Reactive.* Changes at the top of the pyramid are reactive. They consist of quick-fix, fire fighting style problem solving. In bureaucracies, the majority of the organization's energy is focused on this level of change.

2. *Operational.* The second type of change, called operational change, is still essentially problem solving, but it addresses deeper structural sources of the problems (although mostly on a local level). TQM-type continuous improvements are operational changes. Through quality tools such as cause-and-effect diagrams, teams identify the core sources of problems in processes, technologies, and structure, and address them at a systemic level.

3. *Fundamental.* Deep changes to *all* of the ecosystem elements—processes, technologies, structure, and culture—are fundamental changes. Fundamental changes are made on a large scale and seek to change underlying assumptions. Operational change, in contrast, tends to make improvements to the system without challenging existing design assumptions. Business process reengineering, properly executed, is a form of fundamental change.

4. *Transformational.* Changes that reach to the organization's core—its purpose, guiding principles, and/or strategy—are transformational changes. The shift from a bureaucratic to a Quantum Organization is a transformational change because it requires an expansion of the organization's purpose to embrace all of the key stakeholders. Core principles must change to include trust, openness, and other principles, and strategy must change to acknowledge the importance to the organization's survival of flexibility and adaptability.

One of the reasons many change efforts fail is that leaders do not understand the scope of change that is required. TQM offers a prime example. Executives perceived TQM as "incremental changes made continuously by employees throughout the company." They scheduled some training classes, ordered 10 percent improvements over the next year and stood back to reap the benefits. "How hard can this be?" they must have thought. Most leaders suffered a big surprise when these seemingly simple changes failed miserably. Once TQM is implemented, changes at the operational level *are* fairly easy to achieve.

However, the implementation of TQM itself is a transformational change. It requires new core principles (teamwork and quality to name two), as well as repositioning the company's strategy to include quality products and services. Other change initiatives—teamwork, empowerment, and even reengineering— suffer similar fates. This will also be the fate of attempts to shift to a Quantum Organization if companies do not follow the process for transformational change.

The effort, time, and cost of changes increase exponentially from the top of the pyramid to the bottom. But then, so do the benefits. In fact, reactive changes actually weaken the organization because they shift attention and energy away from the fundamental changes required to bring the organization back into balance with the external environment. The longer the deep systemic changes are deferred, the more the organization relies on quick fixes to survive. Eventually, the organization will lose its ability to make the necessary changes: It will fail or be bought out. Obviously, some reactive changes are unavoidable. However, in a healthy company, they are coupled with more fundamental changes to the system.

"Shifting the Burden" Behavior

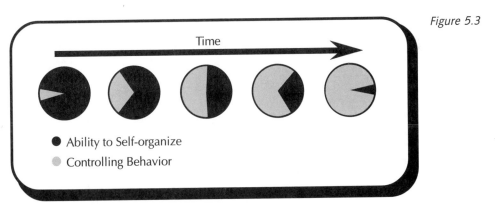

Figure 5.3

Senge describes a system archetype, called "shifting the burden," that illustrates this phenomena. In Figure 5.3, we see where the "burden" of performance is gradually shifted from the deep systemic changes to the quick fixes. Shifting the burden behaviors—which can be equated with addiction—are pervasive in bureaucracies. In the case of addiction, the body comes to rely on a drug for its survival, literally changing its basic metabolism to accommodate it. This not only weakens the body, but it also makes abrupt withdrawal from the drug devastating—even life threatening.

Marc Schwartz, chairman of Spectra Communications Inc. and an executive coach, believes that many people and organizations have relied on quick fixes for so long that they have become addicted to the adrenaline rush that accompanies putting out the fire. "You can really see the effects of the addiction," Schwartz advises, "when you try to take the reactive quick-fix solution away from managers. They resist vigorously, and then find ways to manufacture crises that can only be solved through their own 'heroic' intervention—classic symptoms of addictive behavior." Just as addiction invariably kills the unreformed addict, excessive reliance on quick fixes (or external consultants, which is another form of shifting the burden) eventually spells death for a company.

Integrated Change Methodology

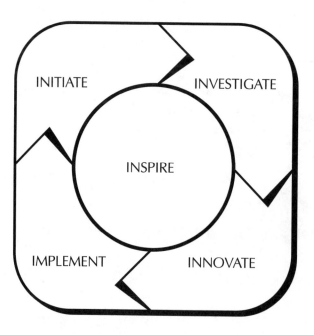

Figure 5.4

My approach to transformational change is the Integrated Change Methodology, pictured in Figure 5.4. The Inspire phase—the heart of any change effort—is a continual process. The remaining elements: Initiate, Investigate, Innovate, and Implement, are the phases that comprise every change project.

Inspire: The Heart of Change

Human-based systems have three interrelated aspects: physical body, mind, and spirit. In an individual person, the physical body is that which can be seen and felt. Mind is the source of a person's conscious and unconscious mental processes. Spirit has many meanings depending on who you ask. In this context, spirit refers to the vital principle or animating force within living beings.

Body, mind, and spirit combine to produce the total functioning of an individual person or a human system. In the Organizational EcoSystem Model, the body correlates with processes, technologies, structure, and cultural artifacts. The mind is comprised of purpose, principles, strategy, cultural beliefs, and memories. The sources of an organization's spirit are the people themselves. Spirit makes the greatest contribution to productivity, followed by mind, and finally by the physical body. For ten thousand years, we have reaped the harvest of human labor. In the past thirty years, and particularly since TQM appeared on the scene, we have realized that employees (not just management) have minds that can contribute significantly to the performance of the company. Spirit, however, is still largely ignored.

Due to the legacy of classical science, we have historically focused almost entirely on the tangible and material aspects of a company. As a result, the "Inspire" portion of Integrated Change—which addresses the mind and spirit of the organization—is disregarded in the majority of companies. This is one of the primary reasons that change fails. By *inspire* I do not mean some sort of "rah-rah" cheerleading efforts on the part of management. True motivation—which is resilient, creative, and courageous—comes from within each person, not from external manipulation. The human spirit is motivated by ownership, participation, fairness, self-reliance, self-determination, and personal meaning. In Quantum Organizations, these characteristics are reflected in the everyday functioning of the company. But in bureaucratic organizations, these conditions are counter-cultural; a tremendous amount of effort has to be put into creating them.

Change Readiness

Contrary to what you may believe, people do not resist change. They resist *being* changed. Few people resist a change when it is their idea; they resist it when it is someone else's idea. The employees that populate the modern organization bear little in common with those of the industrial era. Employees today are educated and aware, and they want more out of their lives than paychecks. They do not want to be told what to do. They want to be partners in the change effort, to be seen as integral to the process instead of a barrier to it. They want to understand the reasons behind the change and feel that they have a legitimate voice in it. This calls for a whole new leadership approach.

> Leading change is an exercise in creating the fertile ground out of which the organization can evolve a new way of operating.

Leading change is an exercise in creating the fertile ground out of which the organization can evolve a new way of operating. The ground is fertile (that is, the organization is ready to change) when the employees are both committed to the change and have the capabilities required to make the desired changes. As shown in Figure 5.5, there are four elements in change readiness. Commitment demands both conviction and will, and capability requires that employees have the requisite skills and enablers.

Commitment to change. Conviction is the intellectual understanding of the reasons that a change should take place. Will is the emotional acceptance of the need to change—the willingness to do what it takes despite personal fears or doubts.

Change Readiness

Figure 5.5

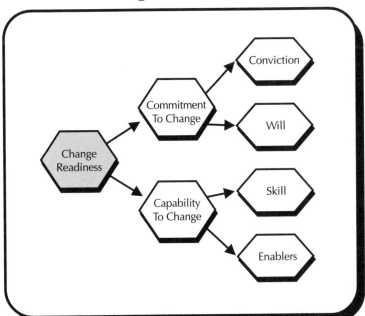

Commitment is a very great power. When people fully commit to making something happen, they will not allow anything or anyone to stand in the way until the goal is met. However, commitment is not easy to achieve. For one thing, commitment cannot be commanded; it must be volunteered. Compliance can be commanded, but it is only a pale shadow of commitment. Bureaucratic organizations are already full of compliant employees. These people do more or less what they are told and little else. The burden on the leaders in this situation is overwhelming. They have to do all of the thinking and problem solving as well as direct the activities of almost every employee—the conditions of "Newtonian despair" as described in chapter 1.

Committed employees, on the other hand, require very little direction. What they need is clarity about their goals so they can make decisions that will advance the organization toward its objective. They also need the resources they deem necessary to get the job done. Committed employees will clear the way to the goal without being told what to do. They will put in the effort needed to succeed, and they will make changes that will actually work in practice. Commitment is the natural state of Quantum Organizations, but it is rare in the typical bureaucracy. Commitment is built on a foundation of trust, honesty, and fairness. It requires openness and the willingness to engage all of the affected employees in the co-creation of the solution. It is difficult to establish, but fairly easy to maintain.

One of the tools in the Integrated Change Methodology, "Stakeholder Analysis," is useful in assessing organizational commitment. A stakeholder analysis is used by the core change team to assess influential people and factions (tribes, castes, departments) as to their relative commitment to the change effort. Three ratings are used:

1. *Enthusiasts.* Enthusiasts voluntarily enroll themselves in the change process. These are truly committed individuals who will do whatever it takes for the change to succeed.

2. *Followers.* Followers are compliant but not committed. Most of them will do at least what they are asked, and often times more, but they do not view the success of the change as their responsibility.

3. *Opponents.* Opponents do not share the vision and do not want to see the changes take place. They usually believe they have something to lose or have a personal vision of how things should be that is different from the new corporate objectives.

A leader's objective is to create the conditions where as many people as possible become Enthusiasts, and as few as possible remain Opponents. Enthusiasts can be leveraged to promote the change effort and to provide feedback to the core change team as to what is really being said and done in the organization.

Followers are not particularly helpful to the change effort. Actions should be taken to encourage Followers to become Enthusiasts—to accept personal responsibility for the change. Many people—both Followers and Enthusiasts—may voice strong opinions that the company should modify certain aspects of the proposed change. Such constructive and supportive comments should be taken into consideration.

Opponents, in contrast, may actively resist the change effort and even attempt to sabotage it—either openly or through passive-aggressive behavior. Such destructive behaviors must be ended (this is the functioning of self-regulation in living systems). As little attention as possible should be given to the resistance to change. Attention is a form of positive reinforcement that can influence people to continue negative behaviors. Instead, focus attention on the actions that promote the desired changes and behaviors.

Capability to change. It is not enough that people want to make a change happen, they also need the skills and enablers required to succeed. The skills required will vary based on the employee groups in questions and the type of change that is desired. Do executives know how to lead change (that is, are they quantum leaders)? Is the change team skilled in teamwork, project management, dialogue, and interpersonal relationships? Will the change require new ways of working or technologies that demand new skills? What new beliefs and behaviors will be required?

Enablers are the resources required to complete the job. These include staff, money, office space, moral support, equipment, computers, and training. The critical point here is that the organization—not the managers—will decide what resources are required. It is the leader's responsibility to make the necessary resources available. There may be cases where the leaders should mentor teams regarding alternative approaches to reduce the resources needed, or guide them to alternatives that would be more effective and efficient. In these cases, the leaders serve as advisors to the team, not as "bosses." The organization has responsibility for the success of the changes, not just the leaders. The leaders are there to offer support, clarify the direction, make resources available, provide feedback and wise counsel, and help the teams connect with other parts of the organization as needed.

Creative Tension: The Impetus to Change

Commitment to any goal makes use of a force called "creative tension." The psychology of creative tension involves dissatisfaction with the current reality coupled with the desire for a future vision. Author and consultant Robert Fritz, writing in his book *Corporate Tides,* used the term "structural dynamics" to describe the function of creative tension. As shown in Figure 5.6, this is the natural tension that results when a desired state varies from the actual state. When creative tension is present, people or organizations follow the path of least resistance, which eventually leads to the resolution of the tension. Fritz explained that when goals are not met, there may be a second structural dynamic at work that is pulling in the opposite direction. As we near one goal, the opposite goal increases in strength until the organization reverses its path and reverts to the original behavior, only to have the cycle repeat again.

This behavior can be seen in the example of a company that resorts to layoffs to improve profits. After the layoff, financial performance will improve at the expense of overworking the remaining employees. Gradually, the need to hire new employees will prove irresistible and costs will begin to increase. When costs have once again reached a critical point, the layoff cycle will start again. The way out of this endless cycle is to weaken or eliminate the opposing dynamic. The creative tension model is very useful, albeit simplistic. The forces at play are always far more complex than the model of just two opposing forces would indicate. Still, the creative tension model can help us in understanding how to gain organizational commitment for a proposed change.

Creative Tension

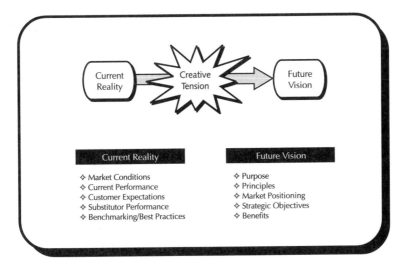

Figure 5.6

Discomfort vs. Fear

It is important to understand what I mean by "dissatisfaction with the current reality." The key word here is *dissatisfaction,* which can be equated with "discomfort" but not with "fear." The difference between discomfort and fear can be demonstrated through a simple exercise. Pick up a key ring with several keys on it. Now, put it under your thigh as you sit in a chair so that your weight rests on it. Very little time will pass before you will become uncomfortable. The keys will begin to dig into your leg and no matter how you shift your weight you will still be uncomfortable. At this point, you are motivated to eliminate the discomfort. You are not afraid of your keys; you simply want to remove them as a source of pain. No one has to tell you to do this; you have your own motivation. In the Integrated Change Methodology, the object is to generate dissatisfaction with the status quo—not fear.

Unfortunately, traditional managers commonly resort to the use of fear as a motivator. This is a terrible mistake. Fear is not only paralyzing, but it also brings out the worst in people—their most basic instincts for survival. Instead of mobilizing people to form a productive and creative response to an external challenge, fear induces destructive and self-protective behaviors. Cooperation breaks down, aggression (both active and passive) increases, deceit and even sabotage becomes more prevalent, and stress and anxiety is increased for almost everyone. These behaviors do nothing to promote the organization's goals and substantially reduce its ability to change.

> Traditional managers commonly resort to the use of fear as a motivator. This is a terrible mistake.

Stress, when formed through fear, is more appropriately called "distress." Distress by itself is enormously debilitating—depleting people's energy, resilience, and ultimately their long-term health. Psychologists note that fear is a motivator only as long as it is present. As soon as the stimulus is removed, the motivation disappears. Companies that rely on fear tactics find that, over time, their threats have to become increasingly extreme to maintain the same level of motivation. This has left many companies in the situation where their employees live in constant fear of losing their jobs. How, I wonder, do these companies expect anxious, exhausted, and angry employees to create exceptional customer satisfaction, high-quality products and services, and rapid and effective change?

Current Reality

People who are content with the status quo are unlikely to feel any reason to want to change it. As a result, creating dissatisfaction with the current reality is a critical element in any change effort. In some cases, the urgency for change will be based on a very real and immediate threat to the organization's existence, such as a large operating loss or rapid deregulation of an industry. In situations such as these, the compelling need for change is obvious. However, there are two drawbacks to such situations. The first is that employees will become fearful under these conditions. The second is that the company will likely find it difficult to obtain the resources (the enablers) required to achieve the necessary changes. In contrast, other companies—particularly those in good financial and competitive shape—may find it difficult to create a compelling argument for making any changes at all. It is ironic that companies that are in the best economic shape to institute dramatic changes are the least inclined to do so. And, those that acknowledge a profound need for change are often in the poorest position to do anything about it.

How do you create the necessary dissatisfaction? "Get all the facts out," advised Jack Welch, CEO of General Electric. "Give people the rationale for change, laying it out in the clearest most dramatic terms. When everybody gets the same facts, they will generally come to the same conclusion." In this, I agree with Welch. In a Quantum Organization, the norm is for everyone to understand the organization's current reality. That is one of the reasons that mobilizing for radical change in these organizations is relatively easy. However, bureaucratic organizations must overcome the legacy of their "need-to-know" information-sharing style, which is not usually an easy thing to accomplish.

> *You have to give people a reason to do something differently.*
>
> — Lawrence Bossidy, CEO of AlliedSignal

In the spring of 1994, Ray & Berndtson first contacted me to assist with reengineering its executive search processes. The CEO, Paul Ray, Jr., was concerned for several reasons. Although the firm was achieving record sales and growth, profitability had remained flat. In addition, he had learned through extensive client research that companies were generally dissatisfied with both the length of time of the average search (the industry average is 160 days) as well as the value equation—the perceived benefits in relation to the cost. (Search fees are charged at an industry standard 33 percent of the new executive's annual salary.)

Ray was concerned not only about the fortunes of his company, in comparison to other search firms, but also about the future of the search industry in general. In our first meeting he pointed out that there was little differentiation between the firms in the industry, and that the process of executive search had not changed significantly in the last twenty years. "When I compared these trends to the rapid changes in other industries," Ray explained, "I knew that it was only a matter of time until a paradigm-busting company emerged and took the search industry by storm. Instead of leaving our fate in another company's hands, we decided that Ray & Berndtson should become the company that reinvented executive search."

Ray & Berndtson is an example of a company that is doing well financially and yet must somehow generate dissatisfaction with the status quo. As a partnership of highly intelligent and ambitious professionals, it has a challenge that most companies do not: The management team could not simply give an order to change, it had to persuade the partners (and the other employees) to voluntarily embrace a radical change effort.

The firm took a number of important steps to gain organizational commitment for the change. It began immediately to employ the three elements of the organic principle of openness: free flow of information, diversity, and interactions among employees. It initially conducted half-day sessions in each office to introduce the reengineering effort, and to begin the dialogue process around the need to change. Two of the most important aspects of these and all later meetings were that they involved everyone (from secretaries to partners), and shared both the refined results and raw data from all of the core project team's work products. These actions sent a message because they demonstrated management's genuine interest in everyone's input.

One of the concerns that managers have with sharing sensitive performance and competitive information with employees is that they do not know how the employees will react. The fear is that bad news will prompt an exodus of the best employees or some other destructive reaction. For Ray & Berndtson, this was a very real concern. All professional services organizations are vulnerable to the defection of partners. In most of these firms, the client base is highly mobile, and it is common for partners to take significant revenue with them when they leave. Management knew that by sharing unadulterated information it increased the risk of employees leaving. Ultimately, the firm decided that

> Traditional organizations must overcome the legacy of their "need-to-know" information-sharing style.

the benefits gained through increased employee commitment far outweighed the risk. (As a post-script, it did not lose a single employee as a direct result of sharing the information.)

Ray & Berndtson began to develop consensus around its new strategic vision in a series of all-day meetings that included every employee. Over the course of the meetings, the management team provided detailed accounts of client surveys and interviews that expressed dissatisfaction with the search industry, along with the changes that clients wanted to see. It described the competitive positioning, strengths, and weaknesses of every major executive search firm. It also introduced potential Substitutors that represented real threats over the long term. The team profiled their company's performance and projected the long-term results if nothing changed. Finally, the team described the new strategic approach that it felt would assure Ray & Berndtson a competitive advantage in the industry. All employees, regardless of rank, were invited to speak frankly in an open dialogue about their questions, concerns, and observations.

At the end of the sessions, the employees had a much clearer understanding about the need to change and the direction the firm was taking. Many employees felt pride and excitement that they had been invited to participate. One executive assistant voiced that she had worked for three executive search firms over twenty years and that this was the first such meeting she had ever attended. She added that this was the first time she understood how the whole business worked. She felt that she would be more effective in her job as a result. The surprise for the management team in all of this was that the more information they shared, the higher employee morale went—even when the information was not flattering to the firm. Carrie Ham, director of change management at Ray & Berndtson, explained it like this: "People already knew most of what was being shared with them. They were excited because management was communicating openly with the firm. This was perceived as such a difference that people began to think that things were different this time."

Of course, not everything went smoothly with this open and inclusive approach. Several people were incensed that the different levels in the organization were all given an equal voice in the meetings. They believed strongly in hierarchy and felt that each level in the organization should have had separate meetings. The internal interview results were presented such that controversial comments and references to individual people were either removed or made generic. Still, some people took offense to some of the feedback and denied its validity—they felt that these comments were the complaints of a few unhappy employees and were not legitimate concerns. Another concern was that the feedback focused on the negative and did not give the organization credit for the positive things that were being done. All of these were normal and expected reactions. The management team did not try to argue these points to prove them right or wrong. They simply acknowledged people's right to their point of view and then moved on. Within a few weeks after the meetings, the focus had shifted—employees had begun to accept the need for change—some even protested that the changes were not happening fast enough!

A Compelling Future Vision

It is not enough for people to be dissatisfied with the current reality. They also need a compelling vision of a better way of operating. If employees gain a clear understanding of the need to change, but do not see evidence of a credible alternative, many of them will move to another company that promises a better future (and the best employees are often the first to go). A future vision provides a new platform for employees to strive for. The change methodology (Integrated Change, in this case) bridges the gap between the old and the new platforms. This is a primary reason that employees need to respect the change methodology. If the organization develops a compelling vision but employees lack faith in its ability to achieve it, the likelihood of failure will be much higher.

> One of the main reasons that transformative change fails is that employees and managers do not see "change" as part of their jobs—they see it as an intrusion.

The second element in creative tension is a compelling future vision; a clear mental picture of a future state. The change effort must develop a vision of the proposed changes that is in harmony with the overall corporate vision. This is a key point. One of the main reasons that transformative change fails is that employees and managers do not see "change" as part of their jobs. Instead, they see it as an *intrusion*, an addition to their normal workloads. They resent the change, do not commit to it, and want it to disappear as soon as possible. This is why organizational change must be woven into the fabric of the company. People need to see it as an integral part of their everyday tasks, not as something separate. When the company's corporate objectives—its strategic vision—includes goals that require organizational change, employees will begin to see the change effort as a means for achieving their personal goals. The efforts required for the proposed change will not be imposed on them, but instead will be something that they need if they and the organization are to succeed.

Techniques for Building Consensus for Change

Here are seven techniques essential for building consensus for change:

1. *Inclusion.* Personal commitment is entirely voluntary. If an organization has any hope of gaining widespread commitment to a proposed change, every employee who is affected by the change should be afforded the opportunity to participate in a meaningful way. The example of Ray & Berndtson's change effort illustrated some of the ways in which people can become involved in a change project.

2. *Openness.* Inclusion and openness are important aspects of the healthy functioning of living systems. Openness in the process of organizational change is very beneficial in reducing confusion, anxiety, and gossip, and in increasing trust and cooperation. Change leaders should understand that the concept of openness goes beyond sharing information; it also speaks to the need for transparency of intention. Hidden agendas and manipulative behaviors are attempts to exploit the employees against their will. These

behaviors, which are contrary to the spirit of openness, further increase both employee cynicism and resistance to change.

3. *Behavior modeling.* How often have we heard about the importance of leaders to walk the talk? One of the primary reasons that change fails in traditional organizations is that leaders exempt themselves from the rules that govern the remainder of the organization. Alfred Bandura, a leading psychologist and social learning theorist, has determined that behavioral modeling (observational learning) has the strongest influence on human behavior of *all* learning techniques. Bandura believes that "the vast majority of the habits that we acquire during our lifetimes are learned by observing and imitating other people." This understanding should amplify our respect for the role of leaders' actions in influencing employee behavior. Through their unilateral authority, leaders in classical organizations have a particularly powerful influence on employee behavior. Employees will do what leaders *do*, not what they *say*. In order for a new culture to take hold, leaders have to embody the new beliefs. They need to become living examples of the desired behaviors and mind-set. The influence of behavior modeling in Quantum Organizations is somewhat reduced for the simple reason that quantum employees take more responsibility for their own behavior.

4. *Communication.* In the context of organizational change, communication is about creating shared understanding. This stands in marked contrast to the traditional view of communication as a one-way message that is expected to be understood and accepted as it was

> *It is no use walking anywhere to preach unless our walking is our preaching.*
>
> — St. Francis of Assisi

intended. This communication style is completely ineffective when used in the context of creating shared meaning. Communication needs to be seen not as a send-and-receive transaction, but as an iterative process in which a field of understanding is developed between two or more people.

5. *Symbolic shockwaves.* Most classical organizations are characterized by a high degree of employee cynicism. Employees have seen so many change programs come and go that they no longer take management's initiatives

seriously. Companies that want to create a quantum culture need to be completely serious about the change or they should not bother to start. But how do leaders convince their disbelieving workforce that they are serious this time around? In part, through a technique called "symbolic shockwaves." These are radical actions that demonstrate unequivocally that the change effort is for real.

For example, in one bureaucratic company that was known for its stifling rules and regulations, the CEO created a big pile of procedure manuals in the company parking lot, gathered all of the employees around, and set the manuals on fire. Then he handed out one page that had all of the rules that any employee needed to know.

The best symbolic shockwaves, of course, are those in which management teams set an example by implementing changes for themselves first. At one company, the CEO eliminated a long-standing perk that had given preferential treatment to management. One day, while the executive team was off-site at a luncheon, he had all of their reserved parking places painted over. When the executives returned, they discovered that they would have to scramble for open parking spots just like every other employee. This demonstrated in a powerful, but humorous way, the company's commitment to equality and teamwork.

6. *Generate quick wins.* Quick wins are important in overcoming employee cynicism. Changes that can be implemented quickly and with minimal effort demonstrate in a definitive way that the proposed organizational design will work. These can be in the form of stories that leaders tell about individual successes, or they can take the form of "learning laboratories"—in which employees participate in computer simulations that demonstrate the operation of the new design.

7. *Persistence.* Fundamental and transformative changes usually take a long time. Many change efforts fail because an organization does not "go the distance" required for the change to succeed. This may happen when

management was not really serious, leaders with new agendas take charge, pressures for short-term quick-fixes take precedence, or unrealistic expectations were held about how long the change would take. Regardless, it is essential to persist even when it is difficult to do so. Ham, Ray & Berndtson's director of change mangement, points out one reason why it is hard to persist in the change effort:

> It takes a lot of stamina—when bad things happen or things don't happen exactly right, or somebody leaves the firm—you just constantly have to keep reassuring people. And sometimes I just get tired, but you just have to put your head down and keep on moving. There have been a couple of times that I felt like the "train might stop" because of the pressure. But it didn't—it takes a lot of effort on everyone's part and it's just your own personal fortitude to keep on going. You have to believe in it—that what you are doing is the right thing for the firm.

Transitioning: Crossing the "Valley of Despair"

Although the following allegory is simplistic, it illustrates many elements of large-scale change in organizations. In it, you will see the action of creative tension; the role of leaders; grief and coping rituals; the anxiety that arises in the midst of the change; how people give up and turn back; the letdown that follows "getting there"; and the eventual stabilizing of the new environment.

Wagons Ho!

When the American frontier was being settled, it was common for groups of people to join together in long wagon trains and head West. The people who decided to go were largely dissatisfied with their current lot. Perhaps the cities were too loud and busy, or the work and pay was lousy, or their families were being forced to live in cramped and squalid quarters. Regardless of the reason, these people were dissatisfied with the status quo and wanted something better for themselves. They had a

glorious vision of the West: All the land that anyone could ever want, gold just laying on the ground waiting to be picked up—truly a "land of milk and honey." So, between their dissatisfaction with their current situation and the beckoning vision of a bountiful land, people took to the trail.

As they set out, hopes and expectations were high. But more than a few people still harbored doubts and, as the last of the familiar sights dropped below the horizon, even the strongest felt some regret over leaving their old lives behind. At night, people gathered to share their sadness and their hopes, telling stories and singing songs, crying a little, laughing a little, and gradually letting go of the past.

The wagon train masters knew the way, but they did not know what surprises might show up unexpectedly, such as Indians, or storms, or broken wagon wheels. Over time, the wagon train incurred casualties to wagons, animals, and even people, and the misfortunes started to accumulate. For some folks, that was enough to make them head back the way they had come. They had wanted the good life the vision promised, but not at that level of work and risk. In some cases, entire wagon trains turned around.

After many weeks in the wilderness, people were tired, afraid, and unsure of themselves. The wagon masters called this part of the trip "the valley of despair," because it was so hard on people. Everything familiar was long gone, and the new land was nowhere in sight. It just seemed that the trip was stretching on forever. This was the point at which the wagon masters were most active in talking with the people. They really could not do much to remove people's pain and problems, so they spent a lot of time just listening to them and even more time reassuring them. They pointed out landmarks to show that the wagon train was on the right track and making good progress. They settled conflicts, helped reallocate resources to people in need, prodded the stragglers to catch up, and kept the group moving.

Finally, in the far distance, the mountaintops that signaled their final destination would creep into sight. Although the trip would still take another few weeks, morale would rise among the travelers. With renewed energy, they would hurry along, no longer needing the support of the wagon masters. And then they finally arrived—only to find that their imagined destination had been far more attractive than reality. The land required a lot of work; any gold that could be found took great effort and a fair share of luck. Still, after the disappointment wore off, people realized that they were much better off than they had been. Not too long after everyone was settled, and life had become fairly routine, some of those folks started talking about the land further west, and how much better it was. . . .

Transition Rituals

In the preceding story, one of the first things that the people experienced was a sense of loss and sadness over the life they had left behind. It did not really matter that they were going on to a better life; they still felt some grief over leaving. The pioneers vented many of these emotions through nightly rituals of story telling, singing, and talking around the campfire. Being together and just knowing that other people were experiencing the same things was very important in helping people to deal with their feelings. In this way, the pioneers were able to work through the process of letting go.

There has never been a beginning that was not accompanied by an ending of some sort. In modern society, we have come to ignore this very important point—much to our detriment. Even when changes are positive, such as getting a new job, having a baby, or winning the lottery, there is an experience of loss. When

> *What we call the beginning is often the end,*
> *and to make our end is to make a beginning.*
> *The end is where we start from.*
>
> —T. S. Eliot

the changes are perceived as negative and beyond control, the loss is even greater. It is not the change itself, but the accompanying sense of loss that creates problems for people if it is not dealt with in a productive way. All important endings have the effect of a symbolic death, with all the attendant emotions and disorientation. One way of understanding this is to recognize that an attachment has been torn away—a connection has been broken. As long as people cling to the broken strands of an old attachment, they cannot fully replace them with new connections. By "attachment," I do not just mean the connections between people. Attachments can be formed with objects, roles, rituals, beliefs—anything that creates stability, predictability, self-worth, or a sense of belonging. Organizational change often severs these forms of attachment. The corresponding grief and loss is inevitable—all that remains is how the organization will choose to deal with it.

Rituals and Grieving. Rituals have been used to help humans through life's difficult transitions ever since primitive people first became self-aware. Rituals help people to create order and assign meaning to otherwise incomprehensible events and experiences. We still see the vestiges of ritual practice in marriages, funerals, bar mitzvahs, and baptisms. But for the most part, our society is scornful toward "ritual" and views it skeptically as superstitious folderol. This attitude would be fine if our society had developed an adequate replacement—but it hasn't. The result is that we have become a society of hurting and emotionally repressed people.

In Western culture, outward displays of grief are discouraged, and emotions are denied or repressed. This is not true of many other cultures. Malidoma Patrice Somé, Ph.D., is a past professor at the University of Michigan and a medicine man of the African Dagara culture. In his book *Rituals*, he describes the detailed grieving rituals his tribe follows. "The Dagara understand the expression of emotion as a process of self-rekindling or calming," Somé stated, "which not only helps in handling [loss] but also resets or repairs the feelings within the person." In his culture, ignoring the need to grieve is lunacy. Somé continues, "People

> Rituals help people to create order and assign meaning to otherwise incomprehensible events and experiences.

who know not the power of shedding their tears together are like a time bomb, dangerous to themselves and to the world around them."

When I first read Somé's books, I was overwhelmed with the recognition of grieving and ritual as something missing not only from my own life, but also from our entire society. This repression of grief and ritual carries a high price, including deteriorating health, anxiety and irritability, emotional instability, extreme unhappiness, and depression.

As hard as it is for Western people to grieve in private, it is infinitely more difficult to do so in a corporate setting. One of my clients, a Fortune 50 company, has gone through several years in which they have instituted repeated cycles of layoffs and restructurings. The employees there are like zombies. No one is allowed to voice pain. Anyone speaking out about the feelings that are going unexpressed, risks becoming the next ex-employee. One person told me that the only way he made it through the day was to take long walks in the surrounding woods during his lunch break. He told me, "It's the only way that I keep my sanity." It is through rituals of grieving and letting go that these emotions are discharged in a healthy way.

> The true source of suffering is not the pain—which usually passes quickly—it is the fear of, and resistance to, experiencing the pain in the first place.

Another reason for the repression and denial of "negative" feelings is that people in our society have developed an extreme aversion to pain. One of the changes that people should make is to reframe pain. It is not something that is "bad" and must be avoided, but a normal and necessary part of the healing process. The reality is that the true source of suffering is not the pain, which usually passes quickly. It is the fear of, and resistance to, experiencing the pain in the first place. How many of us have delayed facing an emotional ordeal—dreading it intensely—only to find that the reality was not very bad after all? There is an old saying that is very apt: "A coward dies a million deaths, but a brave person dies but once." Anytime we have to face our pain, we will have a

natural tendency to fear it. This is when we need to look inside for the courage to move through the experience. Believe it or not, this is a skill that gets easier with practice.

Abuse and Healing. Bureaucracies often have a long history of employee abuse and exploitation that has created a culture of "victimitis," resentment, and deep-seated emotional distress. Repeated rounds of layoffs and years of exercising unilateral, authoritarian power inevitably leaves a wide swath of emotional destruction in its wake. Before such companies will be able to make much progress on the path to becoming a Quantum Organization, they will have to confront these unreleased emotions. It is not only the victims of change who suffer emotionally; the survivors suffer too. In his book *Healing the Wounds*, David Noer describes what he calls "layoff survivor sickness" as "a set of attitudes, feelings and perceptions that occur in employees who remain in organizational systems following involuntary employee reductions." These people experience many of the same emotions as the victims, including anger, depression, fear, distrust, and guilt. In Quantum Organizations, strong and trusting relationships are vital to the success of the company. These are impossible as long as employees carry a heavy load of emotional baggage. No marriage counselor would ever expect a relationship to heal without the family talking through the accumulated feelings. The same is true of relationships anywhere—including business.

> In an organization with a history of avoidance of the soft stuff, the heart-and-soul-stuff, we've now said that not only is the heart and soul stuff important, but it is a prerequisite for taking us where we want to go.
>
> — Dean Linderman, EDS Leadership Development, commenting on the "new" EDS in *Fortune* magazine, *(October 14, 1996)*

Because relationships and feelings are "soft" issues, many people believe that they have no place in business. Somewhere along the way, business became enamored with the image of "toughness." The attitude is: "When the going gets tough, the tough get going!" One of the greatest complements a CEO can get is to be called a "hard-nosed" businessman.

Conversely, the executive who acknowledges the importance of caring and emotions is an instant pariah who earns the scorn of "serious" business people. It is sad to observe executives wriggling like a hooked fish when someone implies that they are "soft." One hears comments like "we aren't doing such-and-such because of ethical reasons; we're doing it becomes it makes *hard business sense*." Part of this is the Newtonian-Cartesian scientific heritage that devalues intangibles such as emotions and feelings. Part of it is the industrial-era management style that glorifies machismo and "chest beating". And part of it is that some executives have become so alienated from their own feelings that they can no longer relate to honest human emotion—they simply do not know how to handle it.

In the business environment, being tough has been confused with being strong. They are not the same thing at all. Mahatma Gandhi, a small, scantly clad man was strong enough to face down the mighty British empire. With his belief in love and non-violence, he could hardly be called tough, but he was strong almost beyond measure. People need to replace being tough with "holding firm convictions." Being tough is about being insensitive; being firm is about staying the course while remaining sensitive to how it affects people.

> *In the business environment, being tough has been confused with being strong. They are not the same thing at all.*

Creating Healing Rituals. In Quantum Organizations, people move through transitions quickly and easily. This is not accomplished through repression or denial. Rather, people use a combination of personal mastery and group rituals to express their feelings and discharge emotions. Common characteristics of healing rituals include:

❋ Rituals need to be a forum for the participants to express their feelings in their own way. It should not take the form of a speech or sermon from a manager. It should come from and speak to the heart, not just the head.

- Rituals should be conducted in a manner where people feel safe about verbalizing their feelings, and where everyone is treated like equals. Some companies are forming "support groups" for this purpose. These are small groups of two or more people who rely on each other as an outlet for expressing pain without any fear of judgment or oppressive caretaking. These groups may meet every couple of weeks, or as often as every day. Some of these groups use exercise, meditation, prayer, and other stress-reduction and calming techniques.
- People often feel a strong sense of shame that they have feelings of grief at all (an outgrowth of our emotionally-repressed society). Part of the healing comes from learning that many people are feeling the same emotions—that a single individual does not have to continue alone in his or her pain. Rituals should create the conditions where this is not only possible, but also encouraged.
- Participants must speak only about themselves and what they are feeling, not engage in blaming other people or outside forces.
- No one may judge whether another's feelings are right or wrong. They are neither right nor wrong; they are just feelings. A safe environment where judgement is completely suspended is essential for people to engage in the necessary self-disclosure.
- No one may try to "fix" others, either through offering advice or by trying to comfort them (unless someone specifically requests it). Our left-brained, male-dominated society has developed a "fix-it" orientation. When someone expresses pain or anxiety, it is very difficult for many people (men and women alike) to resist the temptation to offer advice. But the object of the ritual is to *feel* the pain and then work through it. By comforting someone, you deny them that opportunity. The position to take is the same as if you were visiting a relative who was in the hospital recovering from a painful illness or surgery. There is nothing you can do to change his or her situation—the greatest value you can provide is to listen with your heart and to keep your mouth shut.
- Healing in situations where there is the perception of abuse is a special case that may require the intervention of trained psychologists or counselors.

Types of Healing Rituals

There are many types of healing rituals. They can be elaborate ceremonies, or as simple as a group getting together for a meal or a social gathering. The key with any sort of healing ritual is that it must—even more than a BHAG—pass the "gut appeal" test. The ritual needs to be personal and appropriate for the participants, and it should appeal directly to the organization's collective spirit. One very effective form of ritual that is gaining in popularity in corporations is a "psychodrama." In this technique, people assume roles and act out traumatic events symbolically. The scene may be re-enacted several times with each person playing several different parts in order to experience all of the various psychological perspectives. This is a powerful cathartic technique that engages people's left- and right-brain functions. Some companies use humor to help with healing. This can take the form of skits or other extemporaneous exercises that frame the group's individual and shared pain in a humorous light. Humor is one of the most powerful techniques available for emotional healing—it opens people in a gentle way to look into the heart of their pain.

> Humor is one of the most powerful techniques available for emotional healing—it opens people in a gentle way to look into the heart of their pain.

Stored emotions are not normally accessible to an analytical mind. People cannot usually rationalize their way to emotional healing. This is why it is important to engage in activities that evoke the right-brain functioning of the human mind. Symbolic representations and physical movement are very effective for this. Some of the more innovative approaches involve deep and rapid breathing coupled with evocative music to stimulate right-brain symbolic images; drawing mandalas and interpreting their symbolic meanings; and singing and dancing. Others include dramatic reenactments of an event.

> People cannot rationalize their way to emotional healing.

When the employees of a hospital moved into a new building (a symbolic death), many people felt a sense of loss due to strong emotional ties to the old building, and all of the memories that lingered there. Kareen Strickler, Ph.D., an organizational development expert, described the unique means they had for healing their loss: "They took pictures of themselves in the old work environment, individually and with groups of their closest colleagues. When they moved to the new building, they pinned the photos on the walls of their new offices, and created a bulletin board honoring the old and celebrating the new. In this way, they were able to bridge the gap between the old and the new, and make a clean break with the past."

When Hewlett-Packard's Printed Circuit Board Division closed its doors (another symbolic death), the company took a novel approach to the event. Geoff Ainscow, an organizational specialist who masterminded the process, wanted to create an event that celebrated the transition. "The idea is that all possibilities come from endings," Ainscow said. "One career is ending and another is beginning." He staged a full-blown New Orleans-style jazz band funeral:

> Ainscow organized pallbearers dressed in black robes and caps, a bishop, and musicians playing somber jazz. A procession of 50 marchers began in the plant's cafeteria and wove through the factory, handing out black robes to all who chose to join them and inviting employees to put items that symbolized their time with the division into an open coffin. The procession ended outside at the burial site, where mourners listened to a 30-minute eulogy recounting the division's history and its contributions to the company. Once the coffin was buried, the funeral became a celebration [thus connecting the ending with the new beginning]. Everyone took off their black robes to reveal white T-shirts with vivid images of the phoenix, the mythological bird that rises from its own ashes, and the jazz band launched into Mardi Gras party music.

One of the interesting aspects of both of these examples is the energy that was put into *honoring the past*. There are several advantages to this. Many people feel that a change has become necessary because they somehow failed when they created the old ways of working. When a company honors its past, it is acknowledging the service that past ideas, approaches, people, and places provided the firm. People are helped to understand that the change is not about "failure," it is about letting go of obsolete practices and embracing new ones that are better suited to the current challenges. Another advantage is that it enriches the organization's culture. Every person and organization is the sum total of all that has gone before. It is vital that people understand their past so they can better understand themselves. In traditional cultures, this past-telling role falls to the elders. In modern society, elders—along with any respect for the lessons of the past—are largely disregarded.

> When a company honors its past, it is acknowledging the service that past ideas, approaches, people, and places provided the firm.

One of the tasks in the Ray & Berndtson change effort involved documenting the firm's history in conjunction with a timeline of the whole industry. From this, employees were able to see how the strategies that had made them successful in the past were related to the competitive conditions of the time. They were able to put their old cultural values and practice into context—to see how yesterday's solutions were no longer adequate for current challenges. Also, they saw that the current changes were just another stage in a long history of innovative and daring changes that the firm has undertaken.

In the Valley of Despair

The most critical juncture in any change effort occurs in "the valley of despair"— when the organization has left the "old ways" behind, but has not fully mastered the "new ways." This is when the organization is most likely to lose focus or conviction, and revert to the old ways of doing things. Many factors may come together at once that make this portion of the journey exceedingly difficult. Casualties mount as people leave the company (voluntarily or involuntarily); there are no familiar landmarks for people to judge whether they are moving in the right direction—or moving at all; people are uncomfortable, irritable, and generally miserable; and the trip seems to be stretching out forever. This is the time when Followers are most susceptible to the persuasive arguments of Opponents who talk about how great the "good old days were." Opponents claim that everyone would be much better off if they would just go back to the old ways and try them again, only *harder* this time.

The Opponents are often successful—many change efforts become derailed and abandoned at this point. You can see this happening in today's society, as the old traditions and institutions break down in preparation for the transformation to a higher way of organizing and relating. In America, certain people are calling for a return to fundamentalist religion as a solution for the many problems facing the country. In Russia, the hard-liners argue for a return to the good old days when communism worked so well. "When exactly was that?" most rational people would ask. But the "valley of despair" is not a time when many people are thinking rationally (particularly those who have not learned personal mastery).

> *He who has a* why *to live can bear with almost any* how.
>
> — Nietzche

Leaders have to be very active during the transitional period. This is where they contribute some of their greatest value. Leaders also need to continually seek to reconnect people to the "big picture" (the shared vision), to each other, and to the new environment. Their specific responsibilities include:

✶ *Clarifying and reinforcing the shared vision.* The wagon train leaders of old kept pointing the way forward, reminding people of the great things that awaited them, helping stragglers to catch up, showing wagons that had lost their way how to come back onto the correct path. These are the same actions that modern leaders need to take in stewarding an organization through the "valley of despair." So long as people remain identified with local concerns, they will find countless obstacles and hardships. When people put their attention on the big picture, however, they can transcend personal desires and petty issues, and continue to make progress toward their goal.

✳ *Creating meaning.* In this point in the transition process, people are being assailed by an enormous amount of information. They look to their leaders to help them establish the meaning and relevance of this information. If someone is fired, what does that mean? How should employees understand negative articles in the newspaper or vicious rumors about an impending corporate take-over? What is the meaning of their pain and sacrifice? This is not an exercise in "spin-control" in the manner of issuing a news release with the company's official position. It is an interactive dialogue that helps people to create their own understanding with the input of a leader's broader perspective. Needless to say, the leader should be completely honest, candid, and speak to and from the heart.

✳ *Nurturing relationships.* Long-standing relationships are one of the first casualties of organizational change. Leaders play an important role in helping people to connect with other people, ideas, and methods. Leaders are in a unique position to assist people in weaving the connections that will form the fabric of new relationships.

✳ *Ensuring the rich flow of information.* During times of rapid change, people crave information. More than almost anything else, people want to know two things: (1) what to expect, and (2) whether what they are experiencing is normal. These are two themes that should be addressed continually. Because people are overloaded with activities, the information needs to be shared in easily retrievable and understandable

> *People abhor information vacuums; when there is no on-going conversation as part of the change process, gossip fills the vacuum. Usually the rumors are much worse and more negative than anything that is actually going on.*
>
> — Jeanie Daniel Duck, Vice President, Boston Consulting Group

"packets." However, it is essential that the information not be summarized to the point that it becomes eviscerated of all value—the details should always be made available somewhere.

- *Promoting learning.* As the organization struggles to create the new environment, there will be innumerable experiments in how to make the changes work. It is important for leaders to ferret out the successes and share them with the people who would benefit from this learning.
- *Promoting ownership and self-reliance.* The only way the change effort will succeed is if the employees accept responsibility for the success. A critical mass of people need to become Enthusiasts who will do whatever it takes to succeed. Leaders can promote these behaviors by pointing out examples, celebrating positive results, and constantly communicating with people about what ownership and self-reliance look like in practice.
- *Holding anxiety.* The "valley of despair" is a time of great anxiety. People who have developed personal mastery are more adept at holding their anxiety without negative consequences. However, the people in bureaucracies have normally been socialized into a dependent and reactive mind-set. Leaders have the challenge of helping people experience this anxiety without acting on it destructively (such as reverting to the old ways, becoming hostile, or leaving the company). The techniques described earlier for dealing with feelings of loss are very useful. It is also important for leaders to emphasize that no matter how daunting the challenge may seem, it can be achieved one small step at a time.

New Beginnings

In the wagon train example, we saw that people began to gain energy and motivation as their destination drew nearer and they could see it for themselves. Also, there was an emotional letdown when the reality of the new environment did not live up to people's expectations. These are both common experiences in the "new beginnings" stage of transition. All new things bring with them a certain amount of discomfort. Think back to when you were first married, your first baby arrived, you moved into a new house or apartment—in each case, a period of time had to pass before you became comfortable with the changed environment. All new things require some time for the newness to wear off to become comfortable with the change.

Conducting the Culture Change Project

A classical organization may initially have to use certain command-and-control behaviors to *eliminate* command-and-control behaviors. Soon thereafter, it can start using the quantum principles in the execution of the change effort.

A cultural shift of any kind takes a long time. Some tangible changes will occur fairly quickly, but the transformation of core beliefs will take much longer (companies that have already developed a quantum culture do not share this problem). Small companies (of a few hundred employees) can require at least two to three years to make the

> *Nothing great is created suddenly, any more than a bunch of grapes or a fig. If you tell me that you desire a fig, I answer you that there must be time. Let it first blossom, then bear fruit, then ripen.*
>
> — Epictetus, *Discourses*

change. Mid-sized companies (of a few thousand employees) can expect a five- to seven-year timeline. Gigantic companies (of tens of thousands of employees) may require a decade or more. Because of their size, these very large companies will experience extreme difficulty in achieving the changes. For instance, over a decade after GE launched its intensive cultural change effort, CEO Welch still encounters middle-managers who do not yet "get it." For very large companies, a practical approach is to make the cultural shift at the level of smaller subsidiaries or autonomous divisions.

Initiate: Launching the Project

The shift to a quantum culture is a transformational change project that forms an umbrella under which many fundamental and operational change projects will be conducted. These smaller projects will address changes to processes, technology, and structure. Culture, as you may recall, is the collective beliefs and mind-set of the people in the company. Culture is created through the interaction of inner and outer changes. The inner changes are the intentions that people have to change a belief and learn new behaviors. The outer changes are to the tangible structures through which the beliefs manifest—the "body" portion of the ecosystem. As people begin to see evidence that the new beliefs "succeed," they will gradually adopt them in place of the old beliefs. This is a gradual process that requires constant and consistent reinforcement.

Roles and Governance. All of the organization's change projects need to be coordinated if the company is to prevent total anarchy. There are several different roles that are essential to this process. Each role is briefly discussed below.

- *Sponsor.* In command-and-control organizations, an executive sponsor is key to the change project. The executive should be one hierarchical level above the groups being changed. In the case of cultural change, it needs to be the CEO. The sponsor provides the mandate and inspiration for the change.

  At first, the CEO may be required to use heavy-handed classical management techniques, which may include firing vocal opponents (a symbolic shockwave). However, the CEO (along with everyone else with organizational power or influence) needs to very quickly thereafter begin to operate using the methods of a quantum leader.

- *Steering committee.* A steering committee (or a group of interlocking committees), supports, and coordinates the various change projects. The members of the steering committee should be representatives of the various constituent groups (divisions, departments, processes, teams) who are affected by the change. In bureaucracies, these are usually the top managers in the affected groups. In Quantum Organizations, they will be whoever is most qualified. Traditional steering committees see their role as the "bosses" of the projects; there to pass judgment and hand out orders to the project team. The CEO cannot allow this in creating the Quantum Organization. The steering committee needs to begin to operate immediately using the principles of quantum management. The steering committee members should become an integral part of the projects, with tasks and accountabilities like any other team members. They do not "sit above" the project teams, but are an extension of them. Responsibilities include coordinating and aligning the various projects, providing resources, removing obstacles, monitoring progress, communicating with the organization, and providing feedback and support to the team.

✠ *Champion.* This is an unofficial role that may be played by one or more people. Champions are influential executives who are active and vocal Enthusiasts. They are important as advisors to the project teams, relationship builders, and advocates to the organization wanting change.

✠ *Project leader.* In traditional cultures, project leaders are just like any other command-and-control leaders. However, in a quantum culture, the project team needs to be a living example of the new culture in *every way*. For this reason, the leader should be selected by the project team members. A leader will not be a "boss" to the team, but an equal who the team has given the responsibility to coordinate certain team activities. Every team member serves as leader at different points in the project based on need and relative expertise. Responsibilities of the project leader include: maintaining a global view of the overall project; helping to coordinate task assignments and balance workloads; monitoring progress; supporting team members; and coordinating with the steering committee and sponsor.

> *If you have built castles in the air, your work need not be lost; that is where they should be. Now put the foundations under them.*
>
> — Henry David Thoreau

✠ *Team members.* Each project will be conducted by a team of "core" and "virtual" members. The core members are those who are dedicated to the project over its full life. The virtual members are those who are assigned to the project to provide certain expertise or staff support at various points, but who are only involved periodically. The team members should be Enthusiasts; high performers, risk takers, and big-picture thinkers; they should be trusted and respected by the organization. The team members should be predisposed toward the core competencies of the Quantum Organization—personal leadership, personal mastery, relationship, and dialogue. If possible,

representatives from across the organization (and at all levels) should be selected. At least one should be a senior executive.

Forming the Core Team. Every organization, including a team, is an ecosystem that must have all of the various elements aligned and in place. The core team needs to develop a shared vision that is in harmony with the larger organization. Because this is a project to change the culture, the team should adopt the new cultural beliefs for themselves at the outset. All of the structural components— governance, people, and physical layouts—need to be selected and put into place. Supporting technologies should be acquired. Any processes required for the ecosystem's functioning have to be established. In particular, the organizational change process (Integrated Change, in this example) must be configured in regard to the scope and context of the particular project.

The core team members will provide subject matter expertise and have specific roles in the change process. They will flow between these roles—depending on the circumstances. One of the first responsibilities that the team must tackle is the development of a detailed plan for the change project. The core team members will develop very few of the project work products. Rather, they will engage members of the organization in doing so. This is one of the ways in which participation and ownership is achieved.

Launching the Project. Most employees of bureaucratic organizations are cynical and wary regarding new management initiatives. This project will not be an exception. I advocate a low-key approach to the launch of projects. Big kick- off ceremonies create unrealistic expectations and provoke unneeded skepticism. Likewise, I do not recommend posters, slogans, coffee mugs, T-shirts and the sort—these trinkets are often seen as jokes. The only useful posters are those that have real content, like phone numbers to call if people have questions. The best cure in cynical organizations is for everyone to laugh together, and management will need to laugh the loudest. For instance, a client of mine has employees who issue an "underground" newsletter that parodies everything going on. So far, it has done more to advance the cause and diffuse tensions than any other mechanism.

The project should start slowly, through activities that build creative tension and gradually increase participation and ownership. This will be easy if the first efforts are intended to create the elements of the shared vision. By the time the organization has developed a BHAG, the project will be well on its way, and it can then use the BHAG as its catalyst.

Communication Planning. Most project teams send a few memos and then put a checkmark by the "communicate" task on the project plan. This is one reason that so many of them fail. Communication is critical and should be treated with the same seriousness as the project plan. In fact, it should itself be a detailed plan and define:

1. Key points of the message to be sent

2. The sender of the message

3. The intended audience

4. The communication media to use

5. When and where to communicate the messge

6. Feedback mechanisms that will ensure the message was received

Getting a common message across to many different people is a very difficult task. People interpret information based on their frames of reference, which may be different for each person. This creates a barrier to communication even when people want to hear the message. When they don't want to hear the message—as with transformational change—it is even more difficult. This is the main reason that communications need to be repeated frequently and in many different formats and forums. The rule of thumb that I follow is to communicate the message "seven times and in seven ways." The following passage from a *Harvard Business Review*

> Messages should be communicated "seven times and in seven ways."

article is one of the best that I have found for capturing the essence of communication in the context of organizational change:

> If there is a single rule of communication for leaders, it is this: when you are so sick of talking about something that you can hardly stand it, your message is just starting to get through. . . . From the point of view of leaders, who have been working on the change program for months, the message is already stale. But what counts is the point of view of the organization. Have they heard the message? Do they believe it? Do they know what it means? Have they interpreted it for themselves, and have they internalized it? Until managers have listened, watched, and talked enough to know that the answers to all of these questions is yes, they haven't communicated at all.

Investigate: Know Thy Self

Effective change relies on knowing a great deal about the current configuration, alignment, and performance of the organization's ecosystem elements. The culture change project is challenged with surfacing the company's beliefs and principles-in-action, as well as with profiling the key aspects of structure, processes, and technology. There are several methods for gathering the requisite information, all of which should be used, as appropriate, for painting the most accurate picture possible of the current environment. These methods include:

1. *Interviews.* Interviews are effective for obtaining candid feedback and detailed information. But keep in mind that they are time-consuming and subject to the bias of the interviewer. They can, however, be one of the most useful techniques for documenting the organization's culture.

2. *Assessments and surveys.* These instruments can reach a lot of people quickly to gain statistically accurate data. However, surveys are subject to the bias of the people taking them, and they do not provide a forum for delving into why people answered as they did. Also, summary ratings can be misleading without other corroborating evidence.

3. *Direct and indirect observation*. Observation is an excellent way to gather unadulterated information about the organization. It involves informally observing behavior in meetings and in common areas such as coffee bars. It also includes analyzing the content of memos, policies, marketing brochures and other printed material.

4. *Team mapping and process tracking*. These are two methods for developing detailed process maps. Team mapping involves getting representatives from across the process together to develop a map of the process. This also promotes cross-functional learning. Transaction tracking is about following a transaction step-by-step through the entire process. It is the only sure way to get accurate information about a process, but it is very time consuming and may not be possible for processes that take a very long time.

Intangibles such as *beliefs* and *principles-in-action* cannot be observed directly. However, they are reflected in cultural artifacts that can be observed and used to identify the underlying beliefs. Artifacts include stories and myths, heroes, sayings and mottoes, castes and tribes, symbols, and awards and recognition. They also include the daily rituals of interaction—how people greet each other, interact in various contexts, use unique language, or use body language and gestures. These rituals can be identified through the interview and observation techniques described earlier in this chapter.

One of the strongest ways to integrate new members into the corporate culture is to tell them stories that indirectly teach the cultural norms. If interviewers listen closely, they will catch sayings that are repeated by different people throughout the company. Words are powerful symbols, and sayings and mottoes can reveal a lot about the culture. One of Ray & Berndtson's sayings was "you eat what you kill"—a strong statement about employees' belief in individualism. In bureaucracies, one often hears sayings such as, "It's easier to ask forgiveness than it is to ask for permission." Castes are suborganizations that connote prestige. Examples include the executive, staff, and engineering castes.

Tribes are groups who identify themselves separately from all others and look out for their interests over that of other groups. Tribes can include divisions, departments, or subgroups who share common interests such as political associations or technical backgrounds. Technical professionals tend to associate more strongly with people in their technical tribe (such as other software engineers or accountants) than they do other individuals in their company. Symbols can include anything from corporate logos, to lapel pins, to the size of a person's office. At one firm, the type of dress shirt people wear is symbolic of their station in the company. Finally, the behaviors that companies reward and recognize are clear indicators of what they really value. It is also important to note who rewards whom, and in what venue.

> One of the strongest ways to integrate new members into the corporate culture is to tell them stories that indirectly teach the cultural norms.

Benchmarking and Best Practices. These are two common techniques used for gathering information from the external ecosystem. *Benchmarking* is collecting numerical performance information—usually in regard to Substitutors in the same industry. Examples are invoices processed per accounts payable employee, and the ratio of information technology costs to total revenue. *Best practices* are not numbers, but descriptions of how companies do certain things. Although I am no fan of benchmarking, best practices can be very useful to the change effort.

Benchmarking is time consuming, expensive, and questionable as a source of legitimate and useful information. There is an old saying that there are three kinds of lies: "lies, damn lies, and statistics." The wise person is skeptical of summarized numbers and statistics. From personal experience, I can tell you that there are a thousand ways to make numbers add up to support a particular intention. When comparing the summarized performance numbers of one company against the next, there is no practical way to know how the numbers were derived. They are almost guaranteed to be the equivalent of "apples and oranges." The time and effort put into benchmarking should be redirected to the research of best practices.

The study of best practices both within and outside a company can surface ideas that can be leveraged to create powerful performance improvements. In some cases, the practices can be copied outright, but rarely. The most useful practices are those that provide novel design principles that can be applied in your organization to achieve breakthrough innovations.

My favorite best practices example is the story about how Southwest Airlines developed its unique airplane servicing processes. Southwest Airlines' business strategy requires servicing planes as soon as they arrive at the terminal and then getting them back in the air as quickly as possible. The company could not look to other airlines as examples because none of them did this very well. Instead, it looked outside the industry to a place known for their lightning-fast servicing of vehicles—Indianapolis 500 racing pit crews. Obviously an airline can't service a jet airplane the way a pit crew does a race car, but the underlying principles can be applied. One of these principles was the use of teams of multi-skilled people who did whatever was required to get the car out of the pit. Southwest Airlines has applied this concept, along with others, to become the most consistently profitable airline in history.

Innovate & Implement: From Design to Action

All of the work to this point has been in preparation for the development of a new ecosystem design to meet the organization's goal—which, in this case, is to transform the culture.

Visioning. Although the shared vision will have been developed as described in chapter 4, the high-level design of the remaining elements in the ecosystem should be created in separate "visioning" sessions. These meetings bring together a virtual team of some of the organization's most creative and far-sighted individuals. The success of the session is contingent on bringing in the appropriate people.

> A mistake that many companies make in visioning sessions is to include logical, "down-to-earth" people to reign in the creative types.

Those included should be creative and open-minded, generally respected and trusted by the organization, representatives of a diagonal cross-section of the organization, and a combination of both new and long-time employees. The key

characteristic here is "creative and open-minded." A mistake that many companies make is to include logical, "down to earth" people to reign in the creative types. This causes a breakdown in the process and a deterioration of the creativity of the final product. It is better to have only true "creatives" on the visioning team, and then hand the new design to more practical and detail-oriented people for design validation and implementation planning.

Often, creating such a team means including fifteen to twenty people—far too many for effective brainstorming. The way that I get around this is to divide members into two groups, each of which will develop a prototype design. Then, both groups combine the best of the two designs to create a third alternative that is better than either of the original two. The new design should be a high-level description of the new configuration of each of the elements in the Organizational EcoSystem Model. By "high-level," I mean clearly stated recommendations that are not yet implementable. For example, the group may recommend 360-degree performance reviews, but will not detail what the review looks like or how the conversion to the new method will be accomplished. In the case of "culture," the group will describe the new beliefs that the organization should adopt, along with a description of the artifacts that would support these new beliefs. Structure is one of the most important elements in regard to culture, so the team needs to provide new configurations for each of the three components of structure: governance, people, and physical layouts. The team will also recommend new technologies or changes to existing technologies that are required to achieve the new culture.

Finally, the organization's core processes need to be redesigned. At this level, the visioning team will recommend macro changes such as "align teams around the work to be done instead of by functional expertise." In reality, each of the major processes will require a separate fundamental- or operational-type change project to fully assess and implement the required changes.

Design Action Teams. The visioning session will deliver a "picture" of the new environment as well as a description of each of the major changes required to achieve the new vision. These are called "change actions" and include not only descriptions of the change, but also the expected benefits and a general estimate of the resources required. These change actions are then handed off to "Design Action Teams" (DATs). The DATs are virtual teams that include at least one person from the original visioning session (to provide continuity) and several subject-matter experts. The role of the DAT is to verify the validity of the high-level design, develop a cost-benefit estimate and a risk assessment, and create detailed and implementable design specifications. This is a critical juncture in the project; momentum can seep away until the project stalls and ultimately fails. For this reason, very stringent and aggressive due dates should be established for the DATs to complete their work. I recommend no more than six to eight weeks for this portion of the project.

Implementation. Implementation is a challenge. It is a time when employees are busy running the organization in the old way while simultaneously trying to convert to the new way. Some people describe this as rebuilding a jet while it is flying at 30,000 feet. This is the "valley of despair," and it requires many of the activities described earlier in the section on inspiration. For many people, this will be the first time that the change project has become real to them, so anxiety can be expected to increase. The heavier workload will take a toll on employees' energy and civility. Some companies mistake employees' reactions for low morale during this period. This may not be accurate. People may be experiencing the natural anxiety and grief that comes with endings and new beginnings. This is a time when the skills of personal leadership and personal mastery help tremendously in reducing conflict and increasing cooperation.

After the detailed designs have been completed, the core team needs to establish an implementation plan, grouping the change actions into segments. They can be grouped by scope of effort required, time frame required, the groups impacted, or the ecosystem element. The implementation project will ultimately include several phases. The duration of any one phase should not exceed a year. This "one-year" rule is necessary to prevent the organization from burning out while trying to implement changes. Experience has shown that longer projects have a much higher failure rate than shorter ones, so the overall implementation effort should be broken into short, manageable phases.

The implementation of the new design will be led by a team or teams, but it will involve the effort of all employees affected. The detailed design developed by the DATs must leave ample room for experimentation and refinement by the front-line employees. In the process of making the design work in practice, the employees will need to make many small refinements. The role of the implementation team will be to provide guidance regarding the underlying design principles, and the final vision so that individuals can make effective decisions while customizing the design.

Celebration. Humans have celebrated their accomplishments since they first stood on two legs. However, modern celebrations have lost most of their vitality. They have become logical acknowledgments of a particular achievement. In traditional cultures, the celebrations are emotional and vivid. We would benefit from recapturing some of the drama that accompanies our victories. People love stories, and they are actually one of the most powerful mechanisms for communicating and learning. Teams should begin to celebrate people's victories by having them tell their stories—the more dramatic the better. Soon, people will look forward to these victory celebrations with delight rather than weary resignation.

Modern business people have lost the ability to celebrate. This is one of the factors that has contributed to dehumanizing the work environment. It is vital to celebrate both small and large accomplishments over the course of a change effort. Not only do they break the tedium of the work schedule and help to inspire people, but they also help to establish psychological markers that the organization is making progress through the "valley of despair."

> The loss of our ability to celebrate has contributed to dehumanizing the work environment.

We have also lost the ability to appreciate small victories. We have come to view only those achievements, in excess of aggressive goals, as worthy of celebration. This demotes any lessor accomplishment to a "ho-hum" sort of non-event. Employees may achieve their personal best, but if it is less than someone else's, they are told to try harder. Most of our lives are lived out in the halls of business. If we want to enrich our life experience, we must make changes to the corporate landscape. One of those changes should be to recapture the thrill of accomplishing the small victories—in change efforts and in everyday activities.

PART THREE

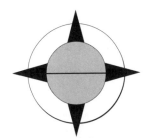

POWERFUL NEW WAYS OF BEING

Come to the edge, he said.
They said: We are afraid.
Come to the edge, he said.
They came.
He pushed them...and they flew.
— Guillaume Apollinaire

Chapter Six
Personal Leadership

This is the true joy in life: Being used for a
purpose recognized by yourself as a mighty
one, being a force of nature instead of a
feverish, selfish little clod of ailments and
grievances, complaining that the world will
not devote itself to making you happy.

— George Bernard Shaw

Part three describes the four meta-skills required in a Quantum Organization:
personal leadership, personal mastery, relationship, and dialogue (see
Fig. 6.1). They are called meta-skills because they are essential for the
effective functioning of the Quantum design concept. Although the skills can
be developed independently, the sequence in which I present them makes a
real difference in the level of mastery that you can achieve. Through *personal
leadership*, people accept full responsibility for their lives; they establish a
sense of who they are, what they want to achieve, and how they will live
their lives. Once they have established ownership of their thoughts and
emotions, they can learn to manage them through the skill of *personal mastery*.
When people have adequately established a relationship with themselves,
then—and only then—can they enter fully into *relationship* with another
person. And finally, once people have mastered the skill of relationship,
they can then achieve the self-disclosure required for creating shared
meaning through *dialogue*.

This chapter addresses the first of the core skills: personal leadership. Our traditional notion of leadership is that it is something that only a few people can do, and these few are uniquely born to it. Leadership, as it has been defined throughout this book, is a *process* in which every person engages. Personal leadership is about people taking responsibility for leading their own lives, for establishing their own authentic identities. It obligates people to be completely responsible for themselves and accountable for the consequences of all their actions. Each of these topics—responsibility, identity, and authenticity—will be discussed in detail over the course of this chapter.

The Four Meta-Skills of the Quantum Organization

Figure 6.1

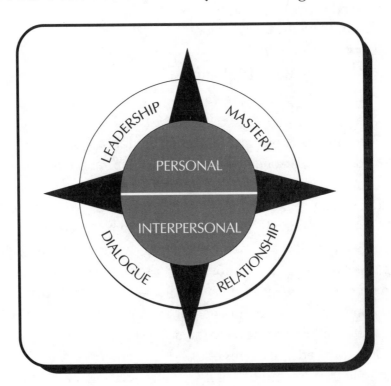

Responsibility: The End of "Victimitis"

Viktor Frankl, a death camp survivor of the Nazi holocaust during World War II, went on to become a prominent psychiatrist. His book, *Man's Search for Meaning*, is a poignant tribute to the triumph of the human spirit over even the worst of circumstances. Frankl observed that the majority of the prisoners believed that they were victims of fate with no power over their lives—

> *Responsibility is not only the ability to respond to what comes toward us, it is also the capacity to stand behind our actions and to be responsible for all that we do or don't do. This means that we do not allow ourselves to be in denial about ourselves, or to be self-indulgent.*
>
> — Angeles Arrian, Ph.D., author of *The Four-Fold Way*

no choice over their actions. As a result, many acted like animals in the single-minded interest of their own preservation. But a rare few did not. These people rose above their circumstances—choosing a different course of action, one of love and service. Frankl wrote of these people:

> We who lived in concentration camps can remember the men who walked through the huts comforting others, giving away their last piece of bread. They may have been few in number, but they offer sufficient proof that everything can be taken from a man but one thing: the last of the human freedoms—to choose one's attitude in any given set of circumstances, to choose one's own way.

People can be victims of circumstances, as Frankl was, but they can never be victims in light of their thoughts and choice of behaviors. A Quantum Organization requires the independent action of every person in accord with the interests of the whole. This can never happen as long as people do not accept responsibility for their lives and for their actions. For this reason, personal leadership requires that all people take complete responsibility for the circumstances of their lives. They need to accept that nobody can make them think, feel, or be anything. Every thought and every action springs from an internal decision chosen by the individual, either consciously or unconsciously.

This is a difficult concept for many people. Western society has a long history of dominance and dependency and has gone to great lengths to convince people that they are not responsible for their actions. Instead, external agents—a

> *To have integrity, we must recognize that our choices bring consequences, and that we cannot escape responsibility for the consequences, not because they are imposed by some external authority, but because they are inherent in the choices themselves.*
>
> — Starhawk, author of *Dreaming the Dark*

capricious god, the "devil," other people, "dumb luck," fate, the competition— are responsible. Irresponsibility is a form of the "shifting the burden" system archetype. This lack of responsibility has become epidemic in the larger society:

- ✠ When a government creates indirect revenue sources (such as excessive borrowing) in lieu of direct taxes, it has acted irresponsibly to shift the burden from the true need—reducing government spending or raising direct taxes. If citizens do not get the direct feedback that government is costing a lot of money, the government will continue to grow and the citizens will still ultimately have to pay—but the bill will be much higher.

- ✠ When employees expect their companies to provide a rich suite of benefits, they have shifted the burden of their own caretaking to the company. The employees do not directly experience the pain of increases in the costs of health insurance and other benefits, and so are not inclined to do anything about them.

- ✠ When companies pollute, they act irresponsibly in shifting the burden of pollution to the public sector. If these companies do not have to pay the full cost of their pollution, they will not be motivated to change anything.

- ✠ CEOs forsake their responsibility when they authorize layoffs and then require *other* people to personally notify employees that they have been fired. This insulates the CEO from witnessing firsthand the human suffering that results from a layoff, and thus prevents them from learning a valuable lesson.

Our language reflects this widespread "victim" mind-set with expressions such as "she made me angry," or "I'm having an anxiety attack," or "with my bad luck I'm sure that I won't get the raise." In each of these examples, the controlling factors of people's lives are attributed to some external entity having power over, and "doing it" to, them. For instance, to say "she made me angry," means that someone else can choose our emotional responses, which is an impossibility. The other person may very well have said or done something offensive, but it is up to each individual to choose a response. One person might get mad, another may ignore the event, a third may laugh at it, and a fourth may feel compassion.

A more accurate statement would be "I allowed myself to get angry because of my interpretation of what she did." Dr. Wayne Dyer, author of several best-selling self-help books, explains this concept using the metaphor of an orange. When you squeeze an orange, juice comes out. It does not matter what kind of orange or how you squeeze it—when you put pressure on the outside of an orange, juice comes out. In the same way, when you "squeeze" a person, the emotional response originates from *within* the person—not from any external source. Personal leadership involves accepting responsibility for deciding what is going to come out when you are squeezed.

Consider the following example. Imagine that you are standing in a hallway at work and someone bumps into you and pushes you aside. When you look around, you see a close friend wearing an amused "Gotcha!" expression. What would you feel and how would you react? With good-natured humor? Now, in the same situation, a total stranger pushes you aside and hurries along without looking back or expressing any sort of apology. What would you feel, and how would you react this time? With anger, resentment, or self-pity? Assume that you did choose to become angry; what if you then discovered that the stranger's wife had been in a car wreck and was in critical condition at the hospital, and he was hurrying to be at her side. What would you feel then? Compassion? A little embarrassment and remorse? In all three cases, the only difference lay in the meaning that *we* ascribed to the event, and the action that *we* chose to take in response. No one made us choose a particular meaning or reaction; we did so wholly on our own out of our beliefs and mind-set. Our reactions are choices. In accepting our responsibility for these choices, we establish power over our lives. The idea that we are, or are not, responsible for our lives is a *belief*. Like any other belief, it can be changed through the techniques of personal mastery, which are described in the next chapter.

Identity: Self-Reference vs. Object-Reference

On a recent vacation to Sedona Arizona (USA), my wife, Connie, and I took an Earth Tour Jeep ride into the surrounding mountains. As soon as we set out, the tour guide turned to us and asked: "Who are you and why are you here?" Most people responded with their job titles and "vacation," or "business." But the driver persisted, saying, "Those are just superficial characteristics. Who are you when you are not any of your roles, and what is your unique reason for being on Earth?" For the cynical, scientific-minded individual, these questions may seem like nothing more than New Age drivel. However, these two questions—perhaps the most fundamental of existential questions—drive to the heart of personal leadership: If you do not know who you are and what you want out of life, how can you take responsibility for achieving it?

> *The most strongly enforced of all known taboos is the taboo against knowing who or what you really are behind the mask of your apparently separate, independent, and isolated ego.*
>
> — Alan Watts, philosopher, author of *The Way of Zen*

Who Are You?

This can be a very vexing question that has profound implications for our sense of personal security and, subsequently, our ability to operate effectively in times of rapid change. If we identify with our outer circumstances, we will constantly be assailed by threats to our existence. Each time something external that we identify with changes, we will experience a kind of symbolic death. For example, if we think we are our job, and then we get laid-off or retire, we will experience a tremendous personal trauma. The same is true if we identify ourselves through any external medium: our income, our relationships, our place in society, or even our beliefs. All of these can and will change, sometimes precipitously. Much of our misery has to do with losing and rebuilding this external sense of identity.

People often have a strong ego, what I call the "small self." Ego-attachment is the most powerful form of object-reference. Ego-attachment makes people both rigid and fragile. Ironically, the people in organizations with the most external power are often the ones most strongly identified with their ego. Ego-identified people view any challenge to their ego as a threat to their very survival—which explains the strong emotional response such threats evoke. This makes for a miserable and paranoiac experience, wherein everyone is seen as a potential threat to the ego's well-being. Ego-identification inevitably leads to people investing a huge amount of their time and energy in boosting and defending their egos—their fragile hold on their identities.

I came face-to-face with my own issues regarding object-orientation in the mid-1980's, and it changed my life. I had started my first business with much hope and fanfare—an on-line mortgage network that would connect real-estate agents with mortgage brokers—only to see it fail a year later. I wrote about this experience in the anthology, *Rediscovering the Soul of Business*:

> On the morning of June 6, 1985, I died. Not a physical death, but a psychological death, what Dr. Stan Grof calls an "ego-death." I had just spent the past year trying to start my own company, spending my life's savings, going deep into debt, and exhausting myself in the process. On that morning, I finally admitted what had been obvious for a while—my company was going to fail. With it went everything that defined who I was to the world. I could no longer say that I "was" my job, because I had none. I couldn't rely on my wealth to create a sense of worth and identity, for I had no money and loads of debt. I could not look to social standing, for a failed entrepreneur has no

social standing. And the failure of my love relationship, a month earlier, ensured that I could not find myself through the love of another. I had nothing, therefore I was nothing. And I died.

Until that point, I had lived my life through the eyes of other people. I had defined myself through object-reference—my sense of identity and my feelings of self-worth were tied directly to the outer circumstances of my life. When my company failed, I faced the most traumatic time of my life—all of these external references were stripped away. When I looked in the mirror, I did not know who I was. For me, the ego-death and subsequent "rebirth" was a wonderfully and powerfully transformative event. I experienced a sort of "awakening" in which I realized in a flash of insight

> *Here lies the cure to racism, greed, violence, and other social ills; people with high self-esteem contribute selflessly to the well-being of others. They are committed to action to a higher good for all.*
>
> — Jack Canfield, co-author of *Chicken Soup for the Soul*

that "I" was not my ego or the external trappings of my life. "I" was still all that had ever been, my true self. Nothing that was real and certain had changed, just superficial aspects of my environment.

Self-Reference Equals Self-Power

Rapid and dramatic changes can upset our lives tremendously. To function effectively, we must base our sense of identity on an internal reference point. Jobs, income, external power, and relationships will come and go, but our *true self* will remain constant through it all.

Not everyone has to "find themselves" the hard way as I did. This awareness can be deliberately nurtured in a gentle process of self-discovery. There are many disciplines available to help with this. One of the most common is meditation— the practice of mental stillness. For many people, meditation conjures negative images of long-haired, wild-looking gurus who force their followers to give up all their earthly belongings. This is an amusing image, but it is a myth. Meditation is a simple practice that involves concentrating intently on a single thought in order to quiet the incessant ramblings of the mind. In this silence, your true self can be experienced directly through intuitive insights and inspirations.

Meditation is best if practiced for at least ten minutes at the beginning and ending of each day. However, in my experience, even a minute or two of mental stillness has enormous restorative and calming power. I have tried many methods, and the one I prefer involves focusing on what the Chinese call the "tantien" (pronounced don-tin). This is the spot (two inches below your navel) where each person's source of power is thought to reside. This form of meditation is called "centering" because it involves finding and holding your "center." The steps are as follows:

1. *Assume a comfortable posture.* I cannot sit in the cross-legged fashion favored by most meditation techniques. Instead, I sit in a firm chair, which works very well for me. Sit erect with your feet flat on the floor, with your hands open and palms facing up on your lap or on your legs. Your back should be straight and not touching the back of the chair. If this posture is hard for you, you may need to lean back or lie on the floor. Holding your back straight will get easier with practice.

2. *Breathe deeply and slowly.* Few people know how to breathe correctly. Most people breathe shallowly from the top of their lungs. This leads to oxygen deprivation and tension throughout the body. (The next time you find yourself tense and stressed, observe your breathing—it will always be fast and shallow.) To learn how to breathe correctly, watch an infant. Observe how the child breathes from the abdomen. To practice doing this, place your hands on your tantien, two inches below your navel. When you breathe in, try to make your hands rise. When the muscles in the abdomen expand, they automatically draw air all the way into the bottom of your lungs. Now breathe out by simply releasing your abdomen and giving a gentle push. The air will be expelled naturally. This natural form of breathing is energizing and relaxing to all parts of your body.

3. *Focus your attention.* Imagine your tantien as a bright light or fire that is radiating warmth. (Some people prefer to imagine this light in their mind or in the area of their heart.) Let your focus slowly drift down from your head through your chest and to your abdomen. See yourself entering the tantien and being surrounded by warm, peaceful, and loving light and energy. Hold your attention there. If your thoughts distract you (which they will) do not become angry or frustrated. Simply release the thoughts and return your attention to the tantien. When you are comfortable with this, imagine expanding this light and warmth so that it gradually fills your whole body. Concentrate like this for the entire meditation period. When it is over, you will feel very relaxed and refreshed. Take a few minutes to enjoy this feeling before jumping back into everyday activities.

Other variations on this exercise include observing your breath as it moves past the tip of your nose, mentally chanting a mantra (a sound such as "Om," or short phrase like "God is love"), or visualizing a desired goal or problem that you are seeking intuitive guidance on. (Jack Kornfield has written a great book on meditation called *A Path With Heart,* which you may find helpful in creating your own practices.)

I usually experience a profound sense of peace and well-being as a result of this centering exercise. Whenever I feel anxious, fearful, or emotionally out of balance, I know that I have shifted to an object-orientation and started to identify with my ego—my "small self." This is a signal that I need to breathe deeply and take a second to reorient myself. Through centering, I can direct my attention within and quickly restore my psychological balance. Letting go of the myriad worries about past and future events is a huge emotional relief, and it frees me to be fully present and aware of the current moment. For the practiced person, this can happen in an instant, but this ability has to be built up over a period of time.

> *I was always looking outside myself for strength and confidence, but it comes from within. It is there all the time.*
>
> — Anne Freud

In addition to feeling peace and calm despite the chaos that is swirling around you, centering has several other benefits. For instance, there are direct and immediate benefits to your health. There is ample evidence proving that meditation reduces blood pressure and the chance of suffering a heart attack. It also enhances your immune system. As you connect more fully with your true self, you will find that you are no longer fearful or feel the need to dominate others. Your power will come from within and can never be taken away from you. Your creativity and intuition will continue to increase as well. And you will notice that people will be attracted to you because you radiate a sense of calm and well-being that is very soothing.

Authenticity: The Hero's Journey

In the legend of the Holy Grail, the knights of King Arthur's Round Table are provided a vision of the Grail (Jesus Christ's chalice from the Last Supper). When the Grail abruptly disappears, the knights set out on a quest to find it. According to legend, each knight enters the forest at the darkest point, where no one had traveled before. The hero of one version of the tale is a young man named Perceval. When he was growing up, Perceval's mother refused to let him learn the ways of the courts. Instead, she raised him to follow his own heart—to live by the dynamics of his own life. Well, Perceval grew into a tall, strong young man, and one day a knight who was riding by spotted him. This gallant knight in his glowing armor and mighty horse overwhelmed Perceval's better judgment, and so he went with him to court where he learned the rules of society.

So it happened that Perceval was one of the knights who rode off in search of the Holy Grail. He, in fact, is the first to come upon the castle where the Grail King resides. The King was ill, and the kingdom itself had become a wasteland. When Perceval first enters the castle, the King is lying on a litter, gravely wounded and barely alive. Perceval is moved by compassion to ask, "What ails you, uncle?" but he refrains. His court training has taught him to never ask unnecessary questions, so he denies his inner wisdom, obeys the rules of society, and the adventure fails. Then, for five years, Perceval struggles through ordeals and hardships until he makes his way back to the castle to ask the question that he wanted to ask the first time. With this simple act of compassion, Perceval invokes the Grail, and the King—and hence the kingdom—is healed.

Joseph Campbell (who tells this story in *The Power of Myth*) explained that "the Grail represents the fulfillment of the highest spiritual potentialities of the human consciousness."

Living Authentically

This powerful allegory has much to teach us about living an authentic life. The principle message is that people must live the lives they were born into—not the ones that society wants them to live—if they hope to achieve the "Holy Grail." The word authentic comes from a root word that means "author." When people live authentically, they become the authors of their life stories—they assume power and authority over their lives. It is the antithesis of living the life of a victim. When the knights ventured forth on their quest, they entered the forest "at the darkest

> *It is good to have an end to journey towards, but it is the journey that matters, in the end.*
>
> —Ursula K. LeGuin, author of *The Left Hand of Darkness*

point, where no one has traveled before." To travel someone else's path would have been inauthentic—the established path is the course of another person's life. It only promises an impoverished existence. The wasteland described in the story is the inevitable consequence of living an inauthentic life. It is hell on Earth, and it shows in the face of everyone caught up in it.

Every person is called to live a unique life, what Joseph Campbell calls the "Hero's Journey." When a person refuses the call of the hero's journey, only misfortune and unhappiness can follow. This is what happened to Perceval when he ignored the urgings of his own heart and did not reach out with compassion to the ailing King. Instead, he did what society said was "right" and subsequently wandered another five years in the wasteland. He finally found the Grail when he followed his heart, and the King and the kingdom were healed.

Finding Your Calling

It is difficult for many people to distinguish between their skills and talents and a calling. Skills make it possible to achieve a calling, but they are rarely the calling itself. For me, the inner urging to pull away from the traditional path was very strong when I was in my teens, and I developed many novel ideas about the life that I would live that were counter to my upbringing. When I entered college, though, I lost my sense of direction. For instance, I changed my major field of study four times in my first two years of college. The courses that really set my

> *Life is either a daring adventure or nothing.*
>
> — Helen Keller

imagination on fire were psychology and anthropology. However, I thought that I couldn't make a living in these fields. So I denied the call. Because I had strong analytical skills, it was easy for me to excel in accounting, so I became an accountant.

I was miserable.

I hated everything about accounting, so within a few months I carved out a niche for myself as a liaison between accounting and data processing for the development of information systems. Over the years, I held many jobs at several different companies and finally found my way to organizational change. Nearly a decade later, I had come full circle—I had found my way back to the "Grail King." As a consultant in organizational transformation, I now use the concepts of psychology and anthropology every day, and I have never been so happy. Just because I was good at accounting did not mean that I should have pursued a career in it—I had no passion for it, and so it was the equivalent of the wasteland for me.

Many people turn away from their calling, as I did, in the interest of making a suitable living. This is the "safe" thing to do, and it might lead to a comfortable life. But it will never lead to true fulfillment—only a person's unique calling can do that. You will find that your comfortable life has come at the price of constant struggle, unhappiness, and a deep sense of emptiness—a sort of "hole in your middle" that nothing can fill up. It takes tremendous courage to defy the social pressures to conform and strike out in your own direction. There will be many trials along your path when you do, and it may be quite difficult for you. However, you will feel fully, vibrantly alive every step of the way. Martha Finney, co-author of *Callings*, comments on the experience of following your heart's calling:

> The Knights of the Round Table, in starting their quest for the Holy Grail, entered the forest at the darkest point. By definition, there can be only one darkest point, so every step after that is a step toward the light. This is a compelling metaphor for the importance of forward movement and the value of simply following one's nose— the inner sense of knowing what's right for yourself. It also helps you appreciate that the position where you are today—even if it is uncomfortable for you—is an advancement along the path to personal fulfillment.

To accept your calling is to live a life of uncertainty—no one can show you the way because this is your unique path. As Dr. Deepak Chopra reminds us:

> Uncertainty is the fertile ground of pure creativity and freedom. Uncertainty means stepping into the unknown in every moment of our existence. The unknown is the field of all possibilities, ever fresh, ever new, always open to the creation of new manifestations. Without uncertainty and the unknown, life is just the stale repetition of outworn memories. You become the victim of the past, and your tormentor today is your self left over from yesterday.

Career expert Barbara Reinhold estimates that 20 million Americans are staying in jobs that they hate in order to keep their health insurance. If that isn't a wasteland, what is? Another reason people stay in jobs they hate is out of a sense of duty to someone or something else. They need the money so their kids can go to the finest schools; they don't want to leave the company in a bind by resigning; or they don't want to disappoint their parents. But because everything in living systems is indivisibly connected, the people who stay in miserable environments are not just hurting themselves, they are hurting every system in which they participate. How many of you (or your spouses) are married to people who hate their jobs and bring a bad attitude home every day to stink up the house with complaining and criticizing? How much damage do you think is being done in the companies where such unhappy employees work?

> *Without uncertainty and the unknown, life is just the stale repetition of outworn memories. You become a victim of the past, and your tormentor today is your self left over from yesterday.*
>
> — Deepak Chopra, Ph.D.

It only takes one step to begin a new life, but that one step may be huge. Many people do not have the luxury of simply quitting their jobs and starting over. If this is your situation, I recommend that you immediately begin to prepare for the necessary life changes. For instance, you could take college classes for the knowledge you will need in a new career, you could begin to accumulate savings to tide you over when you quit, or you could start a new business at night or on weekends until it can support you full-time. Another thing you can do is to learn to live with fewer material goods. If you have already established self-reference based on your true self, you would suffer no loss of self-worth from making less money or from having fewer things. But there is no reason to think that over time you will continue to make less money. Most people actually find that they make more money than they did in their old, inauthentic livelihood.

If you simply cannot make a living following your calling as a full-time vocation, find a way to merge it into whatever you are doing. Scott Adams, the creator of Dilbert, was employed as an engineer at Pacific Bell. He first developed the comic strip for use within his company. His subsequent success is now legion. Robert Fritz, author of *The Path of Least Resistance*, was a professional musician who saw a way to translate the structural patterns of music into a business methodology for improving performance. Your options are endless. Once you accept responsibility for your life, connect with who you truly are, and decide to follow your calling, nothing will stand in the way of you achieving your dreams.

Chapter Seven
Personal Mastery

The real voyage of discovery consists not in seeking new landscapes, but in having new eyes.

— *Marcel Proust*

"Daddy, I'm hungry," my four-year-old son, Ryan, told me. "My food has already gone down into my legs!" In his own way, he had developed a mental model to explain the world of his perception. As he continues to mature, these models will change and grow, becoming ever more accurate and complete. Humans have a benefit over animals in that our ability to change our mind remains plastic. This flexibility is most pronounced when we are young, but with practice, our minds can remain flexible for a lifetime. Creating a Quantum Organization is an inside-out change—it begins with a change of mind. This chapter addresses the elements of personal mastery that are necessary for us to make the mental changes required to operate effectively in a Quantum Organization.

Cognition and Learning

Cognition is the process of perceiving sensory information, attributing meaning to it, and then choosing a response. Perception and reaction happen so quickly that we are usually not even aware that our reactions—our behavior—was chosen at all. We simply know that we responded in a certain way. Human cognition generally follows the steps outlined on the following pages (illustrated in Fig. 7.1).

You may recognize much of this as being similar to the functioning of culture in organizations, which is merely a collective form of cognition.

Human Perception and Cognition

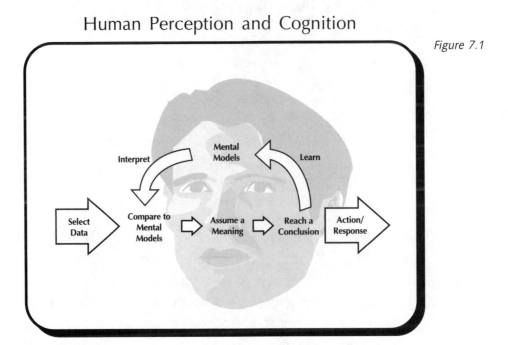

Figure 7.1

1. *Select data.* An external event stimulates our senses, and through the process of perception, we select which information we want to consider further. The amount of raw data available to the human senses is absolutely overwhelming. We naturally filter the information to gain just what is most relevant and important to us. In fact, at least 80 percent of the information that we use in the process of thinking is already in our minds—a meager 20 percent or less of the information is derived from sensory input. The information that we choose to consider is based largely on our beliefs.

2. *Compare to mental models.* Our perceptions are then compared to our beliefs (also called mental models, schemas, and rules). However, the mind is not a

neatly organized file drawer. It is a jumbled up bird's nest of complex interconnections. A stimulus does not match a single belief, but an entire constellation of related beliefs that may stretch back through the years to our earliest childhood memories. You can imagine each of these beliefs as voices from your past, all joined in a confusing chorus of advice.

3. *Assume a meaning.* Based on this constellation of beliefs, we make an assumption about what the information means to us. Of course, the match to an existing mental model is never perfect. So, we must decide whether to modify our mental model or disregard some of the information that we perceive. The stronger a belief, the more likely we are to accept its validity in lieu of the data that contradicts it. This, then, is a second filter of "reality" where certain data—which may have a profound influence on the true meaning of the stimulus—is either ignored or distorted in order to preserve an existing belief.

> At least 80 percent of the information that we use in the process of thinking is already in our minds.

4. *Learn.* Every act of cognition is an act of learning. By *learning*, I do not mean the accumulation of facts, but the *broadening of our understanding of reality*. If we have an existing schema, we may choose to modify it or simply strengthen the belief that is already there. When we choose not to change a mental model even though there is evidence that it is inaccurate, we are participating in *maladaptive learning*, a practice that weakens our ability to function effectively. In the case of a whole new experience where there is no previous schema available, our natural reaction is to postulate possibilities and then experiment. Through this process of discovery, we find what does and does not work. When something works consistently, we adopt it as a belief. We also adopt beliefs about what *does not* work. These beliefs vary in strength based on how certain we are of their "truth." The more the belief is reinforced, the stronger it gets.

5. *Reach a conclusion.* Finally, we choose a reaction based on our repertoire of learned responses and the meaning that we have assigned to the information. Our action then stimulates a new response from the environment—and the cycle continues.

Learning and Mental Models

To an infant, the world is an incoherent, whirling, swirling collage of sensations. Gradually, the baby begins to notice patterns that repeat themselves—mom's face, her smell, her gentle voice. With this recognition comes a symbolic representation of a sensation—a cognitive rule that helps the infant categorize and predict the outer world. These mental models, or schemas, are essential if the infant is to function effectively in the world. Schemas start out as very specific rules and then gradually become generalized to a much wider range of phenomena. For instance, researchers studying parental attachment in infants observed that when a child's mother left the room through an open door, the infant became very agitated. When the mother returned, the infant quickly calmed down. The child's distress was repeated the first few times the mother left and re-entered the room. However, the infant gradually learned the specific rule that "when mother goes through the door she will come back." With this realization, the baby no longer became disturbed when the mother left the room through the original door.

> Mental models create order in our minds by helping us to understand and predict the outer world.

Then the researchers had the mother exit through a *different* door. Instantly, the child became upset again. The infant had no mental model of mom returning through the second door, only through the first one. More quickly this time, the child learned that mom would always return through the second door as well. Soon, the child created a *generalized* schema that "mom returns whenever she goes through *any* door." The infant relied on the generalized mental model to *assume* that "since mom has gone out and returned through other doors, she'll return this time too." This is the functioning of mental models. These schemas create order in our minds by helping us to understand and predict the outer world. Our ability to comprehend the world, then, is tied to how many mental models we have and how accurate these models are.

Mental models are formed directly through personal experiences and indirectly through concepts taught to us by other people. We accept personal experiences because we *know* them through direct observation (although the conclusions that we reached may be erroneous). In contrast, we have to accept social teachings mostly as a matter of faith. Both methods create mental models of what we *assume* to know about the world. The vast majority of our accumulated "knowledge" is actually something that we believe because someone told us it was true. For instance, we accept that the moon is big and round, a long way off in space, without its own source of light—all because someone we trust told us. This acceptance is in spite of our own senses that tell us that the moon is very small, seems to shine by itself, and has many different shapes depending on what time of the month one views it.

Initially, seeing is believing. But later, it is what we believe that shapes what we see. Our minds act to distort our perceptions in order to validate our existing mental models. Psychologists call this "confirmation bias"

> We see what we expect to see, not what is really there.

and "self-fulfilling prophecy." A few years ago, a tribe of stone-age people was discovered living in a dense forest wilderness. These simple people, incredibly, had no knowledge of the outside world. When they were brought to the edge of the forest for the first time and beheld a vast plain with animals scattered all about, they withdrew in horror. Based on their frame of reference, these animals were tiny—the size of ants. They had no previous experience with viewing objects at a distance, and so assumed that the animals had to be tiny. This is the functioning of confirmation bias—we see what we expect to see, not what is really there.

Maladaptive Learning. Very few people doubt their perceptions—in fact they more often defend them to death. The mind is a living system that must remain flexible and adaptive or it will become ineffective in dealing with new challenges. By denying information that contradicts our beliefs and resisting changes to our mind-set, we severely hamper our ability to learn. Children, as we know, form and change their mental models with ease. This plasticity of mind makes children natural learners. Children are constantly being confronted with information (or authorities) that invalidate previous understandings and replace them with new and more accurate teachings. So, one of the beliefs children form is, "beliefs are temporary and subject to change."

As we mature, we gain certainty in our mental models, and increasingly resist changing them. By the time many people attain mid-adulthood, they have a difficult time accepting any challenges to their mind-set. Our society has many sayings regarding this, for example "they are set in their ways," and "you can't teach an old dog new tricks." The original belief in the plasticity of mental

> To know you do not know is best. To pretend to know when you do not know is disease.
>
> — Lao Tzu

models has been replaced by "I know the truth, and any evidence to the contrary is wrong." Part of the reason we cling to our beliefs may be physical—it is physically more difficult to learn as an adult. But more powerful than this are the ideas that we have developed about being "right" and "certain" in our beliefs.

- ✠ Our Newtonian-Cartesian heritage instructs us that knowledge is certain—when you have an answer that fits, no other models should be considered. (This mode of thinking actually has a name: "Occam's Razor" or the "rule of parsimony.")

- ✠ Another reason for resistance is that we identify with our egos instead of our true self, and our ego believes that it *is* the belief. Hence, a threat to a belief is a threat to the ego.

- ✠ In business, industrial-era management practices have created the conditions where managers are expected to know the answers to any and all questions and problems. Any sign of uncertainty is an indication of weakness and even incompetence.

The new science, as we now know, makes it clear that all knowledge is limited. As a result, one of the meta-principles of the quantum culture is:

All mental models are limited approximations
of a constantly changing reality.

By "limited," we mean that all of our ideas about the world are based on a narrow context of environmental conditions—that are observed over a given timeframe—through our particular human way of perceiving. My son's belief that his food "went down into his legs" and made him hungry was based on all of the information available to him at the time. The notions that the Earth was flat, that the sun and stars revolved around the Earth, that kings were divine, that bathing was bad, and untold other beliefs have all fallen as time has passed and we have learned more about the "truth" of the world. However, they did not go easily. As with the Inquisition, there are many examples where the old beliefs were defended savagely and violently.

Beginner's Mind. In order to learn, we must be able to let go of, or modify, outdated beliefs. Consider the story of a Zen master who was visited by a learned university professor of oriental studies. The master received the professor in his private room and had tea served. As soon as he was seated, the professor began to prattle on and on about Zen philosophy. The master merely nodded and continued to pour tea in the visitor's cup. The professor felt quite proud of himself and he rambled on, hardly noticing the Zen master. Then, suddenly, tea began to pour out onto the tatami

> *Always with you it cannot be done. You must*
> *unlearn what you have learned.*
>
> — Master Yoda to Luke Skywalker,
> in the movie *The Empire Strikes Back*

mat. The cup had long since overflowed, and still the master poured more. "Stop, stop, what are you doing?" cried the professor. To which the master replied, "Just as this cup can hold no more tea when it is already filled, how can I give you anything when your mind is already filled?"

Learning requires a beginners mind—the open and inquisitive mind of a child. We need to open our mind so that there is space for new ideas. The essential condition of a beginner's mind is non-judgment. We have to suspend our value judgments—our rush to assign meaning—so that we might see more clearly. Holding a beginner's mind means that we see everyone and every situation as a potential teacher. Obviously, this requires a great deal of humility, which is one reason that personal leadership is a prerequisite for personal mastery. In a Quantum Organization, it is understood that everyone is engaged in a continual learning process. Teachers are not the highest in the hierarchy, but rather the ones with the knowledge—no matter who they are or where they work in the organization.

> Teachers are not the highest in the hierarchy, but rather the ones with the knowledge—no matter who they are or where they work in the organization.

Mindfulness. One of the difficulties that people face in changing their beliefs is that they are mostly unaware of them. The process of cognition as described earlier in this chapter happens in an instant. There are times when such lightning-fast reactions may be necessary to save someone's life or avert some other sort of disaster. But for all practical purposes, they merely keep us from selecting a more thoughtful response to a situation. Learning is predicated on slowing down our thoughts so we can observe the stages of the thought process. This is called *mindfulness*. The practice of mindfulness requires that we be fully present in the current moment. If our thoughts are on some hoped-for future or ruminating over past events, we will have no hope of ever being able to learn. Mindfulness is assisted by the regular practice of meditation.

> *Magical power, marvelous action!*
> *Chopping wood, carrying water . . .*
>
> — Zen poem on Mindfulness

Practicing mindfulness, in relation to eating, provides a powerful example of the difference that being totally aware in the present moment can make to our perception. For instance, can you remember what food you had for lunch yesterday? Do you remember what it tasted like? Was it cold, hot, somewhere in between? What was the texture of the food? Soft? Crunchy? Smooth? Most busy people do not give their food a second thought as they eat. Instead, their minds are elsewhere—on a book or magazine they are reading, on an upcoming meeting, or on a problem at home—everywhere but on the food in their mouths. They mechanically bite, chew, and swallow until the food is gone. At your next meal, I want you to become mindful. Before starting to eat, take a moment to quiet your mind and get centered. Now, select a bite of food. Smell it before putting it in your month. What is the aroma? Roll the food around in your mouth as if it was a swallow of vintage wine. Observe all of the subtle taste sensations, the flavor, the texture, the temperature. After you swallow, take a moment to savor the aftertaste. It may help the experience if you close your eyes. Be sure to put your fork down on the table between every bite. Continue this through the entire meal. You will most likely be astonished by how wonderful the food really tastes, how quickly you get full, and how relaxed and satisfied you feel after the meal. This is what being fully present in the moment feels like.

Changing Our Minds. The realization that we need to change one or more of our beliefs normally arises after we have already had some sort of a negative emotional reaction. Start by becoming centered in the present moment so you can observe your thoughts objectively. You can then follow these steps for changing your mental models:

1. *Take in information from the environment.* We need to consciously seek out information that we have excluded. We can ask ourselves the question: What information is there that we are not seeing or that we are not willing to see? This alone can be enough to allow you to change your initial conclusion, but it has not yet done anything to change the underlying belief.

2. *Compare the environmental information to our mental models.* Once we include more information from step 1, it is easier to see that reality is not squaring with our expectations; we are experiencing negative feelings or

have taken a rigid and inflexible stance on an issue. At this point, we need to suspend judgment and merely observe these differences. It is important to note that by considering information openly, we are not agreeing or disagreeing with it—we are simply observing it.

3. *Examine our beliefs and question whether they are still valid, or if they need to be modified or eliminated.* We can ask such questions as:

   ❋ How did I develop this belief—what were the conditions at the time?

   ❋ Are the conditions still true, and if so, are they true in this circumstance?

   ❋ Are there any other explanations that are equally or more valid in this circumstance and at this time?

   ❋ Do I want to modify my original belief or do I need to replace it altogether?

4. *Choose a response from our repertoire of behaviors.* In Western society, most people have a limited range of alternative behaviors. One important step that each person in a Quantum Organization needs to take is to actively broaden his or her behavioral choices. The more behaviors we have at our disposal, the more flexible and responsive we will be to environmental challenges. Men, for instance, often resort to anger and aggression when their ideas are challenged. Optional responses, though, could be curiosity, compassion, patience, humor; one or more of which might be a better choice.

5. *Actively reinforce the new behavioral response until it becomes a habit.* We can accomplish this through several actions:

   ❋ Visualize what the new behavior will look like when you put it into practice. Set some sort of tangible goal. It need not be measurable from a quantitative sense, but it should at least be observable (such as people feeling that you are being more caring toward them).

   ❋ Practice using the new behavior, and seek frequent feedback from others on how you are progressing.

   ❋ Reward yourself for every step that you take in the right direction.

In the previous chapter, I used the hypothetical example of a total stranger bumping into someone and then hurrying on. We can use this as an example for how to change our mind-set. For the sake of this example, assume that this man bumped me, and I became very angry. I went around for the next few minutes complaining to anyone who would listen.

- My desire to change arose from the realization that my judgements about the other person were actually harming *me*. I was experiencing stress and emotional upset. My preoccupation was disrupting my ability to think clearly and act responsibly.
- As I reviewed the situation, I realized that I had selected only a narrow range of data from the incident—specifically that a stranger bumped into me and continued on without a word of apology. In retrospect, I remember now that I was standing in the middle of the hallway, leaving the man very little room to get by. He had made an effort to get around me without bumping me, but had not succeeded. I also remember glimpsing his face—his look told of his anguish.

> *In vain I have looked for a single man capable of seeing his faults and bringing the charge home against himself.*
>
> — Confucious

- With this additional information, I realize that I must share the blame for the incident because I was standing in the way. In addition, his unique situation justifies his hurry. But I am concerned about *my* response—why was I so quick to get angry, and why did I feel the need to complain? What is the belief that justified my reaction? As I think about it, I realize that I was offended by his pushing me and then not apologizing. The underlying belief is "people are supposed to apologize when they offend someone." Rather than confront this belief, I had responded with righteous indignation.

Is it really true that people should apologize when they offend someone? Who decided that? I realize that although this is a standard that I hold myself to, I have no claim on anyone else's behavior. The way another person responds is really none of my business.

* In the future, what alternate response do I want to choose? One is to simply ignore the event. Another would be to immediately grant the man the benefit of the doubt and assume that there is some reasonable explanation for his behavior.

* I can reinforce this new behavior by sharing my intention with my wife, a close friend, or my personal coach, and ask them to give me feedback on how I am progressing.

Creating Our Own Reality

The world that we see is largely the world that we *expect* to see. In a very real sense, then, we create our own reality. This happens in two ways. First, our beliefs cause us to ignore and distort information that is counter to what we expect. For instance, If we believe in a safe, supportive, and loving world, we will select information from our experience of people and situations that supports this belief. If we believe in a hostile and threatening world of vicious competition, we

> *Luke, you are going to find that many of the truths that we cling to depend greatly on your point of view.*
>
> — Obi-Wan Kenobe to Luke Skywalker, in the movie *Return of the Jedi*

will see it everywhere. The second, and most powerful way that we create our reality is to interact with the environment in a way that attracts people, and solicits responses that validate our beliefs.

For example, if I have low self-esteem and believe at a deep level that I am worthless, I will unconsciously be attracted to people who are predisposed to treat me that way. In addition, these people will be attracted to me because they need to feel superior, and my feelings of worthlessness satisfy their need. These are called "co-dependent" relationships because each person's dysfunction feeds on that of the other in a vicious circle. This co-dependent pattern is why people who leave an abusive relationship always seem to find their way back into another one. Until the underlying belief is changed, the pattern will continue to repeat itself. The same is true for alcoholics and other addicts. To simply stop drinking does nothing to change the underlying beliefs that led to the addictive behavior. This is why Alcoholics Anonymous (AA) has a rigorous twelve-step program. Its aim is to rescript the deep unconscious beliefs.

It is the unconscious mind that is the repository of our beliefs and that initially perceives and interprets sensory input. Our unconscious mind has

> *People need to see the circumstances of their lives as a reflection of themselves, rather than as something that is happening to them. Then they can reclaim power over their lives, and in doing so, will change their world.*
>
> — Jean Johnson, Counselor
> and Business Consulant

some interesting properties that make it possible for us to "reprogram" our beliefs and literally change our lives. For one thing, it cannot distinguish between a real perception and an imagined one. This means that experiences we visualize in vivid detail are as real to the unconscious as an actual experience. Second, the unconscious mind actively seeks to fulfill our beliefs. And third, the unconscious mind has no sense of humor—it takes everything literally. So, when a person says "my job is a pain in the neck," his or her unconscious mind will literally translate this into a real pain in the neck.

As with organizational change, personal change cannot happen until people decide to make the change. This usually happens when things get so miserable in their lives—the proverbial "dark night of the soul"—that they finally breakdown and choose to get better. Once this decision has been made, there are many published techniques that describe ways of reprogramming the unconscious mind. The help of psychologists and counselors is a wise alternative when the beliefs are very strong or evoke emotional trauma. The following method, which is based on elements of many popular techniques, has worked for making powerful changes in my life. If you follow these steps, you should be able to create a substantially better life for yourself.

1. *Set goals for the changes you want to see in your life.* These goals should have the following characteristics:

   ❇ *Be stated in a positive language.* They need to be "for" something rather than "against" something. For instance, do not form a goal such as "I want to quit being poor"—this is negative language. Instead, form a goal such as "I will make $X in annual compensation by the end of next year."

   ❇ *Be definite.* A vague goal will produce vague results. It does not have to be a measurable number, but it does have to be observable. You cannot measure happiness, for instance, but you know when you have achieved it.

   ❇ *Be achievable.* It does not matter whether your goal is related to money, romance, health, or anything else; you can create it for yourself. Of course, some goals—such as lifting an office building with one hand—are impossible. Also, if your goal is extreme, like becoming a millionaire, establish shorter-term stretch goals that move you in the right direction.

   ❇ *Be aligned with your calling.* Every person has a unique path. If your goals are counter to your *calling*, they will not manifest in the way that you want them. It is essential to first set an authentic course for yourself, then set goals along that course.

2. *Create a vision of the change that you want to achieve.* Make the vision that you develop as vivid as possible. What image represents that you have achieved your goal? What will you look like when you have achieved your goal? What will you be doing? What are you saying to yourself and others? What is your physical posture and your attitude? Who is with you? What are

you feeling? What are the colors around you? Can you taste anything? The more real you make your goal, the more convincing it will be to your unconscious mind.

> *Thoughts are things; they have tremendous power. Thoughts crystallize into habit, and habit solidifies into circumstances.*
>
> — Brian Adams
> author of *How to Succeed*

- ✳ *Be open to the outcome.* This means that you are open and accepting of whatever good comes your way. I keep in mind the phrase, "this or something better," as a reminder that my authentic path may take me in ways that I cannot predict. I need to stay open and alert to these opportunities and not become attached to a specific result.

- ✳ *Be clear about what you are willing to give up to make your goals come true.* If you want more money, are you willing to work harder and longer, go back to school, take a risk to move into a new career? If you are not willing to do what it takes to achieve the goal, you should not attempt it.

3. *Create a plan of action.* What do you need to do for your goal to come true? In many cases, you will not know all of the steps. That is okay. All you need to do is to identify the first few steps in the right direction. The next steps will become clear when the time is right.

4. *Take action.* You are responsible for making your vision come true, and this requires that you take the following actions:

- ✳ *Execute the steps in your plan.* As your actions lead you down your path, the next actions will become clear. Also, you may gain information that leads to changes in your goals and/or your vision.

- ✳ *Behave as if your vision had already come true.* Assess all of your behaviors in light of your vision. Are they contributing to it or detracting from it? If your goal is a loving and fulfilling marriage, learn what will be required to achieve it. Then, make sure that all of your behaviors are consistent with creating this goal. Instead of getting angry at your spouse for a small slight, for instance, ignore it or discuss it calmly.

- *Ask for what you want.* People cannot read your mind. If you want something, you need to ask for it. Do not beg, and do not be apologetic. Just be specific and firmly make your request. It also helps to tell a lot of people about your goal. This serves two purposes. It helps you to commit to the goal, and it alerts people who may help you in ways that you could not have asked for directly.

5. *Use affirmations*. These are single sentences that express your desire. Some examples are, "I am prosperous," "I am loving and forgiving," and "I have a fulfilling and rewarding job." Affirmations should be stated in the present tense. Also, they work best when they are repeated many times each day. I recommend 100 times in the morning and another 100 times in the evening for at least thirty days. This is best done when you are centered and focused—during or after a meditation period is preferred.

Emotional Mastery

Our ability to think clearly and learn easily is dependent on our capacity for managing our emotions. Put simply, when people are emotionally upset they can't think straight and they can't learn. As a result, emotional mastery is one of the most important aspects of personal mastery. The four elements of emotional mastery are the ability to identify and understand our emotions, to manage our emotions as we are experiencing them, to recognize other people's emotions, and to empathize with other people. The first two elements are discussed in this chapter, and the final two elements are discussed in Chapter 8.

Understanding Emotions

In his breakthrough book, *Emotional Intelligence*, Daniel Goleman makes the case that emotional mastery is as large a factor in success as conventional intelligence. Goleman's research is clear: Logical thought cannot function effectively independent of emotions. "Emotional aptitude," he explains, "is a *meta-ability*, determining how well we can use whatever skills we have, including raw intellect." Through emotions, humans assign values to differing possibilities. In fact, our emotions enable us to *care* about anything. The goal in personal mastery is not to control or repress our emotions, but to temper them and express them in positive and productive ways.

Emotions are largely misunderstood in our society. We tend to take a dim view of any sort of emotional display, but in particular we frown on any display of "weak" emotions: grief, anxiety, and fear. Our Newtonian-Cartesian heritage has created the conviction that the highest expression of humankind is the unemotional, logical android. People are realizing, though, how impoverished this view of humanity really is. Being emotional is hard-wired into our very being—emotions are not something that can be turned on or off. The only question is how we will handle them—through repression, aggression, or mastery?

> *The sound and fury of an individual's creative life are the elemental waters missing from the dehydrated workday. . . . Adaptability and native creativity on the part of the workforce come through the door only with their passions.*
>
> — David Whyte, author of *The Heart Aroused*

Emotional Repression. Western society has a long history of repressing emotions. Recently, for instance, I overheard a man scolding a crying three-year-old boy by saying, "Do you want to be a sissy? Boys don't cry!" An important aspect of emotional mastery involves learning to experience and express our emotions in a healthy manner rather than repressing them. I use the metaphor of a capacitor to explain the consequences of repressed emotions. A capacitor is a piece of equipment that stores up electrical energy and then discharges it at a later time. Humans have an "emotional capacitor" that stores an emotional charge whenever we repress our emotions. Keeping all of those negative emotions bottled up in our body takes a huge amount of energy. The energy that is being directed there cannot be used in other, more productive ways.

Our emotional capacitor can hold only so much charge. When it becomes saturated, repressed emotions discharge in unhealthy ways. Four of these are described below.

The Emotional Capacitor Overflows

1. *They leak negative energy into our bodies.* Some people turn their repressed emotions inward. When this happens, emotional distress can be expressed through illness. Emotions "leak" into our bodies and cause many different ailments. The medical consequences of unresolved emotional disturbances have been confirmed many times. Heart attacks, cancer, high blood pressure, and susceptibility to diseases are all confirmed consequences. But there are others that are not as debilitating, which include: headaches, back pain, constipation, weight loss (or gain), frequent nagging illnesses such as colds and flu, ulcers, and many others. The emotional capacitor is carried somewhere on the body—the location is different for each person. I carry mine on my shoulders; when it starts to discharge I get aching shoulders and excruciating headaches. Other people carry them in their stomachs and

get ulcers and stomach problems when they overflow. Still others carry them over their hearts and have heart attacks when the charge gets too large. Where do you carry yours?

2. *They are acted out through indirect behaviors.* Acting out our emotions in indirect ways can take many forms. The most common is bickering and "sniping." Many of us have been in, or observed, a relationship that was filled with indirect and almost subliminal messages. I call this behavior "sniping." Bickering is simply a more open version of the same behavior, but it is no more direct regarding the true underlying emotional issues. These relationships maintain a facade of civility, but practically all of the exchanges, both verbal and nonverbal, are sarcastic, critical, or demeaning. These behaviors make for great comedy on television and in movies, but they make for misery and tragedy in real-life relationships. Bickering and sniping may seem fairly benign, but they are one of the highest indicators of the impeding breakdown of a relationship. Indirect acting-out springs from two sources: (1) being unaware of repressed emotions that are giving rise to the behaviors, and (2) being unskilled at communicating your feelings and needs to others.

> Emotional outbursts—contrary to popular beliefs—are not healthy. Venting rage does not relieve emotional distress, but actually adds to it.

3. *They discharge like a lightning bolt in a violent over-reaction.* Have you ever "blown your top" when someone cut in front of you in traffic, or when you were stuck in a traffic jam, or when you missed a flight? Have you or a co-worker ever overreacted and created a huge commotion over some small incident? These are all examples of "emotional flooding"—being overwhelmed by emotions and losing the ability to respond appropriately. Emotional flooding is technically determined by a rise in a person's heart rate. An increase of at least ten beats-per-minute signals the onset of flooding.

Emotional outbursts—contrary to popular beliefs—are not healthy. Venting rage does not relieve emotional distress, but actually adds to it. In addition, outbursts contribute to many of the same health problems described earlier. They are simply unskilled expressions of an overloaded emotional capacitor. Heading off an impulsive and destructive outburst can be accomplished by training yourself to follow the "STAR" approach. STAR is an acronym for Stop, Think, Act, Responsibly. *Stop* your impulse and take time to cool down; *think* about alternative actions; act on your new thoughts and be *responsible* for positive outcomes. Although this is generally used with children, it is just as effective—and necessary—with adults.

4. *They overwhelm us and leave us psychologically numb.* When the burden of an emotion is too intense or overwhelming, some people respond by detaching from their emotions. This response creates a feeling of emotional numbness and listlessness. Other people choose different approaches, including drugs, to distract themselves. The influence behind these feelings and behaviors is the unwillingness to address emotional upset. Instead, people deny them, and try to distract themselves with another stimulus. The key to changing any mood is to choose an action inconsistent with the emotion—for anger, stop and cool down; for sadness or depression, become more active. I have found three approaches that work well for me: (1) let enough time pass and the energy will shift to a more active form, (2) get active doing something, particularly something of service to another person, and (3) confront and diffuse the source of the emotional upset.

Anger. Perhaps the most prevalent of the negative emotions is *anger*. For men in particular, anger is often the only emotion available regardless of the context. In a way, Western society values anger, viewing it as an expression of power and dominance.

Anger and other powerful negative emotions are destructive; they twist a person's attention to their own pre-occupations. Unlike sadness, anger can be energizing, empowering, and even exhilarating. Anger builds on anger. The longer an angry person dwells on an offense, the angrier and more "right"

> *The soul becomes dyed with the color of its thoughts.*
>
> — Marcus Aurelius

the person feels. "Anger is the most seductive of the negative emotions," Goleman states. "The self-righteous inner monologue that propels it along, fills the mind with the most convincing mental arguments for venting rage." Goleman explains that an angry emotional reaction creates an "adrenocortical arousal" that keeps the body at an elevated state of excitement that can last for a few hours or a few days. Any new stimulus, then, simply adds fuel to an already smoldering flame. At some point, releasing the anger ceases to be the objective, and making a point regarding "the principle of the thing" takes over. This is a sure sign that emotional flooding is taking place.

Mastering Our Emotional Responses

Clearing out all of the emotional baggage that accumulates in our emotional capacitor is a lengthy and difficult process. Many of the issues that surface after years of repression require the care and guidance of a professional—a psychologist or a professional counselor. For some people, there is a stigma associated with seeking such help. The common mind-set is that it's okay to see a doctor for ulcer medicine but not to visit a psychologist in order to eliminate the *cause* of the ulcer. There is also the notion that only really mentally ill people go to psychologists. This is simply not true. Even the healthiest people benefit from the guidance of mental health professionals. In my experience, the vast majority of people are merely coping—getting by day-to-day, but not living life to its fullest extent. Getting your emotional capacitor cleared out is an essential step on the path to the full expression of your personal potential.

Most business texts focus on conflict management—resolving issues at the level of events—and avoid the deep psychological underpinnings of these events. From a systems perspective, I am more interested in permanent solutions—rooting out and eliminating the source of our counterproductive emotional responses. Following are several techniques for developing emotional mastery that you can conduct for yourself. Please note that these are not techniques that you should use to analyze or try to "fix" *other* people. These are for *you* to use on *your* emotional issues.

1. *Begin with a commitment.* No one else can make you feel, think, or do anything—you are responsible for these things. So the questions that you need to answer are: How do I want to feel? How do I want to express my emotions? Make a commitment to your answers. Some emotions, such as anger, can give the seductive illusion that you are "right" on an issue. But no matter how much you are in the right, a constant state of anger is a *miserable* feeling. The question is not whether you are right or wrong, but how you want to feel. Anger pushes people away. Do you want to be isolated and alone? Do you want to be "right," or do you want to be happy? The assumption for the remainder of these points is that our goal is to feel emotionally peaceful and loving, and to have a positive outlook on life. When a person ceases trying to be right, and commits to being happy, a whole new range of alternatives opens up.

   > Self-talk is an inner voice that gives expression to your unconscious beliefs—it is full of judgments about yourself, life, and other people.

2. *Learn to notice your emotional reactions as soon as they arise.* If you have a long history of emotional repression, it will be difficult at first to even realize that you are in the grips of a powerful emotion. As you become more aware of when you are having an emotional reaction, you can intercede much earlier in the cycle to head-off emotional flooding. Each time you become aware that you are feeling an emotion, notice your body's reaction. Do you feel tense? Do you clench your teeth or your hands? Do you feel yourself starting to withdraw or shut down? In the future, as you

feel your body responding in these ways, check immediately to see if you are having an emotional reaction, and act to short-circuit it.

An approach called "Think and Prevent" (TAP) can help. The TAP technique involves literally tapping yourself on the leg or arm as you feel emotions being evoked. This is a tangible signal that you need to disengage from the situation and break the impending emotional flooding.

3. *Identify the emotion.* What are you feeling? This may be difficult for some people. Anger, which is one of the most common emotions, is actually a *secondary* emotion. It obscures the primary emotions—hurt, pain, or fear. Because it is a secondary emotion, addressing the anger is ineffective. The primary emotion needs to be surfaced and then the root cause can be identified.

4. *Notice the pattern of your self-talk.* Self-talk is an inner voice that gives expression to your unconscious beliefs—it is full of judgments about yourself, life, and other people. Self-talk is actually the judgments and beliefs that were expressed by authorities in your life, such as parents and teachers, that you have internalized. Self-talk will include messages like "I can't let her get away with this!" or "I am so stupid," or "I can't do this well," or "I'm not likable," or "Men are jerks," or "They shouldn't do that." Once you hear these messages, you can ask yourself what is behind them. For instance, you might ask, "Why can't I let her get away with this?" The answer should be both clear and instantaneous. A typical response might

> *We are not troubled by things, but by the opinions which we have of things.*
>
> — Epictetus, philosopher 55-135 A.D.

be "Because it will mean that you are weak and worthless." This is the real reason for your anger—the fear of being seen as inadequate and worthless.

5. *Explore the root cause of your emotion.* If the source is deeply rooted, you will most likely need the support and guidance of a professional.

❋ Ask yourself, "Who is saying this?" Your self-talk includes messages that you received from infancy to adulthood. It is important to find out where the root belief originated. An image of yourself will eventually emerge— let's say as a four-year-old child (although it can be an image of yourself at any age). It may take a while for you to develop this ability.

❋ Imagine yourself comforting this inner self. Ask the following questions: "Why do you feel inadequate?" "Is it true that you are inadequate?" "What makes 'them' right/wrong?"

❋ Wait for your unconscious mind to answer. The response may be in words or in an image of the original event (or multiple events; sometimes there is more than one cause). In this case, let's assume that you get an image of your father looming over you, shaking his finger in your face and saying "Don't be a sissy. Stop crying and stand up for yourself!" The messages this child got from an early age are: He is weak if he feels hurt, pain or fear; and if he is weak, then the person he loves will be angry at him, reject him, and withdraw love. What a burden to be carrying around!

6. *Discharge the emotion.* Emotions remain stored in your emotional capacitor because you never fully experience them. You minimize or repress them. There are many different therapies, but one common way to diffuse emotions is to re-experience them. This can be a powerful experience. If you doubt your ability to handle this by yourself, seek out a professional. Different people experience and express emotions in different ways. Some may act out violently; others may show little or no outward display.

❋ Let down your guard and allow your body to express the emotions however it wants. This approach requires a safe environment where you can feel uninhibited. Simply relax, call the original image to mind, and let your body react as it will. You may weep, shout, laugh, dance, grimace, tense your muscles, or express your emotion through spontaneous talking. Continue this until you feel "light" and cleared of negative feelings.

✠ Re-enact the scene. This will require the support of other people. This involves staging the original event with a different person playing each part. You are the director. Tell each person what to say and do. Initially, play the part of yourself. What do you feel as you play your part? Ask the others what they felt about the parts they played and what they observed in you. Next, play each part in the scene. What emotions does each evoke in you? What insights do you gain into the motivations and behaviors of the other roles in the scene?

✠ Conduct a dialogue with the person who committed the original offense. Put two chairs facing each other. Sit in one, and ask the other person questions. After you ask the question, move to the other chair and answer as you think he or she would have answered. Ask, "Why did you do that to me?" The answers will begin to reveal what the other person's beliefs and emotional issues may be. Invariably, this exercise results in a deep understanding and compassion for the perpetrator (and for yourself) as you begin to understand how flawed, human, or wounded the offender was.

Forgiving this person is an important element in your healing. Forgiveness is really about you, and not the other person. You are allowing yourself to love the offender despite the hurt that has been inflicted (you are not, though, condoning the offense).

7. *Re-frame the original incident.* Now that you have released your emotions regarding an event, you can re-write it in your unconscious mind. Recall the inner-self who originally revealed this deep psychological wound. Lovingly explain what really happened, and what the offender was feeling. Assure your inner-self that the message received was not true. Using positive self-talk, give yourself new messages, such as, "I am capable," and "I am lovable," and "I am smart." Later, reinforce these messages through affirmations, and by repeating the actions in this step as needed. Eventually,

summoning your inner-self and having similar dialogues will be an effortless and instantaneous process, giving you tremendous power over your emotional reactions.

It is important to note that you were probably not responsible for the original incident, especially if you were a child when it occurred. However, it is solely your responsibility to heal it—no one else can do this for you. The benefits of clearing up your emotional capacitor are extraordinary. Your health will improve markedly. In terminally ill patients, it has been known to cause spontaneous healing that saved their lives.

You will feel lighter and more positive. The world will seem brighter and more vibrant, and all of your senses will seem more acute—sights, sounds, textures, and tastes will all seem more vivid than before. You will find that fewer things upset you; that you are more emotionally stable even in very trying circumstances. And, you will discover that you are able to work through new emotional upsets much more quickly and easily. You will be able to break the patterns of behavior that have kept you locked in destructive relationships, and you will notice improvements in all of your important relationships. The change in your life will be nothing short of remarkable.

Intuition and Logic: Thinking With the Whole Mind

The Newtonian-Cartesian worldview asserts that the only valid way of knowing is through logic and use of the rational mind. As a result, all other forms of knowing are either ignored or ridiculed. The two hemispheres of the human brain have very different abilities. The left brain is the source of logic and language, and it controls the right side of the body. The left brain processes information in a linear, analytical manner. It is excellent for separating and categorizing pieces of a whole. The right brain is the source of creativity, imagination, and sensory input. It controls the left side of the body and it processes information holistically, comprehending it as a single gestalt. The left brain is unemotional and literal. The right brain is emotional and symbolic. The left brain is linguistic; the right brain is visual-spatial. The left brain is rational; the right brain is intuitive.

It should be clear from these descriptions that businesspeople rely almost entirely on left-brain functions. This means that we are quite literally operating our companies with *half a brain*. Intuition is a powerful right-brain function that would benefit us tremendously in the corporate setting. Intuition is no stranger to entrepreneurs who have used their gut feelings in making key strategic decisions. Tom Chapell, CEO of Tom's of Maine, once launched a new product—children's toothpaste—despite piles of painstaking marketing research that predicted it would fail. The product was a success. Chappell describes, in *The Soul of a Business*, his experience of intuition:

> When I have an intuition, it's as if I have an invisible partner working on my behalf, feeding me an idea. In that sense, I view my ability for intuition as a gift not unlike perfect pitch for a musician, or the mathematician's talent for looking at a blackboard full of numbers and seeing a beautiful formula, or a great outfielder's sense of where to run and leap to catch the ball before it flies over the fence.

Intuition is important in comprehending complexity. The wholeness of complex living systems cannot be comprehended by the left brain, which relies on breaking things into parts. The right brain, however, is designed to comprehend vast amounts of disorganized and contradictory information and produce an integrated understanding.

I personally rely heavily on intuition. I feel it as a kind of sixth sense; an inner knowing that has no rational explanation. In writing this book, there were many times when I would go to bed at night with a head full of research, with absolutely no idea how to organize it into an easily comprehended model.

The next morning, I would awake, grab some orange juice, sit down at my computer, and the solution would simply flow from my fingertips. This is quite a remarkable sensation.

> *I never discovered anything with my rational mind.*
>
> — Albert Einstein

Through intuition, we will be able to understand the right action to take in complex situations. We may not be able to say why, but we will know. Intuition and the rational mind make wonderful partners. Each of us is incomplete without the functioning of both. Whereas intuition provides us with creative ideas and the feeling that certain courses of action are right, our left brain validates these and turns them into reality. When we reclaim our intuition and partner it with our mastery of rational thinking, we will function more effectively than we ever before imagined.

Chapter Eight
Relationship

If you want a perfect relationship,
join a different species.

— Pia Mellody,
author of *Breaking Free*

One of our most heartfelt human yearnings is to connect at a very deep level with other people. You would expect, then, that humans would have excellent relationships. Unfortunately, that is not the case. The evidence suggests that we have very little idea about how to get along with one another. Wars rage around the globe, some of which involve genocide on a massive scale. Divorce rates have climbed to more than 50 percent. The legal profession, which serves the role of "undertakers" for relationships, is gigantic. And violent crime—assault, murder, rape—is rampant. People in our global society are in dire need of the simple skills of relating to other human beings in a peaceful and positive way.

This chapter explores the elements that make for successful relationships, focusing on commitment, mutual support, shared goals, communication, and peace making. It should come as no surprise that the first two meta-skills—personal leadership and personal mastery—are essential prerequisites for effective relationships. If individuals have not accepted responsibility for themselves, are not secure in their true identity, and have not learned to manage their thoughts and emotions, they will not be very successful in relating to other people.

Quality Relationships

The success of the modern organization does not depend on the heroic efforts of individuals, but on the effective interaction and collaboration of very diverse individuals in a team environment. Peter Drucker, eminent business advisor and futurist, notes that with knowledge work, "teams become the work unit rather than the individual himself."

> People in our global society are in dire need of the simple skills of relating to other human beings in a peaceful and positive way.

But what makes a team smart and capable? Not raw intelligence or talent, as is traditionally believed. Highly talented individuals can make a significant difference in the performance of a team, *if* the team has achieved a high degree of internal harmony. Otherwise, the presence of a high-performer makes little difference to overall performance. "The key to a high group IQ is social harmony," explains Daniel Goleman in *Emotional Intelligence*. "It is this ability to harmonize that, all other things being equal, will make one group especially talented, productive and successful, and another—with members whose talent and skill are equal in other regards—do poorly."

In Quantum Organizations, the quality of relationships directly translates into organizational performance. For that reason, there must be an explicit commitment to quality relationships. Under the classical management model, there is a tremendous emphasis on accomplishing tasks. This task orientation is, of course, essential to performance. However, it becomes a problem when it is not held in dynamic balance with a relationship orientation. If we are concerned solely with achieving results, almost any abuse of people—within the letter of the law—is justifiable. Men in particular seem to be predominately task-oriented, while women generally favor a relationship orientation. This contributes to many communication breakdowns between the sexes. It also points out that in a male-dominated business environment, making a priority of nurturing and valuing relationships will not be an easy transition. It is, nonetheless, essential to every organization's success.

What makes one relationship successful, and another a dismal failure? Although there is no single answer to this question, the primary elements that can be found in most healthy relationships include:

1. Commitment to a shared vision and common goals

2. Intention and effort to make the relationship succeed

3. Trust

4. Empathy

5. Honoring differences

6. Personal boundaries

7. Self-disclosure

8. Communication

9. Peace making

Understanding the Term "Relationship"

What do we mean by the word *relationship*? This may seem like an obvious question until we try to answer it. Families, teams, and close friendships would certainly qualify as relationships. But what about the people who deliver your mail. Are you in relationship with them? For people who work in very large organizations, are they in relationship with other employees who they have never met?

I believe that an important distinction should be drawn between casual interactions and relationships. A *casual interaction* is characterized by a transaction of some sort that can range from a passing "hello" to the sale of your home. Casual interactions benefit from many of the skills described in this chapter, but they are not relationships. A *relationship*, by my definition, is the commitment of two or more people to supporting each other in the pursuit of a common goal. (Of course, relationships aren't limited to people—they can exist between two or more living systems of any kind.) The key concepts in this definition are "commitment," "mutual support," and "common goal."

Commitment to a Shared Vision

One of the key benefits of a common purpose is that it requires people to transcend their personal interests in the service of something greater than themselves. It binds people together in pursuit of a higher cause. Many differences can be overcome through this shared commitment. The annals of history are full of examples of sworn enemies who join together to combat a common foe. We live together in harmony, not necessarily by resolving our differences, but by accepting them. The thing that makes this possible is a common vision that transcends the differences. One reason that global society does not cooperate more is that we have not created a shared commitment to anything. Individual constituencies have no cause to which they are willing to sacrifice their parochial interests.

> We live together in harmony, not necessarily by resolving our differences, but by accepting them.

An Intention to Make Relationships Succeed

Participants in a relationship—as I have defined it—commit not just to a shared goal, but also to mutual support. They are bound in service to each other and to making the relationship work. This requires them to actively cultivate a positive outlook toward each other. While it is a simple matter to select only the negative aspects of another person and blow them out of proportion, it is just as easy to view these same individuals in a positive light. Without this perspective, the relationship is doomed to constant difficulty and is likely to fail.

Good will—the commitment to seeing our partners in the most positive light—is an everyday responsibility. Consider a simple case: Imagine that your day starts out with a flat tire, or you miss your train, or have some other setback, and arrive at the office in a bad mood. Immediately, a teammate tells you an off-color joke that hits you wrong. How do you respond? Do you take the attitude that this person is a jerk? After all, the evidence is right in front of you—didn't he just commit yet another social blunder? You could reach that conclusion, but the question that you must ask is: Will this thought advance the relationship, or will it contribute to its breakdown? Each person has to recognize these negative thoughts and replace them with positive ones. After taking several deep breaths and centering yourself, you can TAP (Think and Prevent), or STAR (Stop, Think, Act, Responsibly). One alternative reaction would be to see the joke as a well-intentioned, albeit unskilled, attempt to connect with you. Instead of jumping down the co-worker's throat, you could acknowledge a positive intention, even if you did not like the result. Then, if you don't want to hear any more stupid jokes, make your needs known in a positive manner.

Trust

Trust is a fundamental principle of behavior that must exist for relationships to succeed. Trust is total confidence in the integrity, ability, and good character of another person. "Integrity" means being reliable; following through on commitments. "Ability" is about being competent in the execution of responsibilities. "Good character" refers to the emotional and moral qualities of an individual—whether a person is emotionally balanced and consistently chooses "right" action.

> *Trust* is a fundamental principle of behavior that must exist for relationships to succeed.

How is trust between two people developed? This is a chicken-and-egg issue: Does someone's behavior build trust, or is the initial granting of trust what creates trustworthy behavior? The answer is "both." Trust emerges when someone exhibits the qualities described in the previous paragraph. But it is encouraged by the intention to see other people as trustworthy from the outset. This is the power of self-fulfilling prophecy in action. When we look for trustworthy behaviors, not only do we see more of them, but they are also actively encouraged in other people. We help create a field of trust in which other people find it easier to choose trustworthy behaviors and actions. They live up to our expectations.

All of the people in the relationship need to understand trust in the same way. If people have different expectations regarding trustworthy behavior that have not been communicated, the expectations will almost assuredly be violated. People are not mind readers, they cannot know what others expect without being told. Relationships are nurtured through frequent dialogue around issues important to the participants. Trust is a topic that should be addressed in every dialogue session. Has someone failed to live up to a commitment? Is performance of responsibilities falling short? Is someone acting selfishly, or in bad faith to the relationship? Issues such as these cannot be allowed to build up; they need to be addressed immediately. Otherwise, they will continue to fester and will eventually erode the relationship.

Empathy

"Walk a mile in my shoes," the old saying goes, "before you judge me." This adage captures the essence of empathy—the identification and understanding of another person's feelings, situation, and motives. Empathy involves genuinely caring about others' feelings. It is a master skill in attaining emotional intelligence, because it is essential for choosing appropriate behaviors regarding other people. If we can't tell, or don't care what others are feeling, how can we respond appropriately to their needs? Recognizing their emotions is predicated on first being sensitive to your own. This is one reason that personal mastery should precede developing the skills of relationship.

> The difference between empathy and antipathy is the difference, as philosopher Martin Buber explained, between viewing people as "Thou" or "It."

The opposite of empathy is "antipathy," which is having no feeling at all toward others. An individual who cannot share the distress of another person will not be motivated to help. In extreme cases, these people are likely to become sociopaths. Mass murderers, for instance, are often reported to have had no emotional response to murdering their victims. Antipathy reduces other people to objects. They are no longer humans with feelings, hopes, dreams, and the love of their families. They are "Its." The difference between empathy and antipathy is the difference, as philosopher Martin Buber explained, between viewing people as "Thou," or "It." The attitude of "Thou" acknowledges the sacredness of another; "It" reduces people to a discardable "thing." Antipathy is drilled into soldiers going to war. If they were to view the enemy as a "Thou," how could they kill? Likewise, the Nazis reduced Jews to things, and then committed unimaginable atrocities against them.

This is the risk of objectifying others. Abuse is inevitable. Industrial-era management practices, sad to say, encourage antipathy although not to the extremes described previously. The results, however, are similar in principle. How often have you heard, for instance, the expression "people are our company's greatest assets"? This is, in part, a form of antipathy. An asset is a "thing," defined specifically as "a valuable material possession." But people are neither things nor material possessions.

Modern businesses are seen as machines for producing profit. In this light, the needs and interests of employees must be minimized so that profit can be maximized. In this environment, a culture of empathy will be very difficult to develop. Goleman reports that executives find the need for empathy hard to accept:

> A study of 250 executives found that most felt that their work demanded "their heads but not their hearts." Many said they feared that feeling empathy or compassion for those they worked with would put them in conflict with their organizational goals. One felt the idea of sensing the feelings of those who worked for him was absurd—it would, he said, "be impossible to deal with people." Others protested that if they were not emotionally aloof they would be unable to make the "hard" decisions that business requires.

Difficult as it may be, a relationship cannot exist without empathy. The next section offers techniques for developing empathy.

Honoring Differences

John Gray's best-selling book, *Men are from Mars, Women are from Venus*, illustrates the powerful psychological differences between men and women. The very title makes it clear that the sexes are alien to each other. However, Gray did not go far enough with his metaphor. In reality, every single person seems to come from a different planet. Consider just a few of the ways in which people differ:

- There are two different sexes. Males and females have biological differences in how they think, and their socialization leads to very different belief systems and behavioral patterns.

- We are raised in different geographic locations, speak different languages, have different religions, were born in different eras, and have different colored skin.

- We have different parents with unique styles and divergent values.

- Our educational backgrounds are different.

- Our brains work very differently. Some people think quickly, some slowly. Some people are analytical; others are creative. Some people are detail oriented; others are big-picture thinkers. Some people are task oriented; others are relationship oriented. Some people prefer facts; others intuition. Some people are outgoing; some are reserved.

When you consider all of these ways in which people differ, it is a miracle that we can relate to each other at all. Every single person is a marvelous and unique creation. This is the tragedy and the beauty, the curse and the gift, of our differences.

The Tragedy of Prejudice. Humans use mental categories as a way of simplifying the incredible complexity around them. We create labels for people and behaviors that make it easier for us to function, but also lead to distortions and injustice. Labels are a way to prejudge people without having to see them for who they really are. We create a grossly simplified caricature that has little to do with the whole person. We label someone as a "whiner," for instance, and then ignore the many behaviors that bear no relation to whining. We refer to the millions of people who belong to the Democratic party as "liberals," as if every one of them subscribed to the behaviors and ideas that are described as "liberal." We label women as weak and emotional, and then refer to those who are strong and unemotional as "bitches."

> Every single person is a marvelous and unique creation. This is the tragedy and the beauty, the curse and the gift, of our differences.

Labels also create confirmation bias in that we look for the characteristics that we expect to find and ignore the others. In this way, the stereotype is reinforced and we become ever more convinced of how right we are in our judgment of a person or a whole group of people.

Prejudice is an irrational bias toward a group of people. It is a form of labeling that is used to emphasize the superiority of an "in group" over an "out group." Since early times, people have created a sense of belonging by joining together to discriminate against other groups. In some cases, this resulted in warfare; in others it created the subjugation of one or more tribes or castes of people by another. The false sense of superiority that results from prejudice justifies the exploitation and abuse of other people. It reduces the people in the *out group* to objects.

> Ignorance of others is really the only way that prejudice can be sustained.

Prejudice is maintained by "infecting" new generations with biased beliefs and attitudes and by ensuring that the biases are not allowed to be challenged by the facts. Ignorance of others is really the only way that prejudice can be sustained.

Having grown up in the southern United States, I have witnessed prejudice against minorities my whole life. There were times, though, when I was surprised and bewildered to hear a normally bigoted person acknowledge that a particular member of a minority group was "okay." When asked why, the person would say something like, "I work with him every day and know him to be a normal guy like you and me. He's not like the others."

Prejudice is dependent on antipathy. When people get to know each other, they begin to see *people*. The key, then, for developing tolerance is to teach empathy and to create situations where diverse people work closely together toward a common goal. It is also useful to create classes on perspective taking that encourage people to "walk a mile in other people's shoes." One way to do this is to have those involved exchange roles for a time. Perspective-taking can also be learned through exercises and games. In one exercise, the participants must wear a label on their back. They can see everyone else's labels but they cannot see or inquire about their own. One of the labels is designated as a minority and everyone conspires to discriminate against this person. The "minority" is ignored, excluded, laughed at, and avoided—all without knowing what is happening or why. It is a humiliating and humbling experience that provides a small but powerful taste of what it feels like to be the target of focused discrimination.

> As a global society, we can no longer afford the squabbling and warfare over irrational prejudices that have plagued our species for a millennia.

As our world continues to shrink, diverse groups will increasingly be forced into contact with one another. As a global society, we can no longer afford the squabbling and warfare over irrational prejudices that have plagued our species for a millennia. Businesses are already confronting this reality as they seek to create a single corporate identity across multiple countries. In 1996, Texaco was in the news for a scandal that resulted from inflammatory racial comments made by several top executives. Their derogatory and discriminatory remarks were captured on audio tape and then aired repeatedly in the national news. Texaco was painted by the media as a company run by bigoted, white, good-old-boys. Is this an accurate description of the company? Probably not. But the culture of tolerance toward such unacceptable behavior and actions led to the public tar-and-feathering of the whole company. In truth, what happened to Texaco could just as well have happened in any number of corporations that are just as lenient on racism and discrimination.

In the Quantum Organization, there can be no tolerance for discriminatory jokes, slurs, or bias. Companies need to establish and rigorously enforce a no-discrimination policy. It is not possible to force people to change their beliefs, but it is possible to require a change in behavior. And, a change in behavior often stimulates a change in mind.

The Beauty of Diversity. Can you imagine an existence where every person was just like you? Where every day played out in the same predictable way? Where every meal consisted of the same food cooked in the same way? Where every movie featured the same actors and the same plot? I sure can't—that would be a *hell of monotony*. The beauty of diversity is that it creates originality and variety. It makes life interesting. And it has a profound functional role.

In organizations, diversity is a key to strength and adaptability. The more ideas, approaches, and points of view that are expressed, the more options the organization has. Having multiple options dramatically increases flexibility. In this multicultural world, it makes sense for employees in organizations to reflect the ethnic, gender, and cultural mix in the greater society. Diverse people can provide invaluable insights into the values and preferences of various customer segments. In addition, they bring unique perspectives and ideas into the creative mix, further enriching the organization's creative potential.

> In organizations, diversity is a key to strength and adaptability.

Diversity in organizations is not just about race or gender. It is really about diverse ideas and talents. Industrial-age management practices have discouraged creative thought and encouraged homogenous thinking. In Quantum Organizations, this is reversed. Dialogue, another of the meta-skills, is a practice that encourages exploring differing ideas and perspectives. The goal is to create a shared understanding among the participants that emerges when they express their different viewpoints. The result is a much richer and more complete understanding.

Different talents are also essential. John Gardner, a psychologist at Harvard University, has identified eight human intelligences (see Fig. 8.1). Traditional business tends to value just one of these; that of "logical" intelligence. However, each can play a role in organizational excellence. In Quantum Organizations, linguistic, spatial, intrapersonal, and interpersonal intelligences are each as important as logical intelligence.

Gardner's Eight Human Intelligences

Figure 8.1

TYPE	EXAMPLE	DESCRIPTION
1. Linguistic	*Ernest Hemingway* *Maya Angelou*	Communication through language
2. Logical	*Albert Einstein* *Marilyn Vos Savant*	Abstract analytical thought
3. Musical	*Andrew Lloyd Webber* *Barbra Streisand*	Compose or produce music
4. Spatial	*Annie Leibowitz* *Frank Lloyd Wright*	Create visual images
5. Kinesthetic	*Martha Graham* *Michael Jordan*	Physical movement
6. Intrapersonal	*Sigmund Freud* *Carl Yung*	Helps people raise their internal self-awareness
7. Interpersonal	*Mother Teresa* *Mahatma Gandhi*	Awareness of, and responsiveness to, other people's internal states
8. Naturalist	*Jane Goodall* *Charles Darwin*	Insights into Nature

Personality profiles, such as Myers-Briggs or the DISC system, serve to highlight psychological and behavioral preferences. Every person has at least a base-level of competence in each element of these profiles. However, most will have a preference that drives their behavior the majority of the time. A common response is for people to be intolerant of those who have preferences different from their own. An example is creative people denigrating the logical approach of engineers, and vice-versa.

Wisdom would have us leverage the strength of these diverse talents. Let people operate in their preferred mode and appreciate the differences. For example, brainstorming sessions should include people with a high preference for creativity. They are best suited for this particular kind of visioning work. However, a different set of people are better suited for the next stage of work—validating the design. This requires strong analytical skills and attention to details.

Classical management expects the boss to *know everything* and to *do everything* better than anyone else. This has encouraged employees to try to be all things to all people, which is an impossibility and a misuse of talent. As actor Clint Eastwood said in one of his "Dirty Harry" movies, "A man's gotta know his limitations." People need to know both their strengths and non-strengths. Valuing diversity means developing teams around the needed skills and experience, and giving people with the greatest aptitude, responsibility for a particular task. Ultimately, this results in employees making their maximum contribution and enjoying their work. The company benefits by getting the optimal performance from a team.

Personal Boundaries

One of the major causes of problems in relationships is that people do not establish or maintain appropriate personal boundaries. People have different kinds of boundaries, which I have categorized as physical, mental, or spiritual.

- *Physical boundaries* include not only our skin, but also the distance that we prefer to maintain around our bodies. Everyone knows the discomfort that can result from someone standing too close. Physical boundaries also include material things, such as personal possessions, money, time, and energy or effort.

- *Mental boundaries* include our thoughts and beliefs, our emotions, and our intuition.

- *Spiritual boundaries* have to do with our self-esteem, our sense of identity, and our relationship with a higher power such as God.

Boundaries are something that individuals have to decide for themselves. Personal boundaries become dysfunctional when they are either too rigid or too permeable. People who are too rigid avoid others and are excessively independent. They never let anyone touch them at a personal level and refuse assistance from others, preferring to rely wholly on themselves. Those whose boundaries are too loose invade other people's boundaries without regard to or respect for the other's preferences. These people also allow others to freely invade their own boundaries. Feelings of powerlessness and violation result when boundaries are invaded against our wishes. The most evident violations are physical attacks. Mental and spiritual violations are at least as damaging, and maybe more so—they are simply less evident.

Violations of physical boundaries are prosecuted fairly vigorously in our society. Theft, rape, murder, vandalism, and assault are all uniformly denounced as unacceptable behaviors. No one, for instance, would willingly let someone vandalize his or her house by splashing foul-smelling filth on the walls. But many *will* let someone abuse them verbally and psychologically—the equivalent of splashing foul-smelling filth in their mind and soul. The results in both cases are similar. The victim is left to clean up the mess or continue to live in the foul-smelling stench. Many people prefer to live with the stench and simply allow their emotional capacitor to become saturated.

> Feelings of powerlessness and violation result when boundaries are invaded against our wishes.

People have control of their lives and feel powerful when they have effective boundaries, which is when the boundaries are strong but flexible. A healthy inner sense of identity is an important first step in creating effective boundaries. Establishing effective boundaries is essential for taking care of yourself. You take responsibility for your body, mind, and spirit—and do not let anyone trespass those boundaries. You know how to say "no." In business, where boundary violations run rampant, saying "no" is frowned upon. But the happiest people are the ones who do. Excessive overtime is a violation of time and energy boundaries. It also violates employees' family boundaries. Telling people that they don't have a right to feel and appropriately express their emotions, or that their emotions are wrong, is a violation of mental boundaries. Destructive criticizing, yelling, and abusive language are violations of spiritual boundaries.

There is, of course, a right and a wrong way to say "no" to these boundary violations. These are discussed in the section on peace making. Keep in mind, that there is always the chance that saying no will cause other problems, including loss of a job. Regardless, maintaining balance in life requires the ability to say no.

Caretaking. Caretaking is a form of boundary abuse that is usually cloaked under the veil of "being helpful." Caretaking happens when someone does something for another person that the second person could and responsibly would have done. Most of us have heard stories of parents who smother their children by never allowing them to break away and learn to stand on their own. This is caretaking. Caretaking is a fundamental premise of the classical organization, which provides employee benefits and shelters employee salaries against the rise and fall of the company's profitability. The boss is responsible and employees merely have to do what they are told. Caretaking may seem benign, but it is not. It can be just as destructive to self-esteem and psychological balance as any other form of boundary violation.

Projection. Nobody can read another's mind, but that doesn't stop people from trying. A very perceptive person can make consistently accurate guesses about these things, but they are still just guesses. When people assume they know another's motivations, intentions, thoughts, or emotions, they are very likely engaging in a behavior called *projection*. Projection is when one person interprets another person's verbal and nonverbal clues based on personal beliefs and history. They project their own view of the world onto others. This works in the same way that a Rorschach inkblot test works.

A Rorschach blot is a series of abstract images of ink spots on paper. People are shown these blots and asked to describe what they see. Of course, the blots themselves don't depict anything at all, whatever someone sees in them comes from within. Projection works the same way, but the subject is another person's behavior. It is important not to let other people project their inner psychology (eloquently referred to as "their stuff") onto you. Other people can tell you what their perception of you is, but it is up to you to validate whether or not their viewpoint is accurate.

Quantum Organizations rely on effective relationships. Boundary abuses break them down. The quantum employee is expected to demonstrate independence and self-reliance. People who have poor boundary definitions will not be able to do so, because other people run their lives. As a result, Quantum Organizations must create the conditions where personal boundaries are acknowledged and respected.

Self-Disclosure

Relationships cannot develop fully until participants reveal something of their deeper selves to the others in the relationship. Writer and consultant Barbara Shipka explains this through the metaphor of a bead necklace. She equates the beads to individuals on a team (in a relationship). She notes that the beads, which are separate and unique, are held together by an unseen string that passes through the center of each. The beads—joined by this common bond—form a necklace, something that none of them could do alone. The beads, Shipka notes, need to open up on each side in order for the string to pass through and for the common bond to form. It is through *self-disclosure* that these openings are made possible in people.

Self-disclosure is the act of revealing yourself to others—your thoughts, feelings, intentions—telling your story. Another word for self-disclosure is "intimacy." This word is commonly associated with sexuality. But it really refers to familiarity and closeness. Intimacy can be understood better by pronouncing it as "in-to-me-see"—a clear reference to self-disclosure. Why is intimacy so important? It builds understanding, trust, compassion, and commonality—all of which are essential to effective relationships. When you begin to understand other people's stories, your heart softens. You find that their sorrows and joys are similar to yours, and that you have more in common than you ever thought. You draw closer and become more tolerant, more supportive, and more understanding.

Self-disclosure is, for many people, a difficult idea to embrace. The idea of self-disclosure in a business context may seem horrifying to some, and ludicrous to others. These are all responses that are drawn from experiences in traditional organizations and relationships, where there is very little safety and a prevailing environment of hostility and fear. Self-disclosure is something to be approached cautiously. Very few traditional organizations are safe places for self-disclosure. If the corporate environment is not safe, then by no means should you make yourself vulnerable there.

Relationships cannot develop fully until the participants reveal something of their deeper selves to others in the relationship.

True Quantum Organizations, though, must by definition be *safe havens*. It is strong relationships that make these companies work. Anything that advances the development and maintenance of strong relationships needs to be accommodated.

Communication: Reaching Out to Touch Someone

Once you realize that we are all "aliens" trying to find a common language, you can begin to appreciate what a wonder it is that we can communicate at all. The following are a few points that are critical to effective communication:

- *Communication is an end unto itself.* Communication is not just about sending and receiving information. The act of communicating—regardless of the content—is a vehicle for establishing and sustaining relationships.
- *Communication is two-way.* True communication is always a two-way loop—a reciprocal interaction that takes the form of send-receive-confirm.

✠ *Communication is both verbal and nonverbal.* Studies show that the nonverbal content of communication carries much more information than does the verbal.

✠ *Communication contains both fact and feeling.* Most communication is about an exchange of facts. However, there is always a "feeling" element in communications. When it is strong, it will block a person's ability to receive the facts.

Communication Is an End Unto Itself

In business, the prevailing task orientation has led to the use of communication mostly for the exchange of facts. People, however, use communication not just as a means, but also as an end. It is a form of relating that strengthens the bond between individuals. This is true regardless of the content exchanged.

> *Speaking is a skill; communication is a power.*
>
> — Anthony Robbins

In fact, if individuals do not communicate about non-work related topics, it is a safe guess that they will have very weak or nonexistent emotional ties. Women in particular have been noted for their need to connect through talking. However, men do the same thing—they simply choose less personal topics.

In the classical organization, people who are seen standing around talking about matters unrelated to work are seen as wasting time. In our obsession with efficiency, the value of strengthening relationships through casual conversation has been lost. In the Quantum Organization, the importance of this "connect time" is understood and accepted. Since employees are expected to exercise personal leadership, it is their responsibility to choose wisely when to spend time building relationships and when to focus on tasks. Actually, in a healthy organization, the distinction between these become blurred. In the conduct of tasks, it becomes normal to engage in frequent, casual conversation.

Communication Is Two-Way

I have seen numerous examples in business where vitally important information, such as the launch of a major change initiative, is announced through a memo from the CEO. This is supposed to be communication, but it isn't. Communication is a reciprocal exchange that involves one person sending information, and one or more people receiving it and confirming their understanding. In most business communications, the entire focus is on the sending of information—a meager one-third of the complete interaction. This approach is based on the assumption that the receiver has understood what the sender intended. This is a dangerous assumption that is almost never true. Take for instance my use of the word "intimacy" in the previous section. If I had not taken the time to explain my use of the word, can you imagine the misunderstanding that would have resulted? The simple fact is that we cannot know that people understand the words we are using as we *intended* for them to be understood.

> When executives confuse the absence of questions with acceptance and understanding of their message, they have commited a grave error.

Listening is as important to communication as talking. The meta-skill of personal leadership emphasizes the importance of the listener taking responsibility for getting the message. This requires a safe forum where there can be an open exchange between the sender and the receivers of a message. Receivers need the safe-space to ask clarifying and qualifying questions of the sender. A key word in all of this is *safe*. If the sender of a message feels threatened by people questioning the message, the resulting hostility will make for a quick-end to the questions and a breakdown in the communication. Traditional organizations are anything but safe havens for open communication. When executives in these companies confuse the absence of questions with acceptance and understanding of the message, they have committed a grave error.

Communication Is Both Verbal And NonVerbal

All communication contains both verbal and nonverbal information. The nonverbal information derives from four elements of the communication: (1) the body language used, (2) the medium chosen for communicating (a memo vs. a one-on-one conversation), (3) the venue (an auditorium vs. a small luncheon), and (4) the format of the communication (a one-way missive vs. a two-way dialogue). Each of these sends a message of its own, and so should be considered carefully by the sender.

A study by Dr. Albert Mehrabian of UCLA, concluded that 93 percent of the understanding in communication is derived from tone of voice and body language. Body language includes postures (such as being turned toward someone, or away from them), facial expressions (grimacing, smiling), and tonality (for example, speaking loudly, harshly, or with gritted teeth).

> Ninty-three percent of the understanding in communication is derived from tone of voice and body language.

Inconsistency between the verbal message and the corresponding body language create enormous conflict in the listener, particularly if they are children. This creates the situation where the listener does not know which message to believe, and in many cases, causes a double-bind—a damned if you do, damned if you don't situation. An example is telling people that questions are welcomed while sending a bodily message (scowling, frowning, or looking stern) that says "no they are not."

In some organizations, the double-bind is made even more destructive by an injunction against pointing out the double-bind. For instance, it would be completely unacceptable to point out the contradiction between the invitation, "ask questions," and the body language, "don't ask questions." Some people call this behavior "making the unmentionable-unmentionable." This is an insidious disease that completely frustrates any true communication. Esteemed psychiatrist R. D. Laing explains the unmentionable-unmentionable predicament like this: *Rule A:* Do and Don't. *Rule B:* Rule A does not exist. *Rule C:* Do not discuss the existence or nonexistence of rules A or B. Obviously, such conditions cannot continue if a company is to create a quantum culture.

Communication Contains Both Fact And Feeling

In a business context, it is common practice to ignore the fact that humans have emotions. This is a grievous mistake that results in large-scale miscommunication. Humans are emotional creatures. Nothing short of a frontal lobotomy can be done to change that. Feelings will emerge in people, unbidden, any time they experience distress. To ignore this is sheer folly. When strong feelings are invoked, people experience a physiological change in which their ability to think rationally is reduced or even eliminated. If the intention is to communicate successfully, this fact of life must be accepted and made an integral part of effective communication.

Not every communication, of course, provokes an emotional reaction. In such cases, people can focus primarily on sending and receiving facts. However, when feelings do become a factor, the exchange needs to shift from communication to what I call "communi*caring*."

Communicaring is an exchange in which people listen with empathy. It is important to understand that people can have an emotional upset without there being a personal conflict. Executives should understand that change (at least in traditional organizations) always evokes an emotional response. People may not be upset at anyone in particular, and they do not necessarily disagree with the point being made. Communicaring is about helping people get in touch with the upset so they can dispel the emotions that are blocking the communication.

Many people may not see this as their responsibility, and take a "just get over it" attitude. In the spirit of personal leadership and mastery, it *is* the other person's responsibility. However, if *your* goal is to communicate a point and secure another person's

> *I am mystified by the fact that the business world is apparently proud to be seen as hard and uncaring and detached from human values. . . .*
> *I personally don't know how the hell anybody can survive running a business in the nineties without caring.*
>
> — Anita Roddick, Founder of The Body Shop, author of *Body and Soul*

agreement and backing, then it is in your best interest to do what it takes to get the point across. There is one caveat: Although most people who have these upsets get over them quickly—sometimes instantaneously—there are always a few with deep psychological issues who will not respond to communicaring. With these people, you should stop the exchange and, in a separate setting, address your concern about their unresponsiveness despite your repeated efforts to reach out to them. Accept that some people will simply be inconsolable.

When communicaring has been effective, you may see a tangible change in people. They will look lighter, as if a weight has been lifted from them. Their posture will straighten; their face will relax and soften; and they will begin to be more conciliatory and cooperative. Many times people will tell you how much better they feel and will express sincere gratitude and appreciation.

Peace Making: The Care and Feeding of Relationships

Emotional intelligence is probably most important when a relationship must face the crucible of interpersonal conflict. I prefer the term *peace making* over *conflict resolution*, because it encourages action beyond the event in question. It focuses on a desired outcome—peace and harmony—rather than what is not wanted—conflict.

Although it may not seem like it at the time, conflict is a natural and important part of every relationship. It is the mechanism for healing the small "bumps and bruises" that occur in every relationship. Left unhealed, they can escalate to a relationship-threatening level. In fact, the absence of conflict is a clear sign of a relationship in distress.

If there is a problem in your relationship, it is *your* responsibility to address it and restore harmony. It is also the other person's responsibility, but that is not your business—you can only control yourself. It is your responsibility because you have committed to making the relationship work. That means you have decided to place *healing the relationship* as a priority over both the need to be "right" and the desire to avoid the emotional discomfort that conflict causes. This commitment is vital. Without it, peace-making efforts are mostly an endless cycle of acrimony, blaming, fault-finding, denial, and avoidance—conditions that make for "relationship hell."

Sometimes it can be instructive to consider what *not* to do in a relationship. So, I have compiled a list of the top ten actions to take to ensure that your relationship is as *miserable* as possible:

1. Pretend nothing is wrong

2. Be sarcastic and mocking

3. Be defensive

4. Bring up a lot of unrelated issues

5. Insist that the problem is entirely the other person's fault

6. Be self-righteous and convinced you're right

7. Hold a grudge—never forgive, never forget

8. Disregard the other person's feelings

9. Say or do things that are hurtful or cruel

10. Use the silent treatment

Techniques for Peace Making

Even the best relationships run into problems periodically. When this happens, it is important that the people have effective skills for restoring peace and healing the hurt. The ten points above make it clear what not to do. But what are the positive actions a person can take? The following approach can be used to restore harmony in many situations:

1. *State the problem in very specific language.* The person who committed the offense needs to know specifically what behavior caused the problem. In the

heat of emotion, it is common for people to exaggerate with words such as *always* and *never*. Use of this sort of language indicates that the offended person is either not clear why he or she is upset, or is too disturbed, and needs to take more time to cool off.

2. *Explain why it is a problem and how it made you feel.* Once the offender knows what the problem is, they need to know *why* it is a problem. What were the specific consequences? One aspect of this portion of the discussion is to explain how the action made the offended person feel. This is important, because feelings are not something that can be debated. They are neither right nor wrong; they just are. Regardless of whether the offender agrees that the action was inappropriate, amends can be made for what the offended person felt.

3. *Ask for what you want.* The offender also needs to know what the offended person wants to happen in the future. A change in behavior? A task completed or some work redone? An apology? The offender may or may not agree to the request. But without the knowledge of what the offended person wants, there is no chance to make amends.

Consider the example of an exchange between "Steve" and "Sandra." During a meeting, Steve interrupted Sandra several times before she was through talking—so much so that several people commented to her about it after the meeting. So Sandra approached Steve and asked to speak to him in private. Here's a summary of their conversation:

1. Sandra says, "Steve, I noticed that you interrupted me several times while I was talking in the meeting."

2. She goes on to say, "That kept me from completing my thoughts to the group. Also, I felt embarrassed to be cut off like that, and a little bit angry."

3. Then she says, "I need to know if you and I have an unresolved issue that would explain your behavior. Then I want you to quit interrupting me when I am speaking."

4. Steve, who has been listening intently and respectfully, responds: "I realized toward the end of the meeting what I had been doing, and felt bad about it. I wanted to apologize to you. I wasn't really trying to interrupt you. I was simply overly eager to jump into the discussion. I'll be careful in the future but would appreciate it if you could provide me with some ongoing feedback so that I can be sure that the behavior has stopped." At this point, Sandra feels terrific. She thanks Steve, and they go on to talk about other work-related issues.

There are several additional guidelines to follow when using this approach:

✠ *Avoid emotional flooding.* Emotional flooding is common when discussing emotionally charged issues. When this occurs for either party, call a *time-out*. Time-outs are a technique for cooling off. It is a time when everyone should separate and stop thinking about the conflict. Because of the physiological changes that must take place, the time-out period should be as long as is needed to calm down. It is important to note that men tend to flood easier and take longer to cool down.

✠ *Do not become defensive.* This will not help you achieve your goal of restoring peace to the relationship. The opposite of defensiveness is *defenselessness*. Defenselessness helps you to maintain your psychological balance, and increases your ability to think clearly and choose alternative responses. This practice requires detaching from what is being said and not judging it as right or wrong, good or bad. You simply listen and neither agree nor disagree. It can help if you take a moment to center yourself before beginning the discussion.

✠ *Recognize that anger is a secondary emotion.* The issue cannot be resolved until you understand the primary emotion—fear, hurt, or fear of hurt—that the anger is masking.

✠ *Explore to find out why the person feels upset.* If someone is upset at you, you are not necessarily wrong. It could very well be that he or she *personalized* an innocent remark—that is, took a remark or action as having being directed at him or her that wasn't.

✳ *Use "I" language.* This focuses the discussion on what you feel, not what you think the other person thinks or feels. "You" statements are judgmental and threatening, and increase the likelihood of a defensive reaction. Use feeling words in conjunction with the "I" statements. For example, "I felt offended," or "I felt rejected and hurt."

> Relationships skills are no longer a luxury. They are a necessity— both in business and for our global survival.

✳ *Do not tolerate destructive acting out.* Acting out is a dramatization of emotion, such as temper tantrums. Expressing emotions is okay, but only within acceptable limits. It is important for each person to make personal boundaries known and then enforce them as needed.

✳ *Seek win-win outcomes.* Do everything you can to ensure that all of the parties feel good about themselves at the end of the discussion. Extend good will to others—give them the benefit of the doubt. Repeatedly validate that both the relationship and the others' feelings are important to you.

✳ *Criticize the behavior, not the person.* Treat offending people as "Thou." See them in the best possible light, and recognize that it is the behavior that was offensive, not the person.

✳ *Don't sweat the small stuff.* Not all issues are worth bringing up, so pick only the most important to pursue further, and shrug off the remainder.

Although we have covered an enormous amount of material in this chapter, it is only just a beginning for learning about relationships. Some of the ideas presented here may seem daunting when you first read them. Be assured that I have not presented anything I have not learned and put into place in my own life. It has been difficult on occasion, and it has taken a long time. However, the results have been worth it ten times over.

Relationship skills are no longer a luxury. They are a necessity—both in business and for our global survival. I urge you to begin applying these concepts in your life today! Peace on Earth begins one relationship at a time— with you and with me.

Chapter Nine
Dialogue

The test of a first rate intelligence is the ability to hold two opposed ideas in the mind at the same time, and still retain the ability to function.

— F. Scott Fitzgerald

Learning is one of the essential life processes in living systems. Effective learning is based on the ability to see *all* of the available information, change our beliefs and assumptions, and choose new responses. Dialogue is a form of communication that makes this possible. Physicist David Bohm, a major contributor to the resurrection of dialogue as a modern technique, described dialogue in the following way:

> A new kind of mind begins to come into being which is based on the development of common meaning. . . . People are no longer primarily in opposition, nor can they be said to be interacting, rather they are participating in this pool of common meaning, which is capable of constant development and change.

Styles of Communication in Groups

Meetings are ubiquitous in modern organizations. It can seem at times like all a person does is go from one meeting to another—all day long. But what really goes on in these meetings, and what really gets accomplished? If the frustration and dread that people feel toward meetings is any indication—the answer is, "not much." Meetings are a venue for groups of people to share information, make decisions, and learn from one another. In most people's experience, the last of these—group learning—is rarely achieved. As an organization's communication skills mature, the nature of meetings evolves sequentially through four stages. The four stages of group communication include:

1. Open debate

2. Polite debate

3. Skilled discussion

4. Dialogue

Open Debate

There was a beer commercial a few years ago that showed two groups of men arrayed against each other, debating the merits of a particular beer. One group would shout "Tastes Great!" and the other group would shout, just as loud, "Less Filling." Of course, the conflict was never resolved. This is an example of what goes on in many meetings. Each person or faction brings a point of view and personal agenda to the meeting and then forcefully advocates them. The intention is to convert the other people at the table—to "win" the debate. And since this is what everybody else is doing as well, such meetings degenerate into a contest of wills.

Polite Debate

Open debate is characterized by barely controlled pandemonium. Many people talk at once, frequently interrupting each other; the discussion goes off on tangents; participants wander out of the room; a point is decided on and then brought back up repeatedly; and a few people dominate while many sit and watch. These meetings are often openly or covertly hostile. Some companies decide that they will not tolerate such behavior and implement standards of conduct. Meetings then become *polite debates*. Participants talk one at a time, don't interrupt, stay in the meeting, and follow the protocols. It is all really quite civilized. However, the same basic structure is still in place. Each person is still trying to "win" their point of view.

Skilled Discussion

As group communication skills mature in organizations, meetings become more thoughtful and focus more on learning. They take on many of the characteristics of dialogue as described in the next section, and can be very productive. One main difference is that the intention of discussion is to make a decision, whereas the purpose of dialogue is to create a greater understanding. Skilled discussion is an important tool for use in conjunction with dialogue.

Dialogue

Dialogue is the highest form of group communication and the principle tool for group learning. It focuses on developing a common understanding, not on making a decision or taking an action although these often result naturally from the process. In debate, people communicate with the intention of changing *others*, but in dialogue the intention of communication is to change *yourself*—your own mental models and ways of thinking about a topic. In debate, participants assume only one alternative can be chosen as best. Dialogue, in contrast, recognizes paradox as a natural characteristic of human perception. In dialogue, participants recognize that two truths do not need to be mutually exclusive. In the book *Built to Last*, the authors describe this as the "Genius of the AND" and the "Tyranny of the OR." They point out that the best companies have the ability to "embrace both extremes of a number of dimensions at the same time." The "Genius of the AND" is a fundamental competence of the Quantum Organization, and a basic tenet of dialogue.

> Dialogue recognizes paradox as a natural characteristic of human perception.

Creating A Common Field of Understanding

The Sufi tale of four blind men and an elephant is a wonderful metaphor for group learning. The story begins with four blind men who encounter an elephant for the first time. The first grabbed the tail, and exclaimed, "It is like a rope, long and narrow." The second, stumbling into the elephant's leg, said, "You are wrong, it is like a great tree trunk." A third, grasping the elephant's ear, added his perspective, "But I am feeling it too and it is like a great broad leaf!" The last blind man, after grabbing the elephant's trunk, cried out, "You are all wrong—an elephant is like a great hollow pipe!" The parable concludes by observing that "given these men's way of knowing, they will never know an elephant."

The four blind men are like participants in a typical fact-finding or problem-solving meeting. Each has direct personal experience of the problem, and so feels justified in asserting that they know the "truth." Because they are convinced that they are right; each man assumes that it is impossible for any other perspective to also be correct. And since all four blind men are convinced of their own truths, the meeting will remain hopelessly deadlocked. Eventually the Sufi CEO will be forced to make a decision and choose which of the four is the "one right answer." This decision becomes the basis for all future action in regard to elephants. If this were a company deciding on its strategic direction based on such a narrow viewpoint, imagine the difficulties that it would encounter!

The classical command-and-control management style adds another problem to the "debate" approach. Under classical management, once the official viewpoint is adopted, it can no longer be questioned or challenged. When information inevitably surfaces that an "elephant" is much more than a "great tree trunk," for instance, employees are forced to ignore this information—to continue on as if this discrepancy did not exist. It is no small wonder, then, that problem solving is frequently futile. It is impossible to solve a problem that arose because of an error in perception by trying to make an "ear" (the new information) become a "leg" (the official position). These are some of the factors that explain why companies get so far out of sync with the marketplace.

It is easy to see how absurd it is to think that an elephant has only one of the four characteristics. Since you and I have seen and comprehend the whole elephant, we know that these blind men are only seeing smaller parts of the bigger picture. Their different perspectives stem from experiencing only the small piece of the elephant that is available from where they stand. Their error is in assuming that they alone know the truth about elephants.

It is not so easy, however, to recognize similar absurdities in our own thinking. When we are in the place of the Sufi blind men, we do not have the perspective of the whole, and so we fall into the same trap that they did. The function of dialogue is to create a field of understanding so a comprehensive view of the elephant can emerge.

Barriers to Dialogue

Classical organizations were specifically designed to restrict the flow of information, interaction, and diversity. It is obvious that dialogue, which requires all three of these conditions, will be counter to the prevailing culture. Some of the barriers to dialogue in traditional companies include:

✳ *Internal competition.* In classical organizations, the people who get promoted are often the ones who "win" the most in meetings. They are seen as smarter and more capable than other people. The winners are granted more informal influence, and confirmation bias ensures that their ideas continue to be favored. To admit being wrong is a sign of weakness, so people advocate their positions strenuously. After all, their careers may depend on it.

✳ *Ego-identification with ideas.* Few people in bureaucratic organizations have mastered personal leadership. Instead of realizing that their true self is separate from their ideas, they believe that they *are* their ideas. This is reinforced by the common practice of judging people by their ideas. When the rejection of your idea becomes a rejection of you personally, your motivation to "win" becomes extreme, and "losing" becomes a major blow to your self-esteem and confidence.

- *Belief that truth and knowledge can be certain and complete*. The belief of the Newtonian-Cartesian worldview is that knowledge is certain and absolute. When people feel certain about their knowledge, there is no tolerance for contradictory information.
- *Belief that the "boss" knows everything*. The industrial-era belief that the boss is the smartest person and is always right is still alive and well in many companies. This mind-set stymies further learning.
- *Hierarchy limits who can contribute*. In command-and-control organizations, employees are expected to know their places in the hierarchy. Many people are justifiably afraid to speak up in meetings where senior managers are present. I am constantly approached in the hallway after meetings by participants who say, "I was afraid to say this in the meeting, but I want to you to know . . ." Such limitations on the sharing of information make for ill-informed decisions and poor organizational performance.
- *Certain implicit rules are unmentionable*. In classical organizations, many of the most dysfunctional and destructive rules cannot be mentioned. Who would question an egotistical CEO about the rule that states he or she is always right? Everyone continues on knowing full well that the rule is invalid and damaging but seemingly powerless to do anything about it.
- *The existence of unmentionable rules is unmentionable*. The clincher is that no one is allowed to mention that unmentionable rules even exist. This crushes any hope that the underlying rule will be changed or eliminated, thus trapping the organization in rigid and maladaptive behaviors.

Creating Dialogue

The objective of dialogue is to create a new level of understanding that is shared by all of the participants and that transcends each of their individual viewpoints. Dialogue brings together the meta-skills of personal leadership, personal mastery, and relationship in a group learning environment. The ingredients for successful dialogue include:

- Openness and self-disclosure
- Defenselessness
- Suspending assumptions and judgments
- Diversity of opinions and perspectives
- Equality of ideas
- Thoughtfulness and careful consideration
- Expert facilitation

Dialogue entails every participant sharing a unique perspective on a matter. Everyone is expected to contribute as equals, with the focus being on the ideas, not on the contributors. If hierarchy is still prominent in the organization, it should be suspended during the course of the session. Everyone understands at the outset that every perspective is a valid—albeit limited—view of a greater whole. Two or more contradictory points may be held as true, with the awareness that their validity relies on where one stands to view the issue.

> Dialogue entails every participant sharing a unique perspective on a matter.

Statements are made to the center of the group rather than to specific individuals. This helps the group focus on the ideas being presented and away from personalities. It also reinforces that this is a process that belongs to the whole group. As people share a viewpoint, they are expected to identify and explain the assumptions on which their points are based. This requires a great deal of self-disclosure, of "in-to-me-see," that participants need to be confident enough to provide.

Others in the group will openly inquire into the assumptions. In doing this, they should avoid judging people for their ideas, a practice that would quickly destroy the field of trust and openness that is necessary for dialogue to succeed. The responsibility of the participants is not to analyze the ideas from their own viewpoint, but to take another person's standpoint to see the issue. Group inquiry serves to clarify the source, meaning, and validity of the assumptions underlying the various ideas presented. Having a group of people scrutinize your rationale can be a threatening experience. It is important for all participants to exercise defenselessness. They need to be able to view their ideas objectively—to stand aside from them and observe them unemotionally. By relinquishing ownership and treating ideas as belonging to the whole group, people can become merely participants inquiring into an idea—even though they initially contributed it.

Disagreement is an essential aspect of dialogue. The suppression of differences with the intention of preserving the peace, which is so common in "group-think," is anathema to the dialogue process. Dialogue thrives on diversity—the whole idea is to gain the broadest possible perspective on an issue. Obstructions to the flow of information will undermine the effectiveness of the overall process.

> Dialogue thrives on diversity—the whole idea is to gain the broadest possible perspective on an issue.

Dialogue differs from debate in that it has a much slower pace. Silence is more prevalent as people consider new ideas and understandings. In comparison to temperature, debate is "white hot" and dialogue is "cool blue." In facilitating these sessions, I often note that the "temperature" of the interactions is rising, and that a cooling-off period is needed. Skilled facilitators are important, particularly in the early stages of learning the new skills. Their primary role is to reflect the group back to itself. This feedback helps the participants learn new behaviors and responses. While guiding the session, facilitators both teach the principles of the four meta-skills and provide a model through their conduct.

The Potential for Dialogue

Dialogue is a powerful tool for shaping well-rounded comprehension of complex issues. It promotes collaboration and increases collective intelligence. The benefits for business are increased effectiveness and responsiveness. The use of dialogue also raises the level of shared understanding and trust. This contributes directly to the organization's ability to respond quickly and effectively to new challenges. The depth of the thinking involved provides the participants with a much wider range of alternatives that can be brought to bear in everyday decision making.

In a broader social context, dialogue benefits any groups that are engaged in win-lose struggles. These polarized conflicts are pervasive in our society:

- Pro-choice vs. Pro-life
- Conservative vs. Liberal
- White People vs. People of Color
- Rich vs. Poor
- First-World Countries vs. Third-World Countries
- Environmentalists vs. Industrialists
- Management vs. Labor
- Religion vs. Religion
- Gun Control Advocates vs. The National Rifle Association
- Gay Rights vs. Religious Fundamentalism

None of these conflicts need remain this way. As a society, we can choose peace over our need to be right on these points and join together to find new alternatives that break the age-old stalemate in these either-or contests. Dialogue—the creation of common understanding—is a light that we can use to find our way out of the dark hole of misunderstanding and strife that we have dug for ourselves. We have the power to change, but we must choose to use it. In the words of John F. Kennedy, "If not now, when? If not us, who?"

EPILOGUE

*You see things that are and say
"Why?" But I dream things that
never were and say "Why not?"*
— George Bernard Shaw

Chapter Ten
For Our Children

*We must be the change we wish
to see in the world.*

— Mahatma Gandhi

Recently as I stood watching my four year-old-son sleep—peacefully snuggled
into his blankets—I wondered to myself, "What kind of future are we creating for
him and the other children of this world?" I thought about the hopes that I have
for him, how I want him to:

Be loved ✳ Be happy and healthy and safe ✳ Be free ✳ Experience
the beauty and majesty of Nature ✳ View life as interesting and
exciting ✳ Make a meaningful contribution to the world ✳ Know
that his life matters ✳ Feel connected to other people and to know
that he belongs ✳ Earn enough money to afford a comfortable
lifestyle ✳ Have fun and enjoy life ✳ Experience peace

These are not just my individual yearnings. I know that all parents have similar
hopes for their children. No matter who they are—what job title they hold, how
wealthy they are, how old they are, whether they are married or single, black,
white, or yellow—their hopes for their children are basically the same.

Because we all share such aspirations, they form our collective hopes and dreams. People join together in communities in order to bring their aspirations to life. At some deep level we have always known that when people come together they create something more than the sum of the individuals involved. A group forms a new consciousness; a new life. These collective forums—our organizations and institutions—are living systems. An organization's mind is the collective mind of the people in it; its heart the collective heart; its dream the collective dream. It should follow then that our institutions—the collective "us"— want the same things that we as individuals want.

Why, then, are we making the world what it is? The social conditions I see are not those of my personal vision. Are they yours? Who among us wishes for war, widespread poverty and drastic income disparities, a hundred-million starving children, heart disease and cancer, a drug-addicted society, governmental bureaucracy and ineptitude, widespread environmental devastation and pollution, exploding population levels,

> *The greatest challenge of the day is to bring about a revolution of the heart, a revolution that has to start with each one of us.*
>
> — Dorothy Day

teenage pregnancy and suicide, or epidemic levels of crime, fear, and anxiety? If we want to produce different conditions in our society—to achieve our hopes and dreams—we must accept that we will have to make fundamental changes in ourselves, in our organizations, and in our institutions.

Our global society is at a bifurcation point—the point in which living systems operating at the edge of chaos either leap to new and novel forms of order and stability or disintegrate into complete disorder. Left to run its course, there is no way to know how the results of this "quantum" leap will turn out. However, human systems are not governed by the "hard wiring" that biological organisms are. We can consciously influence our future—we can "stack the odds" so to speak. We will only hurt ourselves by continuing with the mind-sets, approaches, and practices that put us in this situation to start with.

The concepts emerging from the science of living systems hold tremendous promise for the future of humankind. For the first time, we have a viable alternative to the machine metaphor that has dominated our collective worldview for the last three centuries. The new metaphor is that of a web—a web of life—a dynamic, interconnected network of relationships in a never-ending dance of co-creation and co-evolution. The full integration of these concepts into society will provide the foundation for humankind to evolve to a higher level of being. We will have the legitimate opportunity to achieve a new order, to fully realize our unexpressed potential. In the words of Dee Hock:

> We are at that very point in time when a 400-year-old age is dying and another is struggling to be born—a shifting of culture, science, society and institutions enormously greater than the world has ever experienced. Ahead, the possibility of the regeneration of individuality, liberty, community, and ethics such as the world has never known, and a harmony with nature, with one another, and with the divine intelligence such as the world has never dreamed.

I have confidence in the human spirit and faith in Nature's processes. I thrill to the possibilities of what lies just over our time horizon. I cannot help but think that the emergence of the quantum worldview at this time in our history foreshadows our evolutionary path. We stand poised at the edge of chaos, and the universe holds its breath.

The Wonders of Quantum Physics

Science has come full circle. Prior to the scientific revolution, and in many non-Western cultures even today, people lived in an "enchanted" world, filled with consciousness, purpose and meaning. Rocks, trees, rivers and clouds were all seen as wondrous and alive. It was a world of relatedness and connection, and humankind was a full and active participant. In this worldview, nature was unknowable, magical and mysterious, dangerous and supportive. People were at times fearful of nature, but they were never in any way *alienated* from her, or from their own spiritual heritage. Then, in the 1600's, the architects of Newtonian-Cartesian thinking ended all that. Their world was that of a deterministic machine—lifeless, purposeless, filled with inert objects "hurrying around endlessly and meaninglessly." These machine objects could be taken apart, studied, and put back together again with nothing lost—they were the sum of their parts, nothing more and nothing less. Humans, and everything else, were separate, isolated, unrelated in any way but by coincidence, possessing neither spirit nor consciousness. Nature became ours to exploit, to "torture" into doing our bidding. She had absolute properties of space, time and matter that were mathematical, linear and predictable. It was a hostile world where we must constantly struggle to survive, and where everything teeters on the verge of collapse—held together only by the strength of our will.

With the findings of the new science, we have returned to our nature home. In this new/ancient worldview, nature is vibrantly, dynamically alive, constantly changing, unpredictable, intrinsically unknowable. It is shape-shifting energy dancing a never-ending tribute to life. Human consciousness has an integral part in this cosmic dance, participating actively and joyfully in bringing the universe into being. Life is steeped in meaning and purpose and it is we who put it there. Nature is characterized by dynamic balance, by flow, by improvisation and by an intrinsic urge to evolve to higher levels of complexity. She finds her own way, keeps her own schedules, and moves in circles.

We will begin our journey into the wonder-filled world of quantum science with Albert Einstein's discoveries, because it was his theories of relativity that catapulted physicists into the exploration of the atomic world with all of its innate strangeness.

Every "Thing" Is Energy

"Do you know what Einstein discovered?" I remember being in fourth grade and posing this question to Beth (the most beautiful girl in the school) in an effort to show off. She just stood there, looking at me the way cows look at passing cars. "$E=mc^2!$" I enthusiastically answered for her. She was *not* impressed... neither with me nor with that little bit of trivia. Of course I didn't have a clue what the equation meant, but I knew Einstein was important, so "$E=mc^2$" must have meant something important too. "Important" was a gross understatement. Einstein's famous equation heralded the beginning of a new age for science and foreshadowed the end of the Newtonian-Cartesian worldview.

Michael Faraday and Clerk Maxwell were the first people to go beyond Newtonian physics when they investigated the idea of a new kind of "force field." In 1873, they originated the theory of *electrodynamics,* which is based on the concept that *fields* were real in their own right, without reference to material bodies. These ideas culminated in the thought that light was a rapidly alternating electromagnetic field that moved through space in the form of a wave. Their conclusions led through the years to Albert Einstein who developed the theory of relativity, one of the two pillars of modern physics (the second being quantum mechanics).

Newton, the father of classical physics, based his laws of motion on three assumptions involving the absolute, fixed and separate properties of space, time, and matter. Einstein's Special and General Theories of Relativity showed that on very small and very large scales, these assumptions were *invalid*. With this discovery, three of Newtonian science's foundation stones crumbled to pieces. Relativity proved that space and time were actually related characteristics of the same phenomena. There wasn't space *and* time, but a four-dimensional continuum, *space-time*. It also contributed the now famous theory of the interconvertibility of mass and energy, $E=mc^2$.

The theory of relativity was as earth-shattering for Newtonian science as Newtonian science had been for the Church in the 1600's. However, it is important to note one very significant difference. The Newtonian-Cartesian model ruled out the previous world view entirely, claiming to be the only true model—complete without reference to anything else. Advocates of the Newtonian-Cartesian worldview set out to methodically destroy every last vestige of the organic, god-centered view that preceded it. A dogmatic and repressive Church view was replaced by a dogmatic and repressive Newtonian view.

The new science, in contrast, incorporates the Newtonian science, it does not discard it. Despite certain of Newton's assumptions being invalid, his science is still essential for putting people on the moon (and getting them back). It is basically useless though, for understanding the behavior of large groups of agents in complex living systems.

Atomic Shock Syndrome

Einstein's Special Theory of Relativity included the mathematical formula that I tried so hard to impress Beth with, $E=mc^2$. In this formula, energy (E) is equivalent to mass (m) times the speed of light squared (c^2). (If you ever wondered how splitting something as small as an atom generates the power of a nuclear explosion, it will help you to know that the speed of light squared is almost *35 billion* mi./sec. That's a *lot* of energy.) We are all familiar with the idea that the electricity that makes our computers work is energy. Quantum physics says that in addition, you, the chair you are sitting on, the air you're breathing and this book are all fields of energy—great clouds of it. In fact the only thing that really exists are these fields of energy, pervading all of space. It seems like a rather large leap of faith to accept that all of these tangible things around us, not to mention our own bodies, are really energy just because some abstract mathematical formula says so. I call this disbelief "atomic shock syndrome"— these ideas are just too alien to both our classical worldview and our experience of the macro-world to accept them without resistance. It will help our understanding if we start with a review of what we know about atoms.

Most of us were taught in science class that the nucleus of an atom is made of hard balls of protons and neutrons, and that spinning closely around the nucleus are hard little balls of matter called electrons. Well, you can forget all of that. Atoms are actually very strange. To start with, atoms aren't made of anything solid. They are made of energy and are almost entirely comprised of empty space. The following description, based on Fritjof Capra's metaphor, illustrates the current understanding of an atom and its components.

If we could blow an orange up to the size of the Earth, the atoms in it would be the size of cherries, and they would be packed in very densely. But that's nothing compared to how tiny the elements of an atom are. We would have no hope of seeing the sub-atomic elements in that cherry-sized atom. We would have to blow the atom up to the size of a large auditorium, like the Sydney Opera House in Australia. In an atom that big, the nucleus would be the size of tiny pebble. The electrons, which are 200 times smaller than the nucleus, would be no bigger than a dust mote, and they would be circling way out there at the edge of the building. All of the rest of the atom is just space, there is practically no mass (matter) at all in an atom.

When I first learned this, my immediate reaction was to ask, "If atoms are made up of all that empty space, why does everything seem so solid? Why can't we just put our hand through solid doors or walk through walls?" The answer points to a trick of perception. If you have a ceiling fan, you know that when it is not moving, you have no difficulty putting your arm up through the empty space between the blades. There is plenty of room, at least 75 percent of the area covered by the blades is empty space. However, if you turn the fan on its highest setting, it will begin to look like a solid disc. If you (foolishly) try to put your arm up through the spaces between the blades, your fingers would bounce off as if it were a solid surface. This is what happens with atoms. The electrons in an atom are moving very fast—600 miles per *second*—making them appear as if they are a rigid, solid sphere. Even more astonishing, the particles in the nucleus are moving at the much faster speed of 40,000 mi./sec.! It is these speeds that approach the velocity of light that bring the theory of relativity into play at the atomic level.

Atomic Particles Are Indestructibly Destructible

We will never be able to see actual images of an atom. In order for us to see something, photons must bounce off the object and then strike the retina in our eye. When photons encounter an electron, it is like pool balls crashing together at a thousand miles per second, they are knocked about or smashed to pieces. In fact, it is through just this act of destruction that one of sub-atomic physic's most interesting events take place.

Atoms have two kinds of energy: that which is stored as mass in the atom and the energy associated with movement, called *kinetic* energy. When two particles collide one or both may be smashed to bits. The purpose of those huge, expensive, donut shaped "particle accelerators" is to crash particles together at high speeds to see what kind of sub-particles will result. (Approximately 200 of the of these particles have been identified thus far.) It is not surprising that the particles break into pieces, what is amazing is that the pieces are *not any smaller than the original particles*. "But," the astonished reader may ask, "how can that be? When something breaks into parts, the parts have to be smaller!" True, but not when we are talking about atoms. The reason for this is $E=mc^2$ (energy and mass are interconvertible). The original particles are destroyed, but their *kinetic* energy is converted to *mass* to form new particles of equal size.

These atomic collisions are going on constantly. Particles from the atoms in your body are colliding with and exchanging energy with everything around you in your environment. Cosmic rays, showering down on the earth's atmosphere create a rain of high speed particles that both destroy and create particles in collision after collision—a ceaseless dance of birth and death, creation and destruction. This is the death/rebirth motif at its most fundamental expression. Everything is lost, nothing is lost. Everything changes, nothing changes. What a beautiful counterpoint to our usual fear and apprehension regarding the destructive aspect of change!

Something From Nothing and Then Back Again

Space isn't really empty. It is actually filled with atomic particles/fields. In quantum field theory these are called "virtual particles," and they are symbolized through "vacuum diagrams." These particles have a unique behavior in that they come into existence from nowhere and then disappear just as quickly back into nowhere. The "empty void " is actually filled with atomic particles that cannot be separated from the space that surrounds them. These particles wink into and out of existence . . . all of the time . . . everywhere . . . in a dynamic, rhythmic dance of cosmic potentialities.

A World of Paradox

Now that we know that electrons aren't the solid little particles of matter circling a nucleus that we were taught, we are left with the question: "What are they?" Well, as a matter of fact, no one knows for sure *what* they are. Physicists uncovered the first quantum paradox in the 1920's. An international group of distinguished scientists determined that sub-atomic particles have a dual aspect which depended on how we look at them. The "dual aspect" that the scientists discovered refers to the nature of sub-atomic phenomena to have the characteristics of both particles *and* waves. This was supposed to be *impossible*. Particles are confined to a small area and can be thought of as objects. Waves are spread out like clouds over a large region of space. Nevertheless, the famous "split screen experiment" demonstrated beyond a doubt that a single photon of light behaved like a particle in one experiment, and like a wave in another experiment. With these findings, three more foundation stones of Newton's classical physics came crashing down. These included:

✠ The belief in a universe populated by lifeless matter

✠ That the scientific method could reveal the universe with absolute certainty

✠ That humans were objective (non-participating) observers who did not influence in any way what was being observed.

In the split screen experiment, a single photon of light is fired through a screen that has two slits in it. When only one of the slits was open, the photon went through like the particle that it was thought to be. When both slits were opened, the scientists expected the particle to go through one *or* the other of the slits, since a single particle could only go through one of them. Instead, the photon spread out and went through *both* slits, a wave behavior.

This was a perplexing development. Nothing in the physicist's models of the universe accounted for this paradox. In addition, a new question was raised, How did the photon *know* when only one slit or when both slits were open? How did it know to manifest one time as a particle, and another time as a wave? The answer—as strange as it sounds—was that the photon manifested the characteristic that the scientists were testing for! Saying this differently, it was *the scientist's expectations and method of measuring* the photon that determined whether it would be a particle or wave.

This is a *staggering* discovery. Somehow, the particles manifest in the manner that is expected by the observer. No longer can we pretend to be objective observers of our universe. Our very act of observing *changes* what is being observed, and may even *create* it. We are active participants in the cosmic dance and it is our consciousness that in large measure determines the world that we see.

Heisenberg's Uncertainty Principle

Not only does the wave/particle duality present a paradox, it makes it impossible to ever fully know what is happening in quantum events. Quantum phenomena have pairs of characteristics such as wave-particle and position-velocity. It seems that in the quantum world, the more you know about one characteristic in the pair of attributes (such as "position"), the less you can know about the other (in this case, "velocity"). You can know where a particle is, but not how fast it is going; or how fast it is going, but not where it is. Werner Heisenberg contributed a set of mathematical equations, called the *uncertainty principle*, to calculate the trade-off between these pairs of characteristics. In essence, Heisenberg has affirmed that science *can no longer be certain and absolute*, and that the true nature of reality is intrinsically *unknowable*. For quantum physicists, the answer to every question could quite easily begin with "It depends."

Of course, the wave-particle dilemma really isn't a paradox. We see a paradox because of the limitations of our system of perception and thought— we simply do not have a mental model that explains the reality of the sub-atomic world. Niels Bohr has stepped in to help reconcile the paradox of duality through his concept of *complementarity*. Using this approach, he treats each view as equally valid but limited to only part of the total picture. "The particle picture and the wave picture [are] two complementary descriptions of the same reality," he explained, "each of them only partly correct and having a limited range of application."

Schrödinger's Cat

Quantum science gets even stranger. As we have seen, there are no particles, there are only fields of energy. But they aren't really fields of energy either. They are only *probabilities*, because we cannot calculate when or where the sub-atomic event will occur (Heisenberg's uncertainty principle). So, they aren't real things in a classical sense, they are abstract concepts with "tendencies to exist" which scientists call "probability waves" (or "wave functions"). One of the characteristics of these probability waves is that they do not seem to come into existence *until they are measured*. It is the act of observing them that causes them to manifest. Prior to being measured, all of the possibilities still exist. However, the instant they are measured (observed), one outcome manifests and all of the other potential probability waves "collapse." (Another theory, called the "Many Worlds Interpretation" is that all of the potentialities manifest and each splits off into an "alternative universe.")

Erwin Schrödinger illustrated this dilemma with his famous thought experiment, "Schrödinger's Cat." A cat is placed in a closed box. A mechanism is set to release poisonous gas based on a random event—either the gas will be released or it won't, there is no way to know ahead of time. Then, the moment passes and the cat's fate is sealed—either it is dead or alive. Or is it? According to quantum physics, the wave functions for both outcomes exist at the same time. The cat is both dead *and* alive. Neither of these potentialities manifest until an observer opens the box. Then one of the wave functions comes into being, and the other collapses.

Our universe is one of infinite potential. I am reminded of all of the business decisions that I have witnessed where the decision was cast as an "either/or" choice between two alternatives. "Either I'm right or he is," or "either we centralize or decentralize," or "either we lose money or we layoff 5,000 employees." The concept of wave functions helps me to see with new eyes the power contained in our act of choosing. Before we decide, our choices are infinite and varied, not limited to just two with an "either/or" guillotine hanging over them. It is not until we finally choose that all of the other possibilities collapse and just the one remains. At the same time, this choice gives rise to an infinite number of alternatives for our next choice.

A Single Unified Web of Life

The wave functions that held Schrödinger's Cat's fate are not really probabilities of "things." They are probabilities of *interactions*. It seems that *interconnections* are the fabric of the universe. Particles themselves are abstractions whose properties are, as Niels Bohr explains, "definable and observable only through their interactions with other systems." In this way, it is the *whole* that gives rise to the behavior of the *parts*—a complete reversal of classical science which holds that the properties of the parts give rise to the whole.

The End of "Cause and Effect"

And quantum science is stranger even yet. The interconnections at the sub-atomic level which we have just discussed are both local and *non-local*. By non-local, we mean that a probability wave can be connected to anywhere else in the universe. And here's the topper—the connection is *instantaneous*, what is called "action-at-a-distance." Einstein couldn't accept this. Nothing was supposed to travel faster than light, which although extremely fast, still takes time to travel. These non-local connections, however, happen instantly, no time transpires between the two interactions, no matter how far apart they are!

Einstein protested bitterly, exclaiming in a famous debate with Niels Bohr that "God does not play dice!" To prove it, he developed the renowned EPR thought experiment. In this experiment, two atomic particles are correlated, which means they are given opposite spins such that the sum of their spins equals zero. At this point, the experimenter knows that the particles are spinning in exactly opposite directions, but not what axis the particles are spinning on. They could be spinning up and down vertically, left or right horizontally, or in any other direction. The particles are then separated by a distance that could theoretically be completely across the universe. When the experimenter measures the spin of one of the particles, she will have chosen an axis. Instantaneously, across the universe, the second particle would have to show an opposite spin along the same axis. But how would the second particle know—from so far away—*which* axis the experimenter chose to measure?

Unfortunately for Einstein, in 1964 physicist John Bell constructed a mathematical proof (Bell's Theorem) of these non-local correlated connections. Then, in 1982, French physicist Alain Aspect devised an experiment which demonstrated that "elementary particles are, indeed, affected by connections that exist unseen across space and time." With this conclusion, the Cartesian notion of definite causes and effects, which had already been eroding, finally collapsed.

The Bootstrap Approach

Can it be, then, that the universe really is a single unified whole? In the early 1960's, Geoffrey Chew proposed just this with his philosophical foundation for "S-matrix" theory. Other scientists were still on a "cowboy safari" in search of nature's basic building blocks. The formulations they developed (such as Feynman Diagrams) are principally concerned with the identity and behavior of individual particles. Chew's theory, also known as the "bootstrap" approach, takes the position that nature cannot be reduced to fundamental entities but instead must be understood entirely through self-consistency. The properties of any part of the "web" follow from the interrelations with other parts of the web, and "the overall consistency of their interrelations determines the structure of the entire web." S-matrix diagrams represent only the *interactions*, not the particles— "the dance rather than the dancers is of primary importance."

At the sub-atomic level, we find a universe of interconnections connecting to other interconnections, a vast web of relationships connecting all of the universe, instantaneously. It is scary to think of our leading scientists sitting with new age pop idols chanting "all is one," but that, in fact, seems to be the scientific reality of the universe. If the central metaphor of classical physics is that of a clock, the central metaphor for quantum physics is that of a web. This web is comprised of interrelated and interpenetrating patterns of dynamic, living energy engaged in a constant dance of creation and destruction.

Flowering "Fields" of Thought

From a business management viewpoint, one of the most exciting concepts to emerge out of quantum science is that of *energy fields*. For instance, what is it that gives different companies (or homes, churches, communities and other institutions for that matter) their distinct feel? I pay particular attention to the "feel" of a company when I first walk into their offices. That is the point at which it is most discernible for me. Every company that I have encountered has its own ambiance, its own atmosphere. Some are energetic and upbeat, some are serious and others fun, some are anxious and fearful and some are relaxed, and some are mortuaries of the living dead. I can perceive this before ever conducting the first interview. Many people have had this experience. "Shelly," a public relations consultant, describes one of her clients as being "energy vampires." She describes an environment in which everything drags along, energy is low, there is no enthusiasm or resilience. At the end of the day at this company, she goes home exhausted, with all of the energy drained out of her, "Although I usually stay up until past midnight on most evenings with no problem, after a day with that company, I collapse in bed exhausted by nine o'clock." This "atmosphere" that organizations develop can be thought of as an energy field, one which pervades every aspect of the organization.

Physicists have postulated four kinds of energetic force fields: strong, weak, gravitational and electromagnetic. Strong interactions are the glue that holds the nucleus of atoms together and, as the name implies, it is the strongest of the forces. Weak and electromagnetic forces have to do with interactions of other kinds of atomic particles. Gravity, as we all know, involves the attractive quality of large masses of matter.

According to quantum field theory, fields exist everywhere at the atomic level. These are not really "fields" as we think of them, they are (like all atomic phenomena) *interactions*. Atomic elements are in a constant dance in which they collide with each other, take on energy, and give off energy in the form of photons (or their equivalent). Particles both emit and reabsorb these photons and absorb those of other particles. These interactions either attract particles to each other or repel them from each other. These exchanges are what we call "electrodynamic forces" but in fact are *energetic interactions*—a unified web of atomic relationships.

Holographic Fields

David Bohm, an eminent physicist, saw fields as whirlpools in a single cosmic ocean. It is the unity of this cosmic ocean that explains the non-local connectedness of quantum events. Bohm imagined a "deeper order of existence, a vast and more primary level of reality that gives birth to all the objects and appearances of our physical world." The lenses of our perception draw from this unseen order manifestations which we experience as our external reality. He calls this hidden realm the *implicate* or "enfolded" order, and the external reality the *explicate* or "unfolded" order. In his view, our "perceptual lenses" are constantly changing, and so different aspects of the enfolded order are constantly unfolding to us. The following example illustrates this concept.

Recall the tale of the Sufi elephant from chapter 9, "Dialogue." This elephant is the implicate order. All of the potential characteristics of this elephant (a leaf, a rope, a tree, a pipe) already exist, but they are enfolded, they do not manifest until we turn our attention to them. When we approach the elephant from one perspective, the tail "unfolds" from the totality of the elephant, and we see the elephant as a rope. When we approach from another angle (use a different perceptual lens), the ear unfolds from the totality of the elephant, and we see the elephant as a great leaf. The elephant has never changed, only our way of viewing it has. In effect, we are "blind"—unable to see or ever know the full reality of the elephant—so we have only our direct and limited experience of it.

Bohm uses the metaphor of a *hologram* to explain the functioning of this deeper level of reality. George Lucas' movie, *Star Wars*, has a scene in it in which Luke Skywalker's robot, R2D2, projects a miniature 3-dimensional image of princess Leia delivering a plea to Obi-wan Kenobi for assistance. That image was a hologram. Holograms have some very interesting and very strange characteristics. When you view a holographic projection, it is a three-dimensional image that looks different from every angle that you view it, just as a person looks different as you walk around them. Holograms are created with the use of lasers by creating interference patterns on a holographic plate. The plate itself (like Bohm's implicate order) has no discernible images in it, just a bunch of concentric circles "like when a handful of pebbles is tossed into a pond." The hologram only comes into existence when a laser beam (the equivalent of our "lens of perception") is shone through it. But there is one important distinction in the properties of the holographic plate. Unlike a piece of photographic film, if you break the holographic plate into two pieces, both pieces can still reproduce the *entire* original image! Moreover, no matter how small a piece is broken off, every part of the plate contains the whole image. Each small piece of the film contains all of the information of the whole, the only difference is that the smaller pieces are hazier and less defined.

A holograph is a static image—like putting princess Leia's message on "pause" and viewing a single "frame." Bohm recognized that life is not static but a constant movement and so amended his metaphor. He coined the term *holomovement* to "convey the dynamic and ever active nature of the incalculable enfoldings and unfoldings that moment by moment create our universe." (Actually, quantum science implies that it is *our* thoughts that cause aspects of the universe to manifest, it does not simply unfold by itself.) As we learned in regard to the functioning of guiding principles, the power of this metaphor is very useful for application in a business context.

Morphogenic Fields

British biologist Rupert Sheldrake, in a theory highly consistent with Bohm's implicate order, believes that "morphogenic fields" shape the form, development, and behavior of organisms—even if there are *no conventional forms of contact between them.* Through *morphic resonance*, fields are "built-up" over time by the repetitive actions of animals (or people) of the same species. When a certain number of the members of the species learn the behavior, it is automatically acquired by the other members of the species.

Sheldrake has proven the action of morphogenic fields experimentally with both animals and such elementary phenomena as the growth of crystals. The implications of this concept are profound. Morphogenic fields and the action of morphic resonance give us a way of understanding the unifying power of shared vision in organizations. It can be seen as a form of the mental visioning process that many people use to both help them through personal change and to achieve their goals. In addition, it offers another explanation of the operation of the self-transformation (positive feedback) process in systemic change and Stephen Jay Gould's punctuated equilibria theory of evolution.

The idea of invisible fields influencing material objects is not wholly new to any of us. We all have seen how invisible fields from a magnet cause patterns to emerge in iron filings. And none of us question how radios and televisions can pluck invisible pictures and sounds out of thin air and reproduce them so perfectly. It is really only a matter of extending these experiences for people to be able to accept the notion of morphogenic fields or the existence of Bohm's implicate order. Once we gain a degree of comfort with these concepts, we can begin to deploy them to our advantage in our everyday activities. As yet, we have not even *begun* to plumb the depths of potential that these concepts hold for us.

Bibliography

Ackoff, Russell L. *The Democratic Corporation: A Radical Prescription for Recreating Corporate America and Rediscovering Success*. New York: Oxford University Press, 1994.

Adams, Scott. *The Dilbert Principle: A Cubicle's Eye View of Bosses, Meetings, Management Fads & Other Workplace Afflictions*. New York: HarperBusiness, 1996.

Arrien, Angeles. *The Four-Fold Way: Walking the Paths of the Warrior, Teacher, Healer, and Visionary*. San Francisco: HarperSanFrancisco, 1993.

Ash, Mary Kay. *Mary Kay: The Success Story of America's Most Dynamic Business Woman*. New York: Harper Perennial, 1987.

Barnard, Chester. *Organization Management: Selected Papers*. Boston: Harvard University Press, 1948.

Barta, Carolyn. "A Bridge to Where?" *Dallas Morning News*, December 15, 1996.

Bartlett, John. *Bartlett's Familiar Quotations*. Boston: Little, Brown and Company, 1992.

Berman, Morris. *The Re-enchantment of the World*. Ithaca, New York: Cornell University Press, 1981.

Block, Peter. *Stewardship: Choosing Service Over Self-Interest*. San Francisco: Berrett-Koehler, 1993.

Byrne, John A. "Paradigms for Post-Modern Managers." *Business Week*, Reinventing America, 1992.

Caldwell, Bruce. "Missteps, Miscues." *Information Week*, June 20, 1994.

Campbell, Joseph. *The Lost Teachings of Joseph Campbell*. Redmond, WA: Zygon International, 1993. Audiotape.

Campbell, Joseph, with Bill Moyers. *The Power of Myth*. New York: Doubleday, 1988.

Capra, Fritjof. *The Tao of Physics*. Boston: New Science Library, 1975.

———. *The Turning Point: Science, Society, and the Rising Culture*. New York: Bantam Books, 1982.

———. *The Web of Life: A New Scientific Understanding of Living Systems*. New York: Anchor Books, 1996.

Carlin, Peter. "How to Make a Decision Like a Tribe." *Fast Company*, Premier Issue.

Case, John. "A Company of Businesspeople." *Inc.*, April 1993.

Chapell, Tom. *The Soul of a Business: Managing for Profit and the Common Good.* New York: Bantam Books, 1993.

Chopra, Deepak. *The Seven Spiritual Laws of Success: A Practical Guide to the Fulfillment of Your Dreams.* San Rafael, CA: Amber-Allen, 1994.

Collins, James C., and Jerry I. Porras. *Built to Last: Successful Habits of Visionary Companies.* New York: HarperBusiness, 1994.

Connelly, Julie. "Have We Become Mad Dogs at the Office?" *Fortune*, November 28, 1994.

Covey, Stephen R. *The Seven Habits of Highly Effective People.* New York: Simon and Schuster, 1989.

Davenport, Thomas H. "Why Reengineering Failed." *Fast Company*, Premier Issue.

Deal, Terence E., and Allan A. Kennedy. *Corporate Cultures: The Rites and Rituals of Corporate Life.* Reading, MA: Addison-Wesley, 1982.

Defoore, Bill, and John Renesch, eds. *Rediscovering the Soul of Business.* San Francisco: Sterling and Stone, 1995.

Duck, Jeanie Daniel. "Managing Change: The Art of Balancing." *Harvard Business Review*, November-December 1993.

Dwyer, Paula, et al. "Tearing up Today's Organization Chart." *Business Week*, November 18, 1994.

Eisler, Riane. *The Chalice & The Blade: Our History, Our Future.* San Francisco:HarperSan Francisco, 1987.

Estes, Ralph. *The Tyranny of the Bottom-Line: Why Corporations Make Good People Do Bad Things.* San Francisco: Berrett-Koehler, 1996.

Fields, Rick, et al. *Chop Wood Carry Water; A Guide to Finding Spiritual Fulfillment in Everyday Life.* New York: Tarcher/Putnum, 1984.

Finegan, Jay. "Unconventional Wisdom." *Inc.*, December 1994.

Fishman, Charles. "Can't Anyone Here Play This Game?" *Fast Company*, Premier Issue.

———. "I Want My Ford TV." *Fast Company*, Premier Issue.

———. "Whole Foods Teams." *Fast Company*, April-May, 1996.

Bibliography

Frankl, Viktor. *Man's Search for Meaning: An Introduction to Logotherapy*. New York: Touchstone, 1984.

Fraser, Derek. "Industrial Revolution." *Grolier Multi-Media Encyclopedia*, 1994.

Fritz, Robert. *Corporate Tides: The Inescapable Laws of Organizational Structure*. San Francisco: Berrett-Koehler, 1996.

Goleman, Daniel. *Emotional Intelligence*. New York: Bantam Books, 1995.

Gould, Stephen Jay. "Creating the Creators." *Discover*, October 1996.

Gray, John, Ph.D. *Men Are From Mars, Women Are From Venus: A Practical Guide for Improving Communication and Getting What You Want in Your Relationships*. New York: HarperCollins, 1992.

Grof, Stanislav. *Beyond the Brain: Birth, Death, and Transcendence in Psychology*. New York: SUNY, 1985.

Hamel, Gary, et al. "Collaborate with Your Competitors—and Win." *Harvard Business Review*, January-February, 1989.

Handy, Charles. *The Age of Paradox*. Boston: The Harvard Business School Press, 1994.

Harvey, Eric, and Alexander Lucia. *Walk the Talk . . . And Get The Results You Want*. Dallas: Performance Publishing, 1995.

Hayward, Susan. *A Guide for the Advanced Soul: A Book of Insight*. Little, Brown and Company, 1984.

Helgesen, Sally. *The Web of Inclusion: A New Architecture for Building Great Organizations*. New York: Currency-Doubleday, 1995.

Hock, Dee. "A Conversation With Keynote Speaker Dee Hock." *Pegasus Communications: The Systems Thinking in Action Conference*, October 3, 1996. Audiotape.

————. "Birth of the Chaordic Century: Out of Control and into Order." *Pegasus Communications: The Systems Thinking in Action Conference*, October 3, 1996. Audiotape.

Hofman, Mike. "Forget the Organization, Says Management Guru." *Inc.*, November 1996.

Huey, John. "The New Post-Heroic Leadership." *Fortune*, February 21, 1994.

Jackson, Phil. "Spiritual lessons from a Hoops Master." *The New Leaders*, March/April 1996.

Jaworski, Joseph. *Synchronicity: The Inner Path of Leadership*. San Francisco: Berrett-Koehler, 1996.

Jeffreys, Michael. *Success Secrets of the Motivational Superstars*. Rocklin, CA: Prima Publishing, 1996.

Jones, Patricia, and Larry Kahaner. *Say It and Live It: 50 Corporate Mission Statements That Hit the Mark*. New York: Currency-Doubleday, 1995.

Katzenbach, John. *Just Cause*. New York: Ballantine Books, 1992.

Kornfield, Jack. *A Path With Heart: A Guide Through the Perils and Promises of Spiritual Life*. New York: Bantam Books, 1993.

Kotter, John P., and James L. Heskett. *Corporate Culture and Performance*. New York: The Free Press, 1992.

Madrick, Jeffrey. *The End of Affluence: The Causes and Consequences of America's Economic Dilemma*. New York: Random House, 1995.

Magid, Lynn H. *A Guide to Dallas Private Schools*. Chelsea, MI: BookCrafters, 1996.

Manning, Anita. "How to Cope If Work Is Killing You." *USA Today*, June 4, 1996.

Matson, Eric. "The People of Hewlett-Packard v. the Past." *Fast Company*, Premier issue.

Mitchell, Russell, et al. "The Schwab Revolution." *Business Week*, December 19, 1994.

Myerson, Mort. "Everything I Thought I Knew About Leadership Is Wrong." *Fast Company*, April-May 1996.

Noer, David M. *Healing the Wounds: Overcoming the Trauma of Layoffs and Revitalizing Downsized Organizations*. San Francisco: Jossey-Bass, 1993.

Nonaka, Ikujiro, and Hirotaka Takeuchi. "Tacit Knowledge is Key to Japanese Success." *The New Leaders*, September/October 1995.

Oakley, Ed, and David Krug. *Enlightened Leadership*. New York: Fireside, 1991.

Owen, Harrison. *Spirit: Transformation and Development in Organizations*. Potomac, MD: Abbott, 1987.

Osbon, Diane K. ed. *The Joseph Campbell Companion*. New York: HarperCollins, 1991.

Pennar, Karen. "Economic Anxiety." *Business Week*, March 11, 1996.

Renesch, John, ed. "CEO Champions Open Book Management." *The New Leaders*, November/December 1995.

Bibliography

————. "Odwalla Does the Right Thing." *The New Leaders*, Jan./Feb. 1997.

Rifkin, Glenn. "Nothing but Net." *Fast Company*, June-July 1996.

Roddick, Anita. *Body and Soul*. New York: Crown, 1991.

Rubin, Harriet. "Thank You Ma'am, May I Have Another?" *Fast Company*, June-July, 1996.

Rummler, Geary A., and Alan P. Brache. *Improving Performance: How to Manage the White Space on the Organization Chart*. San Francisco: Jossey-Bass, 1990.

Santrock, John W. *Life-Span Development*. Dubuque, IA: Wm. C. Brown, 1983.

Schaef, Anne Wilson, and Diane Fassel. *The Addictive Organization*. San Francisco: Harper & Row, 1988.

Schwartz, Peter. *The Art of the Long View: Planning for the Future in an Uncertain World*. New York: Currency-Doubleday, 1991.

Semlar, Ricardo. *Maverick: The Success Story Behind the World's Most Unusual Workplace*. New York: Warner Books, 1993.

Senge, Peter M. *The Fifth Discipline: The Art and Practice of the Learning Organization*. New York: Currency-Doubleday, 1990.

Senge, Peter M., et al. *The Fifth Discipline Fieldbook*. New York: Currency-Doubleday, 1994.

Shaffer, David. *Social and Personality Development*. Pacific Grove, CA: Brooks/Cole, 1988.

Sherman, Stratford. "A Master Class in Radical Change." *Fortune*, Dec. 13, 1993.

————. "Secrets of HP's 'Muddled' Team." *Fortune*, March 18, 1996.

Somé, Malidoma Patrice. *Ritual: Power, Healing and Community*. Portland: Swan/Raven, 1993.

Stacey, Ralph D. *Complexity and Creativity in Organizations*. San Francisco: Berrett-Koehler, 1996.

Stack, Jack. *The Great Game of Business*. New York: Currency-Doubleday, 1992.

Stamps, David. "Corporate Anorexia." *Training*, February 1996.

Stewart, Phyllis L., and Nancy L. Wityak. "Bureaucracy." *Grolier Multi-Media Encyclopedia*, 1994.

Stewart, Thomas A. "Reengineering: The Hot New Managing Tool." *Fortune*, August 23, 1993.

Talbot, Michael. *The Holographic Universe*. New York: HarperCollins, 1991.

Vaill, Peter. *Learning as a Way of Being: Strategies for Survival in a World of Permanent White Water.* San Francisco: Jossey-Bass, 1996.

Waldrop, M. Mitchell. *Complexity: The Emerging Science at the Edge of Order and Chaos.* New York: Touchstone, 1992.

———. "The Trillion Dollar Vision of Dee Hock." *Fast Company*, October-November 1996.

Webber, Chris M. "XBS Learns to Grow." *Fast Company*, October-November 1996.

Wheatley, Margaret J. *Leadership and the New Science.* San Francisco: Berrett-Koehler, 1994.

Wheatley, Margaret J., and Myron Kellner-Rogers. *A Simpler Way.* San Francisco: Berrett-Koehler, 1996.

Whyte, David. *The Heart Aroused.* New York: Currency-Doubleday, 1994.

Youngblood, Mark D. *Eating the Chocolate Elephant.* Richardson, TX, Micrografx, 1994.

Zohar, Danah. *The Quantum Self: Human Nature and Consciousness Defined by the New Physics.* New York: Quill/William Morrow, 1990.

Zukav, Gary. *The Dancing Wu Li Masters: An Overview of the New Physics.* New York: Quill/William Morrow, 1979.

Notes

Chapter 1: A New Order

4   *"It is the mode"* – Susanne Langer as quoted in Berman, *The Re-enchantment of the World,* 183.

5   *"this marvellous science"* – René Descartes as quoted in Capra, *The Turning Point,* 57.

5   *"The modern scientific paradigm"* – Berman, *The Re-enchantment of the World,* 23.

6   *"Can nature possibly"* – As quoted in ibid., 76.

6   *"We have not"* – Wheatley, *Leadership and the New Science,* 140-141.

6   *"It is foolish for"* – Thomas Jefferson as quoted in the movie *Mindwalk,* by Fritjof Capra.

8   *"We're talking about"* – Dwyer, et al. "Tearing up Today's Organization Chart."

8   *I too can feel* – Wheatley, *Leadership and the New Science,* 44-45.

11   *[People] talk about* – Vaill, *Learning as a Way of Being,* 15.

12   *"Newtonian despair"*– Wheatley, *Leadership and the New Science,* 44.

14   *"most companies are ill-equipped"* – Youngblood, *Eating the Chocolate Elephant,* 4.

14   *"The problem for most executives"* – Duck, "Managing Change: The Art of Balancing."

14   *"Thriving in this fast-paced"* – Dwyer, et al. "Tearing up Today's Organization Chart."

14   *"Change is not something"* – Ronald E. Compton as quote in Byrne, "Paradigms for Postmodern Managers."

16   *"Eighteen months after"* – Rummler and Brache, *Improving Performance,* 12.

16   *"a recent poll by consulting firm Arthur D. Little"* – Caldwell, "Missteps, Miscues," 50.

16   *A similar study by CSC Index* – Davenport, "Why Reengineering Failed," 71.

17   *Two-thirds or more* – Caldwell, "Missteps, Miscues," 50.

17   *Fast Company magazine reported* – Fishman, "Can't Anybody Here Play This Game?", 18.

18   *a five year study* – Stamps, "Corporate Anorexia."

18   *"ten years of downsizing"* – Pennar, "Economic Anxiety."

18   *there is more stress* – Manning, "How to Cope if Work is Killing You."

18   *An international airline* – as reported on the Oprah Winfrey Show, October 24, 1996.

Notes, Chapter 1: A New Order, cont'd

18 *A 1993 study* – Connelly, "Have We Become Mad Dogs at the Office?"

19 *"the prison of our"* – Chopra, *The Seven Spiritual Laws of Success*, 86.

20 *"the most efficient method"* – Stewart and Wityak, "Bureaucracy."

21 *"The decisive reason"* – ibid.

21 *There were six elements* – ibid.

21 *"If this system"* – Madrick, *The End of Affluence*, 51.

22 *"that observation, measurement"* – Fraser, "Industrial Revolution."

22 *So-called scientific management* – Madrick, *The End of Affluence*, 50-51.

23 *"Workers are adults"* – Semler, *Maverick*, 67-68.

24 *Because of the low retail* – Youngblood, *Eating the Chocolate Elephant*, 21.

26 *"This is the end"* – Gerald Celente as quoted in Barta, "A Bridge to Where?"

27 *"the mechanical worldview"* – Zohar, *The Quantum Self*, 234.

27 *R. Kaku, chairman* – Jaworski, *Synchronicity: The Inner Path of Leadership*, 165.

28 *You can tell what's* – Campbell, *The Power of Myth*, 95-96.

28 *"order for free"?* – Stuart Kaufman as quoted in Waldrop, *Complexity*, 124.

29 *three factors that drive* – Stacey, *Complexity and Creativity in Organizations*, 99.

32 *The "dynamic connectedness" of* – Helgesen, *The Web of Inclusion*, 16-17.

Chapter 2: The Way of Living Systems

33 *"I am convinced"* – Heinz Pagels as quoted in Waldrop, *Complexity*, back cover.

34 *"feed on a continual flux"* – Capra, *The Web of Life*, 48.

36 *"exhibiting most of"* – Capra, *The Turning Point*, 271.

42 *"the tendency to associate"* – ibid, 278.

44 *"there is no way"* – Berman, *The Re-enchantment of the World*, 283. Berman elaborates in a footnote that some species—such as wolves—do have a power hierarchy, but there is no evidence that it carries over to the relationships of humans.

44 *"as a real tree"* – Capra, *The Turning Point*, 282.

46 *"Any system that maximizes"* – Berman, *The Re-enchantment of the World*, 243-244.

47 *The only thing* – Chris Turner, as quoted in Webber, "XBS Learns to Grow," 115.

Notes

Notes, Chapter 2: The Way of Living Systems, cont'd

48   *"looking at the facts"* – From a private conversation.

48   *all of the pieces contain the whole* – If you break a holographic plate into two pieces, both pieces can still reproduce the entire original image. Moreover, no matter how small a piece is broken off, every part of the plate contains the whole image—each small piece of the film contains all of the information of the whole. The only difference is that the smaller pieces are hazier and less defined.

48   *"Boids learned to flock"* – Stacey, *Complexity and Creativity in Organizations*, 73.

50   *"$1 [invested] in"* – Collins and Porras, *Built to Last*, 4.

50   *The principles they uncovered* – ibid., entire book.

52   *"The ethics of optima"* – Gregory Bateson as quoted in Berman, *The Re-enchantment of the World*, 255.

52   *"Contrary to business school"* – Collins and Porras, *Built to Last*, 55.

52   *"profit is like oxygen"* – ibid., 55.

54   *At this bifurcation point* – This behavior is equivalent to Stephen Jay Gould's punctuated equilibria model of evolutionary development, and the behavior of morphic resonance in morphogenic fields as described by Rupert Sheldrake.

57   *Feathers may have first evolved* – Gould, "Creating the Creators."

59   *"Nothing we have created"* – Wheatley, *A Simpler Way*, 39.

59   *"it is critical levels"* – Stacey, *Complexity and Creativity in Organizations*, 81.

60   *A flower, a rainbow* – Chopra, *The Seven Spiritual Laws of Success*, 67-68.

60   *in statistics there are two* – Handy, *The Age of Paradox*, 73-75.

61   *"Western managers"* – Nonaka and Takeuchi, "Tacit Knowledge is Key to Japanese Success,"4.

62   *"Information chastity belts,"* – Wheatley, *Leadership and the New Science*, 105.

63   *"The more people know"* – Stack, *The Great Game of Business*, 71.

63   *"so why pretend"* – Fishman, "I Want My Ford TV," 18.

63   *"A business should be"* – Stack, *The Great Game of Business*, 72.

63   *"We never would"* – ibid., 72.

65   *"I realized that if "* – Bob Buckman as quoted in Rifkin, "Nothing but Net," 124.

67   *Dee Hock, speaking at* – Hock, " A Conversation with Keynote Speaker Dee Hock."

68   *"form and function engage"* – Wheatley, *Leadership and the New Science*, 91.

68   *Information, as odd as* – The concepts presented here are drawn in part from the ideas put forth in Wheatley, *Leadership and the New Science*, Chapter 6.

Notes, Chapter 2: The Way of Living Systems, cont'd

68 *"all matter, including ourselves"* – David Bohm, as quoted in Zukav, *The Dancing Wu Li Masters*, 323.

69 *"Everything flows; only process is real."* – Heraclitus as quoted in Berman, *The Re-enchantment of the World*, 145.

Chapter 3: The Quantum Organization

75 *"The study of complexity"* – Whyte, *The Heart Aroused*, 253.

75 *"Reengineering is so hot"* – Stewart, "Reengineering: The Hot New Managing Tool."

84 *"You know you have a rockin'"* – Adams, *The Dilbert Principle*, 38.

85 *Tom Chappell, CEO* – Chappell, *The Soul of a Business*, 50-52.

85 *Odwalla, a fresh juice bottler* – Renesch, "Odwalla Does the Right Thing," 10.

87 *Trammell Crow estimates* – Jones and Kahaner, *Say It and Live It*, 61.

88 *"money is not the"* – Anita Roddick as quoted in Helgeson, *The Web of Inclusion*, 7.

88 *"money motivates neither"* – Dee Hock as quoted in Waldrop, "The Trillion Dollar Vision of Dee Hock," 75.

88 *We are in the business* – Jones and Kahaner, *Say It and Live It*, 167.

88 *The Southland Corporation exists* – ibid., 213.

90 *"The most enlightened companies"* – Ed McCracken as quoted in Hofman, "Forget the Organization, Says Management Guru," 20.

90 *Out-of-balance behavior creates* – Reinforcing feedback loops *always* reach a point where they return to dynamic balance. This takes one of two forms: the systems fall into disorder—the equivalent of dying, or it self-transcends to a new level of complexity that is more stable and balanced. Self-transcendence is limited in physical organisms—running a human's heartbeat up to 500 beats per minute will kill the person; they will never self-transcend by creating a second heart to carry the load, or by suddenly reconfiguring the fiber of the heart muscle such that it can beat at that rate. Human organizations, which are systems of *ideas*, have the ability to move in either direction.

91 *"valuing all key constituencies"* – Kotter and Heskett. *Corporate Culture and Performance*, 50.

91 *We try never to forget* – George Merck III as quoted in Collins and Porras. *Built to Last*, 48.

92 *One must speak for* – Carlin, "How to Make a Decision Like A Tribe," 105.

Notes, Chapter 3: The Quantum Organization, cont'd

96 *"Big Hairy Audacious Goals,"* – Collins and Porras. *Built to Last,* Chapter 5.

93 *A BHAG of increasing the stock price* – The exception to this is when all employees have enough stock to make the goal personally meaningful—that is, that people could correlate their own efforts with a significant increase in their own wealth. Having a handful of shares in a corporate ESOP is not enough.

97 *"Collaboration is second best."* – Hamel et al. "Collaborate with Your Competitors—and Win."

99 *In 1994, the company won* – Finegan, "Unconventional Wisdom."

100 *Discount brokerage firm Charles Schwab* – Mitchell, et al. "The Schwab Revolution."

100 I did not coin the terms Substitutor or Complementor. I originally saw them in a *Harvard Business Review* article but I have not been able to locate the original article.

100 *SRC has spun off seventeen* – Renesch, "CEO Champions Open Book Management," 3.

103 *"There's an old expression"* – Dr. Carl Sorensen as quoted in Oakley and Krug, *Enlightened Leadership,* 99.

105 *"Leaders must learn"* – Warren Bennis as quoted in Huey, "The New Post-Heroic Leadership," 44.

108 *"Everything I thought I knew"* – Myerson, "Everything I Thought I Knew About Leadership is Wrong," 72.

108 *As Rianne Eisler explained* – Eisler, *The Chalice and the Blade,* entire book.

109 *the board is often essentially impotent* – Estes, *Tyranny of the Bottom Line,* 63-67.

110 *self-help expert Stephen Covey* – Covey, *The Seven Habits of Highly Effective People,* Habit 4.

110 *"Maybe the country's entire"* – Rubin, "Thank you Ma'am, May I have Another," 59.

111 *Dee Hock describes one* – Hock, "The Birth of the 'Chaordic' Century."

111 *"Just ask the fired heads"* – Huey, "The New Post-Heroic Leadership."

112 *"There's considerable evidence"* – Case, "A Company of Businesspeople," 86.

112 *The leader is often* – Huey, "The New Post-Heroic Leadership," 48.

112 *"The community creates"* – Block, *Stewardship,* 42.

113 *"Leadership is a verb"* – Bill Gore as quoted in Huey, "The New Post-Heroic Leadership."

113 *Teams at Whole Foods* – Fishman, "Whole Foods Teams."

114 *In the process of devising* – Helgesen, *The Web of Inclusion,* 10.

Notes, Chapter 3: The Quantum Organization, cont'd

116 *"America is used to killers"* – Katzenbach, *Just Cause*, 375.

119 *Author and leadership expert Peter Block* – Block, *Stewardship*, 178.

120 *"If you are trying"* – John Mackey as quoted in Fishman, "Whole Foods Teams," 110.

120 *John Mackey, CEO* – John Mackey as quoted in ibid.

121 *According to psychologist* – Shaffer, *Social and Personality Development*, 325.

121 *figure 3.3* – Carol Gilligan, a leading psychology researcher, criticizes Kohlberg's model for understating the importance of *caring* to moral development. She believes this is a result of the bias toward "male" values in modern society. In her model, the conventional morality has a much higher emphasis on being responsible and caring for others, and her postconventional level stresses interdependence much more than does Kohlberg's model.

122 *"The day-to-day reality"* – Block, *Stewardship*, 169.

123 *"Everyone likes the idea"* – ibid., 172.

123 *"One of the most frightening"* – Adams, *The Dilbert Principle*, 101.

123 *"The consequences"* – From a private conversation.

125 *"When people are free"* – Sherman, "Secret's of HP's Muddled Team," 116.

127 *"Nothing seems more medieval"* – Semler, *Maverick*, 69.

129 *Depending on your status* – Adams, *The Dilbert Principle*, 24-25.

135 *"There is no mission"* – Vaill, *Learning as a Way of Being*, 191.

135 *A Montessori education* – Magid, *A Guide to Dallas Private Schools*, 533.

Chapter 4: The Power of Shared Vision

137 *One study of a group* – As quoted in Talbot, *The Holographic Universe*, 88.

138 *"I've learned that the"* – Jackson, "Spiritual Lessons from a Hoops Master," 1.

139 *"In the absence"* – Robert Fritz, as quoted in Senge, *The Fifth Discipline*, 209.

139 *"People want to be bound"* – Barnard, *Organization Management: Selected Papers*.

143 *It's been my experience* – Ash, *Mary Kay*, 79.

144 *"Our efforts to do a better job"* - Harvey, *Walk the Talk*, 131.

146 *"Without a pull"* - Senge, *The Fifth Discipline*, 209.

147 *I think people were receptive* – From a private conversation.

Chapter 5: Transforming Corporate Culture

147 *As you go the way* – As quoted in Osbon, *A Joseph Campbell Companion*, 26.

155 *Senge describes a system archetype* – Senge, *The Fifth Discipline*, 104-113.

156 *"You can really see"* – From a private conversation.

162 *"structural dynamics"* – Fritz, *Corporate Tides*, 19.

165 *"Give people the rationale"* – Jack Welch as quoted in Sherman, "A Master Class in Radical Change," 84.

165 *"You have to give people"* – Lawrence Bossidy as quoted in ibid., 84.

165 *"When I compared these trends"* – From a private conversation.

167 *"People already know"* – From a private conversation.

170 *"the vast majority of"* – Alfred Bandura as quoted in Shaffer, *Social and Personality Development*, 65.

170 *"It is no use walking"* – St. Francis of Assisi as quoted in Fields et. al, *Chop Wood, Carry Water*, 240.

172 *It takes a lot of stamina* – From a private conversation.

174 *"What we call the beginning"* – T.S. Eliot as quoted in Fields et. al, *Chop Wood, Carry Water*, 2.

175 *"The Dagara understand"* – Somé, *Ritual*, 96-97.

177 *"a set of attitudes,"* – Noer, *Healing the Wounds*, 13.

181 *"They took pictures"* – From a private conversation.

181 *"The idea is that"* – Geoff Ainscow as quoted in Matson, "The People of Hewlett-Packard v. the Past," 26.

181 *Ainscow organized pallbearers* – ibid., 26.

183 *"He who has a why"* – Nietzche as quoted in Frankl, *Man's Search for Meaning*, 84.

184 *"People abhor information vacuums;"* – Duck, "Managing Change: The Art of Balancing," 110.

186 *"Nothing great is created suddenly,"* – Epictetus as quoted in Bartlett, *Barlett's Familiar Quotations*, 108.

188 *"If you have built castles"* – Henry David Thoreau as quoted in Fields et. al, *Chop Wood, Carry Water*, 119.

191 *If there is a single rule* – Duck, "Managing Change: The Art of Balancing," 111.

Chapter 6: Personal Leadership

203 *We who lived in* – Frankl, *Man's Search for Meaning*, 75.

203 *"Responsibility is not only"* – Arrian, *The Four-Fold Way*, 19.

204 *"To have integrity"* – Starhawk as quoted in Arrian, *The Four-Fold Way*, 5.

206 *The most strongly enforced* – Alan Watts as quoted in Fields et. al *Chop Wood, Carry Water*, 12.

207 *On the morning of June 6* – DeFoore and Renesch, *Rediscovering the Soul of Business*, 172.

208 *"Here lies the cure"* – Jack Canfield as quoted in Jeffreys, *Success Secrets of the Motivational Superstars*, 293.

212 *"It is good to have"*– Ursula K. LeGuin as quoted in Hayward, *A Guide for the Advanced Soul*.

212 *"The Grail represents"* – Campbell, *The Power of Myth*, 196-198.

213 *"Life is either"* – Helen Keller as quoted in Hayward, *A Guide for the Advanced Soul*.

214 *"The Knights of the Round Table"* – From a private conversation.

214 *Uncertainty is the fertile ground* – Chopra, *The Seven Laws of Spiritual Success*, 86-87.

215 *Career expert Barbara Reinhold* – Manning, "How to cope if work is killing you."

Chapter 7: Personal Mastery

218 *a meager 20 percent or less* – Wheatley, *A Simpler Way*, 48.

221 *A Few Years ago a tribe* – Campbell, "Joseph Campbell – "The lost Teachings."

222 *To know you do not know* – as quoted in Fields et. al, *Chop Wood, Carry Water*, 24.

224 *Magical power, marvelous action* – as quoted in Fields et. al, *Chop Wood, Carry Water*, xi.

229 *"People need to see"* – From a private conversation.

231 *Thoughts are things* – Brian Adams as quoted in Hayward, *A Guide for the Advanced Soul*.

233 *"Emotional aptitude"* – Goleman, *Emotional Intelligence*, 36.

233 *"The sound and fury"* – Whyte, *The Heart Aroused*, 7.

235 *one of the highest indicators* – Goleman, *Emotional Intelligence*.

235 *Emotional flooding is technically* – ibid., 139.

236 *Venting rage does not relieve* – ibid., 64.

Notes, Chapter 7: Personal Mastery, cont'd

237 *"The soul becomes dyed"* – Marcus Aurelius as quoted in Fields et. al, *Chop Wood, Carry Water*, 183.

237 *"the self-righteous inner monologue"* – Goleman, *Emotional Intelligence*, 59

239 *"We are not troubled"* – Epictetus as quoted in Fields et. al, *Chop Wood, Carry Water*, 182.

243 *When I have an intuition* – Chapell, *The Soul of Business*, 109.

244 *"I never discovered anything"* – Albert Einstein as quoted in Senge, *The Fifth Discipline*, 169.

Chapter 8: Relationship

245 *"If you want a perfect"* – From a seminar, notes in author's possession.

246 *"teams become the work"* – Peter Drucker as quoted in Goleman, *Emotional Intelligence*, 159.

246 *the presence of a high-performer* – ibid., 161.

246 *"It is this ability"* – ibid., 160.

251 *A study of 250 executives* – as quoted in ibid., 149.

260 *Barbara Shipka explains this* – DeFoore and Renesch, *Rediscovering the Soul of Business*, 57-58.

264 *Esteemed psychiatrist R. D. Laing* – R.D. Laing as quoted in Berman, *The Re-enchantment of the World*, 228.

265 *"I am mystified by the fact"* – Roddick, *Body and Soul*, 16.

Chapter 9: Dialogue

271 *"The test of a first rate"* – F. Scott Fitzgerald as quoted in Collins and Porras, *Built to Last*, 45.

271 *A new kind of mind* – David Bohm as quoted in Senge, *The Fifth Discipline*, 241.

272 *The four stages of group* – Based loosely on Senge et. al, *Fifth Discipline Fieldbook*, 386.

273 *the "Genius of the AND"* – Collins and Porras, *Built to Last*, 44.

274 *"given these men's"* – As quoted in Senge, *The Fifth Discipline*, 66.

Chapter 10: For Our Children

283 *"We must be the change"* – Mahatma Gandhi as quoted in Oakley and Krug, *Enlightened Leadership*, 99.

Appendix A: The Wonders of Quantum Physics

287 *"hurrying around endlessly"* – as quoted in Berman, *The Re-enchantment of the World*, 45.

290 *Fritjof Capra's metaphor* – Capra, *The Tao of Physics*, 65.

294 *"The particle picture"* – Niels Bohr as quoted in *ibid*, 79.

296 *"definable and observable"* – Niels Bohr as quoted in *ibid.*, 80.

296 *"elementary particles are"* – Wheatley, *Leadership and the New Science*, 40.

297 *"the overall consistency"* – Capra, *The Turning Point*, 93.

297 *"the dance rather than"* – Zukav, *The Dancing Wu Li Masters*, 262.

299 *"deeper order of existence"* – David Bohn as quoted in Talbot, *The Holographic Universe*, 46.

299 *"like when a handful of pebbles"* – ibid., 15.

300 *"convey the dynamic"* – David Bohm as quoted in ibid., 47.

300 *Sheldrake has proven* – Grof, *Beyond the Brain*, 63.

Index

Index

Consulting Services

CREATING QUANTUM ORGANIZATIONS

***The decision to create a Quantum Organization can be both exhilarating
and terrifying—so much potential and yet so much risk!***

It can be helpful at times like this to seek the counsel of those who have traveled this road before. At Quay Alliance, Inc., helping companies through the large-scale transformational change that is required to become a Quantum Organization is the heart of our business. Mark Youngblood is joined by experienced and knowledgeable consultants who see their role as supporting and transferring skills to our clients. And we walk our talk: We pride ourselves in exemplifying the principles described in this book.

If you are interested in learning more about the services available from Quay Alliance, Inc., complete this form and return it to the address shown below, or call us toll-free at:

1-800-991-1981

Yes, contact me about:

❏ Consulting
❏ Training:
    ❏ In-House
    ❏ Public
❏ Speaking Engagements

Name: _____ Title: _____

Organization: _____

Address: _____ _____

City: _____ ST: _____ Zip: _____

Phone: (   ) ___ - _____ Fax: (   ) ___ - _____ E-mail: _____

Mail to: Quay Alliance, Inc.   Phone: (800) 991-1981
          9330 LBJ Freeway Suite 900   Fax: (972) 783-2040
          Dallas, TX 75243-3443   E-mail: QuayAll@aol.com

COME VISIT OUR WEBSITE AT

WWW.QuantumOrg.Com

- **Excerpts from selected chapters plus additional material not included in the book**

- **New articles by Mark Youngblood**

- **Discussion Forum**

- **Links to related web sites**

- **Reading Room featuring relevant magazine articles and reviews of related books**

- **Information on consulting services and public speaking topics offered by Mark Youngblood**

- **Book ordering**

For additional copies of

Life at the Edge of Chaos

To order, call toll-free 1-800-992-6320
or contact us on the internet at
http://www.QuantumOrg.Com
E-mail: QuayAll@aol.com

Pricing per book*	**Shipping Options***
1-9 . . . . $27.50 each	Single book rates:
10-24 . . . . $24.75 each	Book rate . . . . . . $5.50 (allow 10 days)
25-99 . . . . $22.00 each	UPS Ground . . . $7.50 (allow 7 days)
100-499 . . . . $19.25 each	Next day rush . . $23.50
over 500 — Contact Publisher	(Add approximately $1 for each add'l book)

We accept: **Mastercard – Visa – Amex**

Invoicing: **Available to qualified businesses for orders over $100**

Contact Publisher Regarding:

✔ **Special rates for bulk orders over 500 books**
✔ **College textbook/course adoption use**
✔ **Consultant reseller discounts**

*Terms subject to change without prior notice.